W9-AMX-279

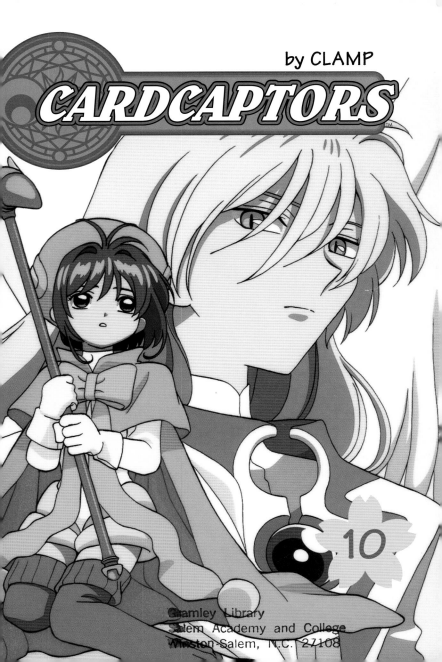

by CLAMP

CARDCAPTORS™

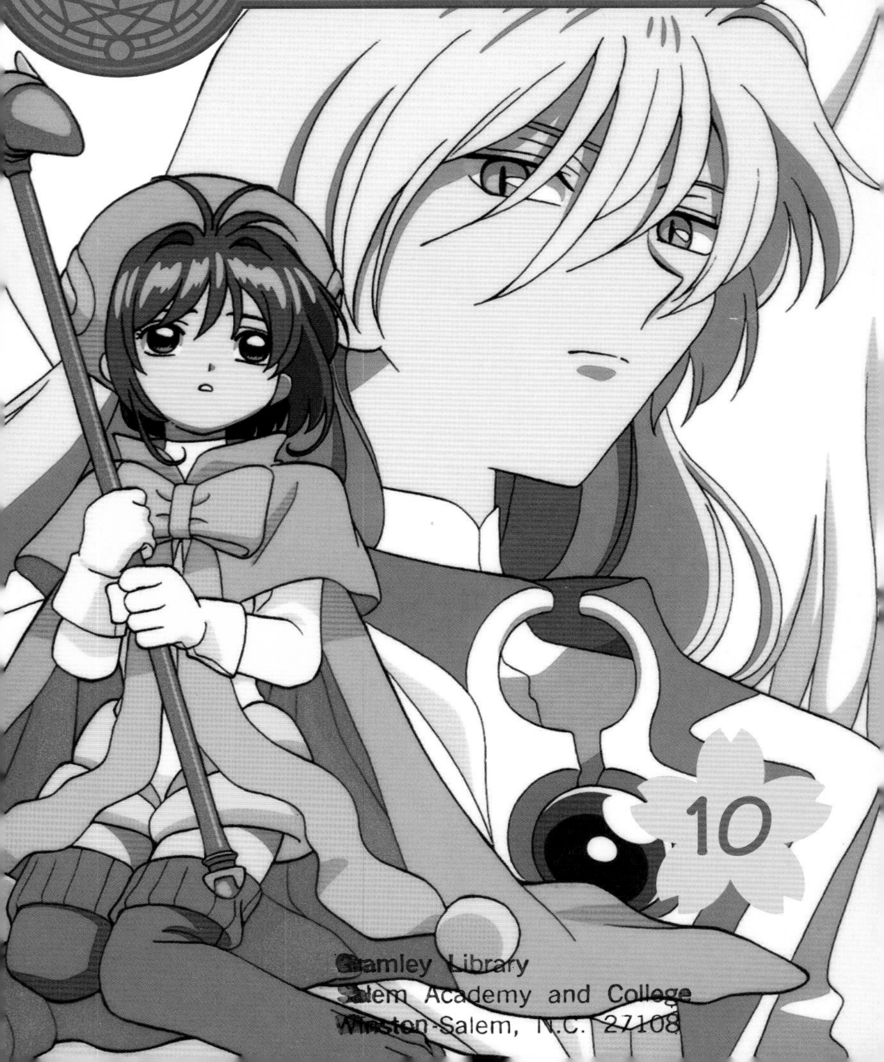
10

Translator – Kong Chang
English Adaptation – Carol Fox
Copy Editors – Bryce Coleman, Paul Morrissey
Layout – Michael Hanson
Graphic Designer – Anna Kernbaum
Senior Editor – Jake Forbes

Production Manager – Jennifer Miller
Art Director – Matt Alford
VP Production – Ron Klamert
President & COO – John Parker
Publisher – Stuart Levy

Email: editor@TOKYOPOP.com
Come visit us online at www.TOKYOPOP.com

A TOKYOPOP® book
5900 Wilshire Blvd. Ste. 2000, Los Angeles, CA 90036

ISBN: 1-59182-049-9

First TOKYOPOP priting: December 2002

10 9 8 7 6 5 4 3 2 1

Manufactured in the USA.

CARDCAPTORS

Contents

CARDCAPTORS™

Big Introduction of Characte

These are all of my fellow Cardcaptors and friends who appear in this s

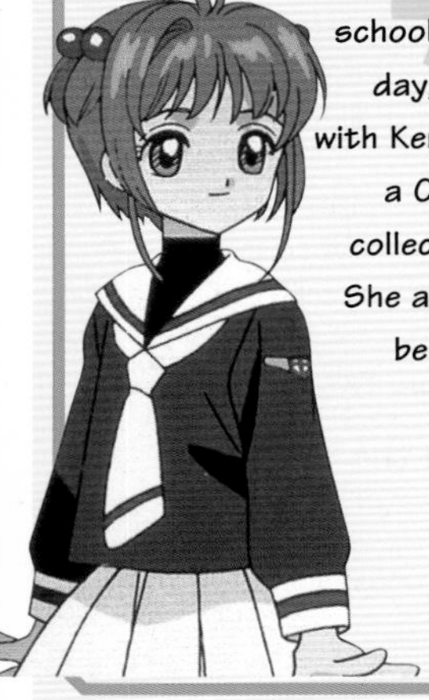

SAKURA AVALON

A healthy and bright fourth year elementary school student. One day, after meeting with Kero, she became a Cardcaptor who collects Clow Cards. She always does her best with a smile for everybody.

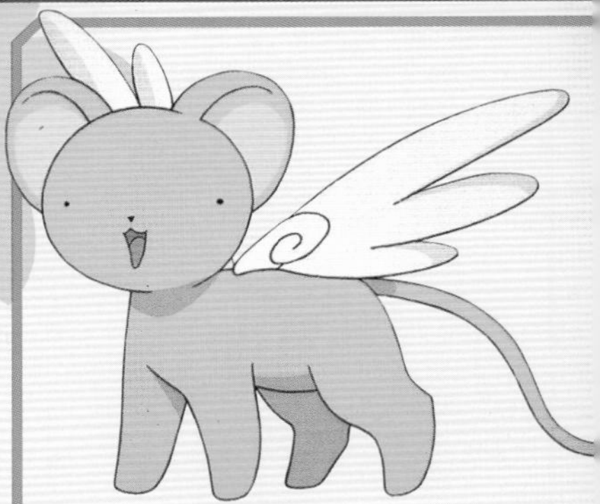

KERO (KEROBEROS)

He is the Sealing Beast who protects the Clow Cards, but for an ancient, magi creature, he sure does talk funny! He's Sakura's reassuring partner.

Friends Who Collect Clow Ca

MADISON TAYLOR

Sakura's best friend. She collects cards and helps out with various things. She makes costumes for Sakura and videotapes all of the action.

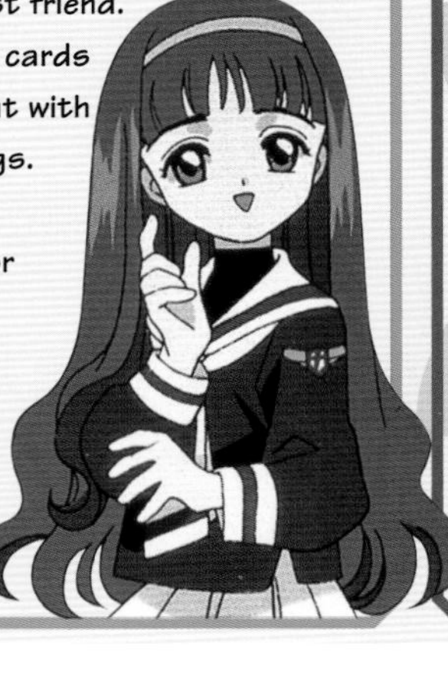

LI SHOWRON

A boy who transferred from Hong Kong. He is in the same class as Sakura, and he's also searching for the Clow Cards. He used to be Sakura's rival, but now he's a trusted friend.

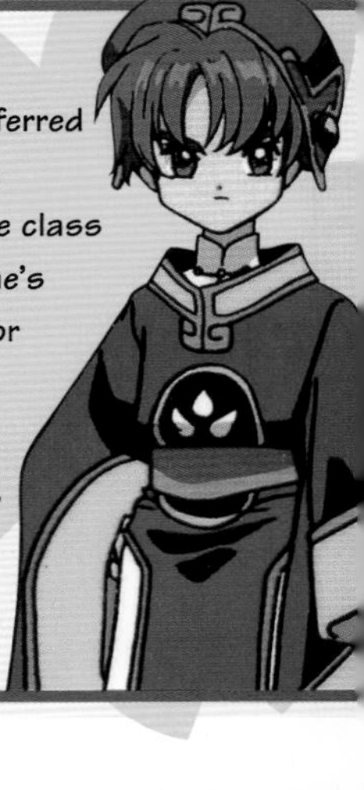

PEOPLE WHO WATCH OVER SAKURA

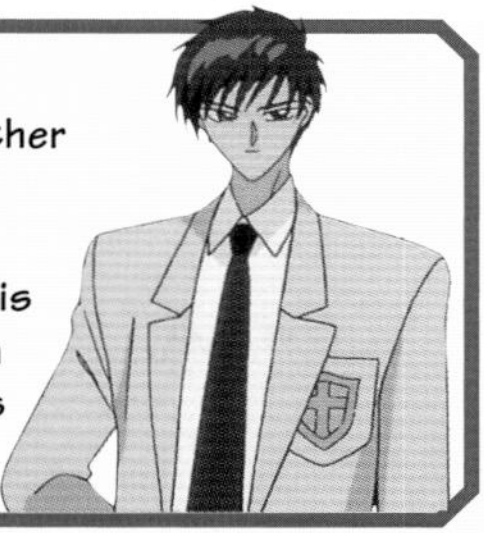

:I AVALON
ura's older brother
a high school
homore. He's
ays picking on his
er, but beneath
l, he truly cares
her.

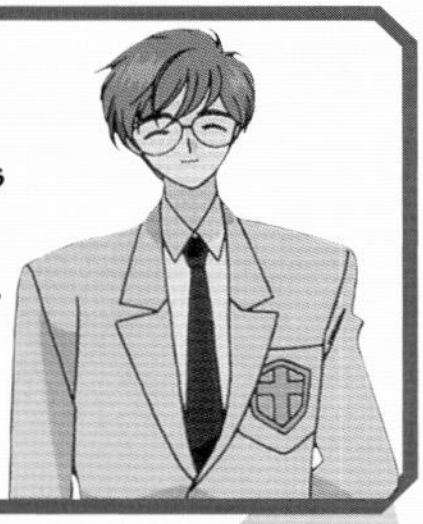

.IAN STAR
i's best friend and
object of Sakura's
ection. Julian is
art, athletic, kind...
all-around
at guy!

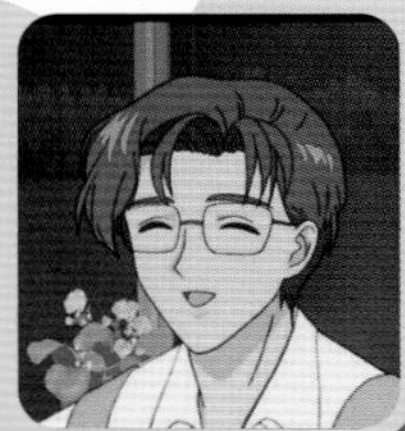

EN AVALON
ura's father
hes archaeology
he university. His
xes are good,
his cooking is
notch.

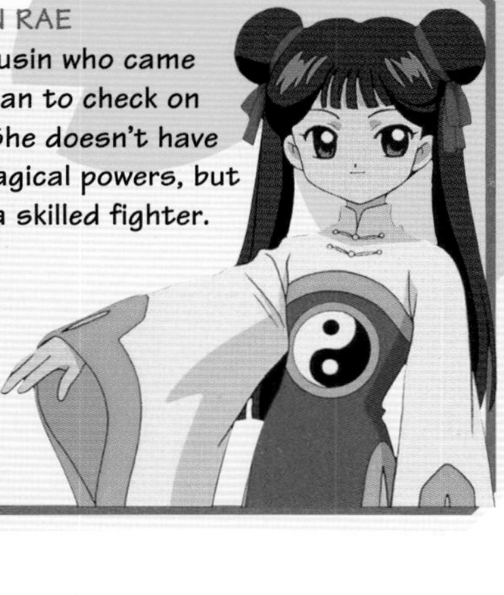

LIN RAE
cousin who came
'apan to check on
. She doesn't have
magical powers, but
s a skilled fighter.

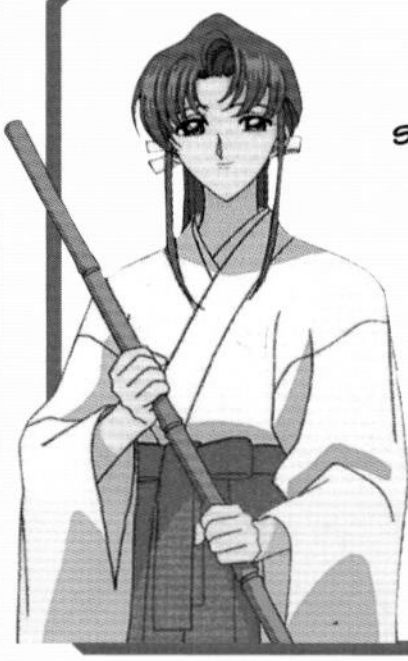

LAYLA MACKENZIE
Ms. MacKenzie is the substitute math teacher for Sakura's class. She also helps out at her father's shrine. She seems to have a magical aura about her. Li doesn't trust her, but Sakura really admires her.

Everyone in the Fifth Year, Second Class

SAKURA'S CLASSMATES

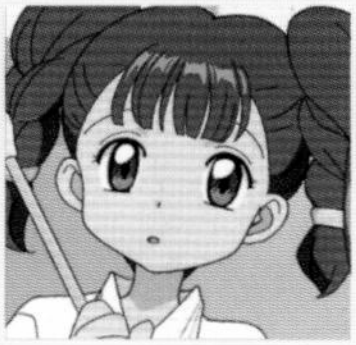

CHELSEA
A bright and healthy girl. She's very close friends with her childhood friend, Zachary.

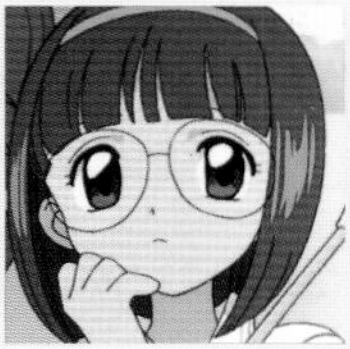

NIKKI
Quiet, composed, and always down-to-earth. She loves scary stories and is well acquainted with myths and legends.

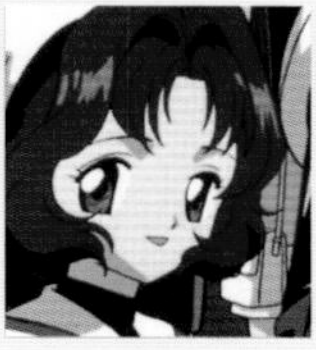

RITA
Beautiful, refined and mature for her age. She's a true friend.

Episode 43

Meilin's Story

CARDCAPTORS

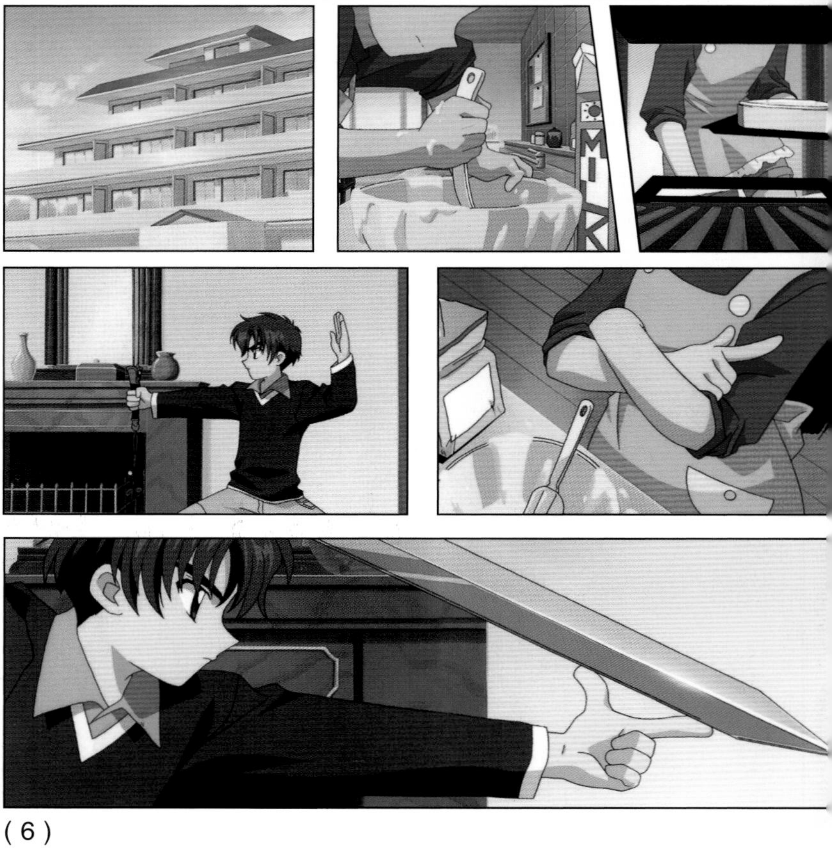

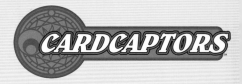

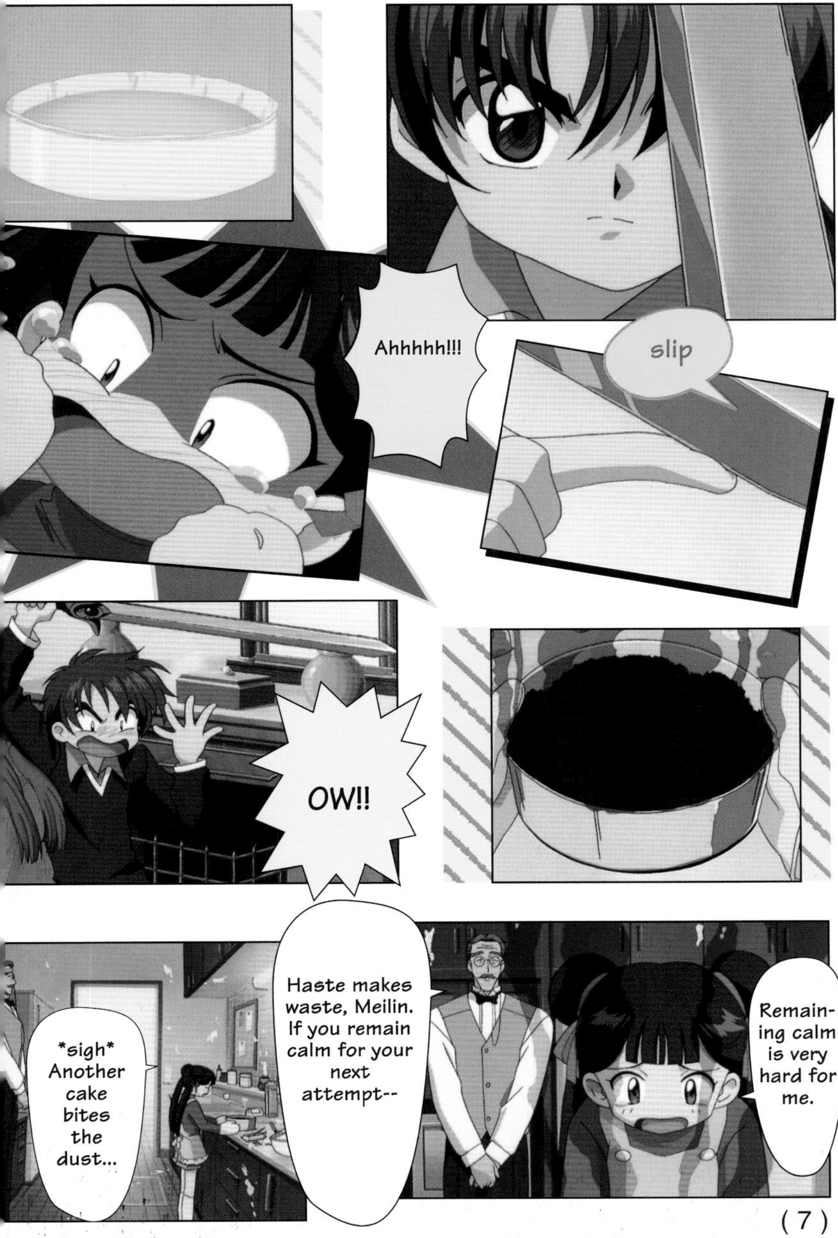

Ahhhhh!!!
slip
OW!!
sigh Another cake bites the dust...
Haste makes waste, Meilin. If you remain calm for your next attempt--
Remaining calm is very hard for me.

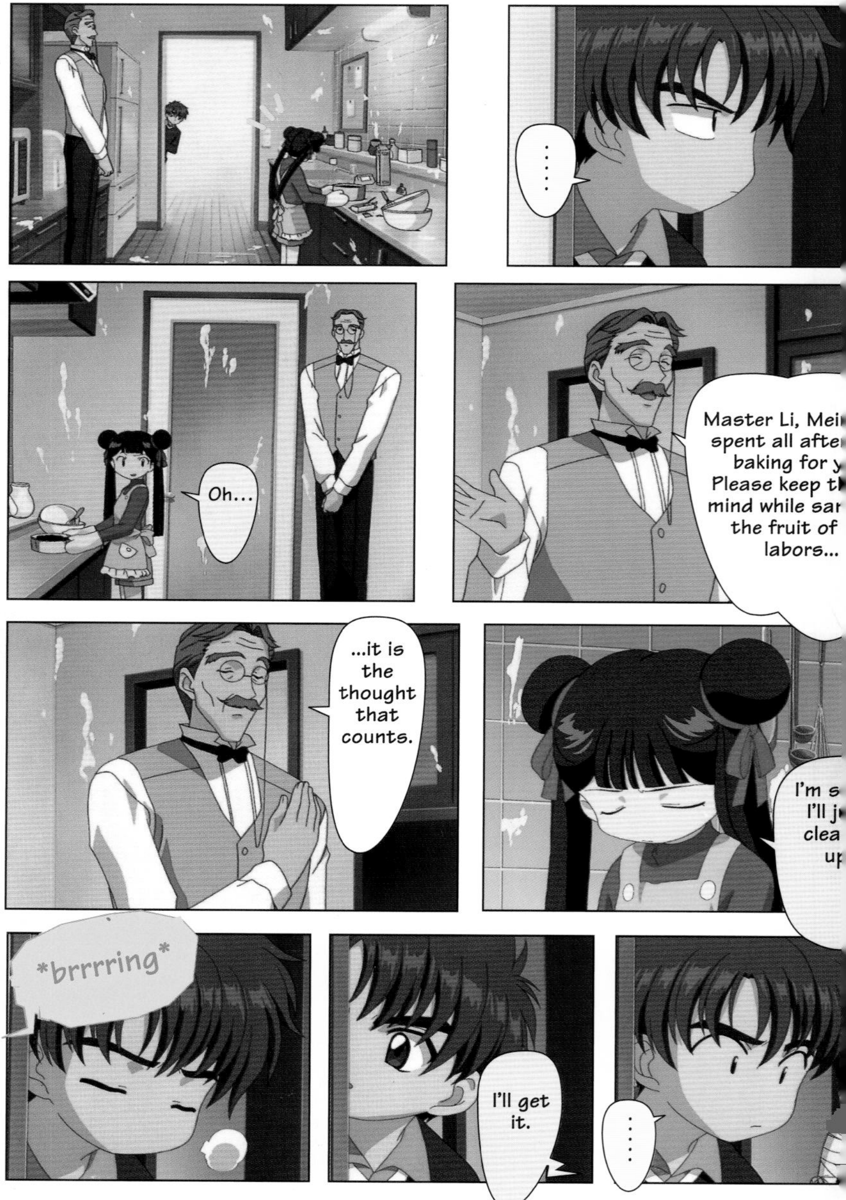

......
Oh...
Master Li, Mei spent all afte baking for y Please keep t mind while sa the fruit of labors...
...it is the thought that counts.
I'm s I'll j clea u
brrrring
I'll get it.
......

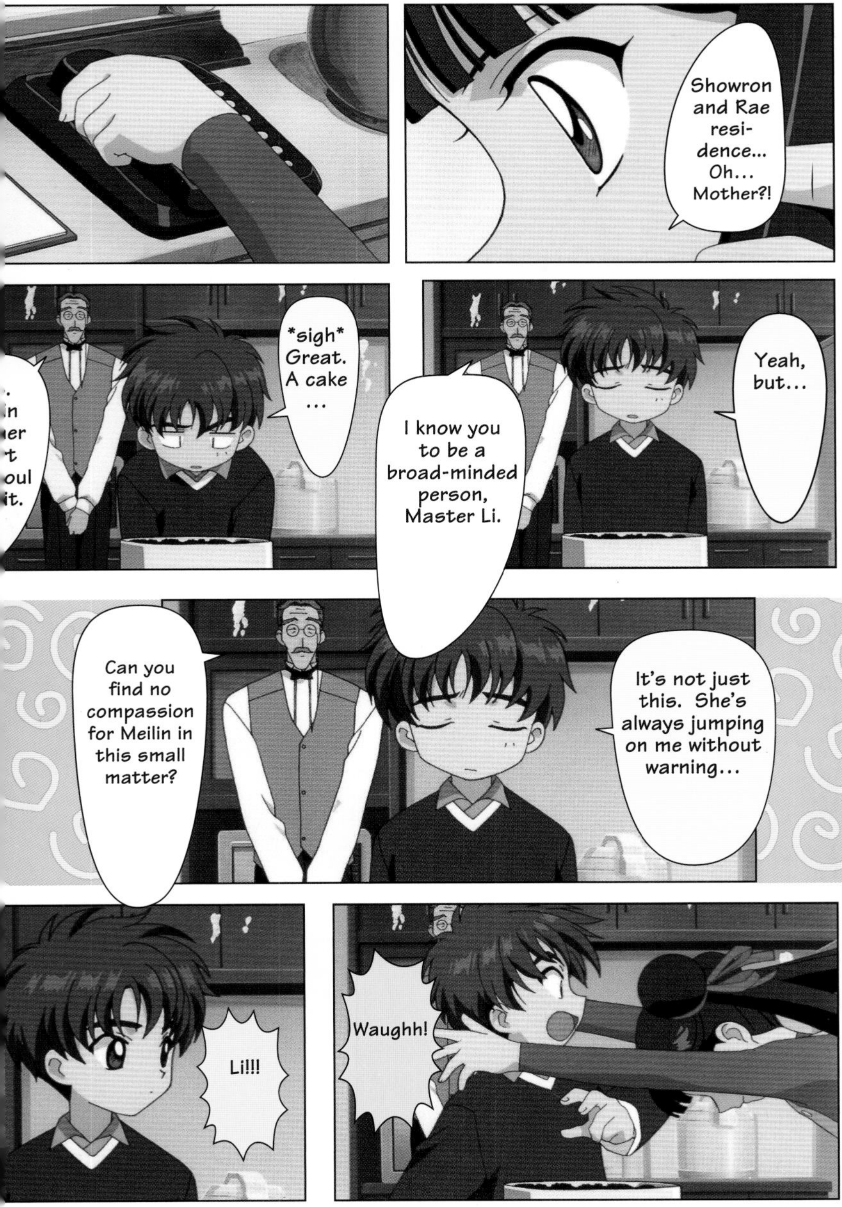
Showron and Rae resi-dence... Oh... Mother?!
sigh Great. A cake ...
I know you to be a broad-minded person, Master Li.
Yeah, but...
Can you find no compassion for Meilin in this small matter?
It's not just this. She's always jumping on me without warning...
Li!!!
Waughh!

That hurt!

Meilin! How ma[ny] times ha[ve] I told y[ou] not to [do] that?!

...What's wrong?

Meilin?

......

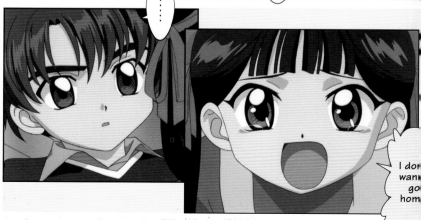

I do[n't] wann[a] go hom[e!]

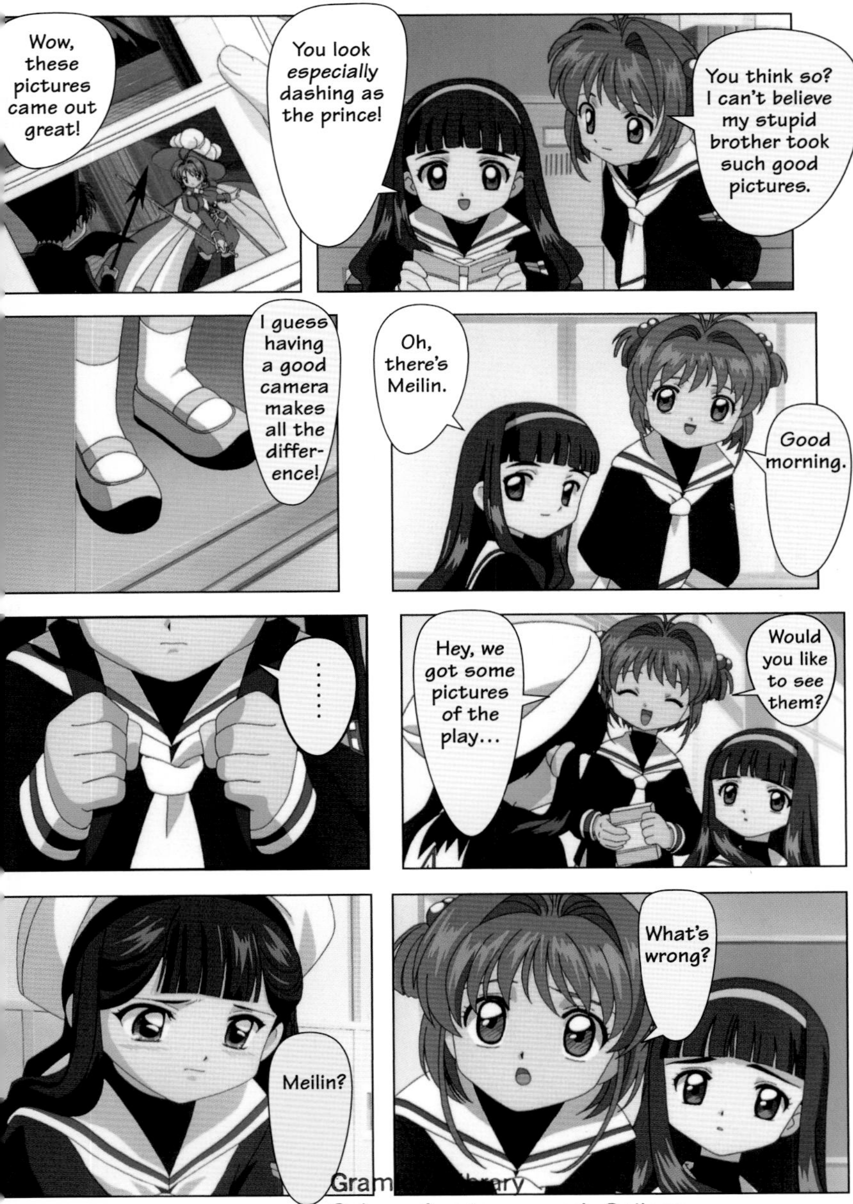
Wow, these pictures came out great!
You look *especially* dashing as the prince!
You think so? I can't believe my stupid brother took such good pictures.
I guess having a good camera makes all the differ-ence!
Oh, there's Meilin.
Good morning.
......
Hey, we got some pictures of the play...
Would you like to see them?
Meilin?
What's wrong?

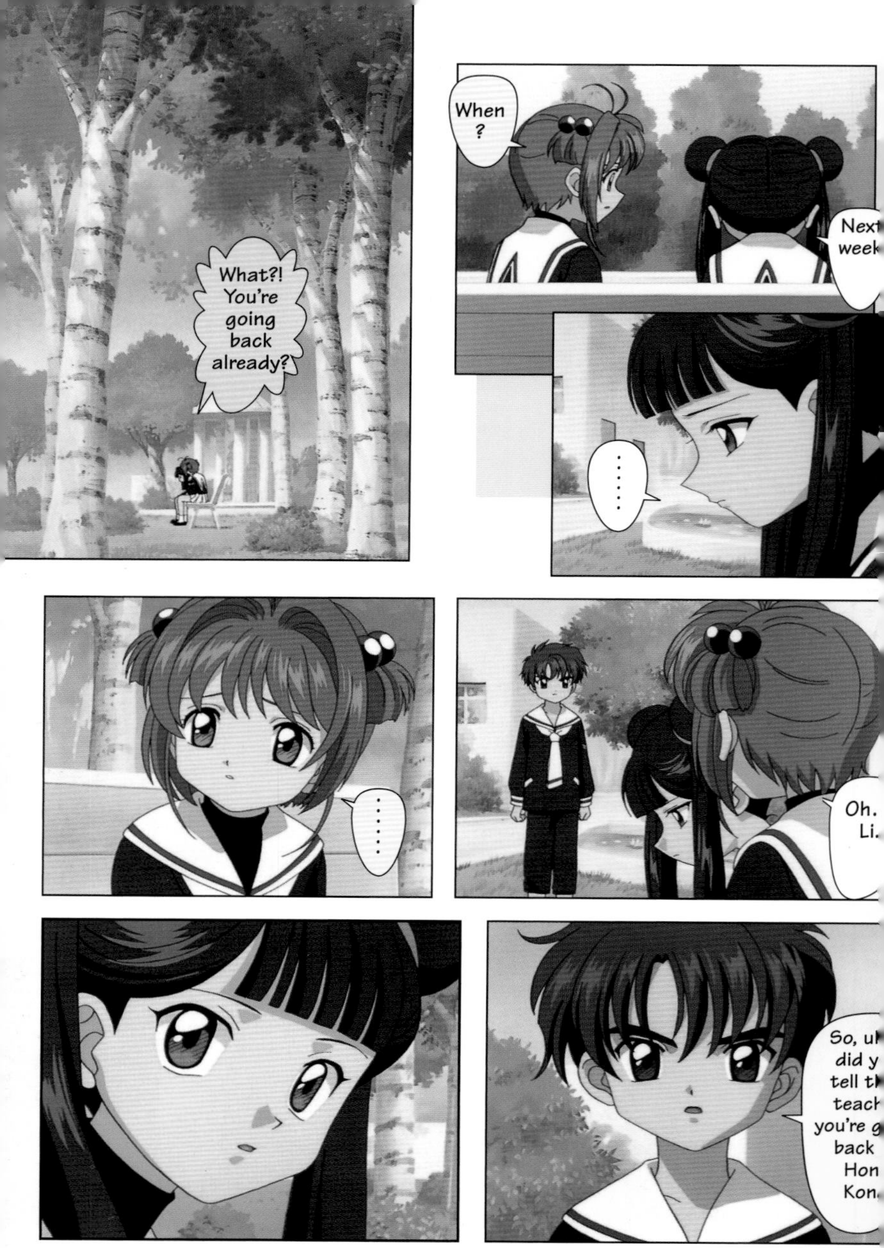

What?! You're going back already?
When ?
Nex wee
......
......
Oh. Li.
So, u did y tell t teach you're g back Hon Kon.

. . . . .

You should. Leaving a [co]untry is a big [d]eal, Meilin. [I]f you don't [t]ake all the necessary steps—

It can't be helped. Auntie says you need to go back.

...Can't be helped, huh?

You're glad I'm leaving! Aren't you?

[Whe]n I in [y]our [w]ay, [Meil]i?!

Huh?

It's true. I've been in your way since I got here, haven't I?

You're such a moron, Li!!

I never said that...

Hey, Meilin!

Meilin?!

sigh

Yeah.

So, she really is going home...

(14)

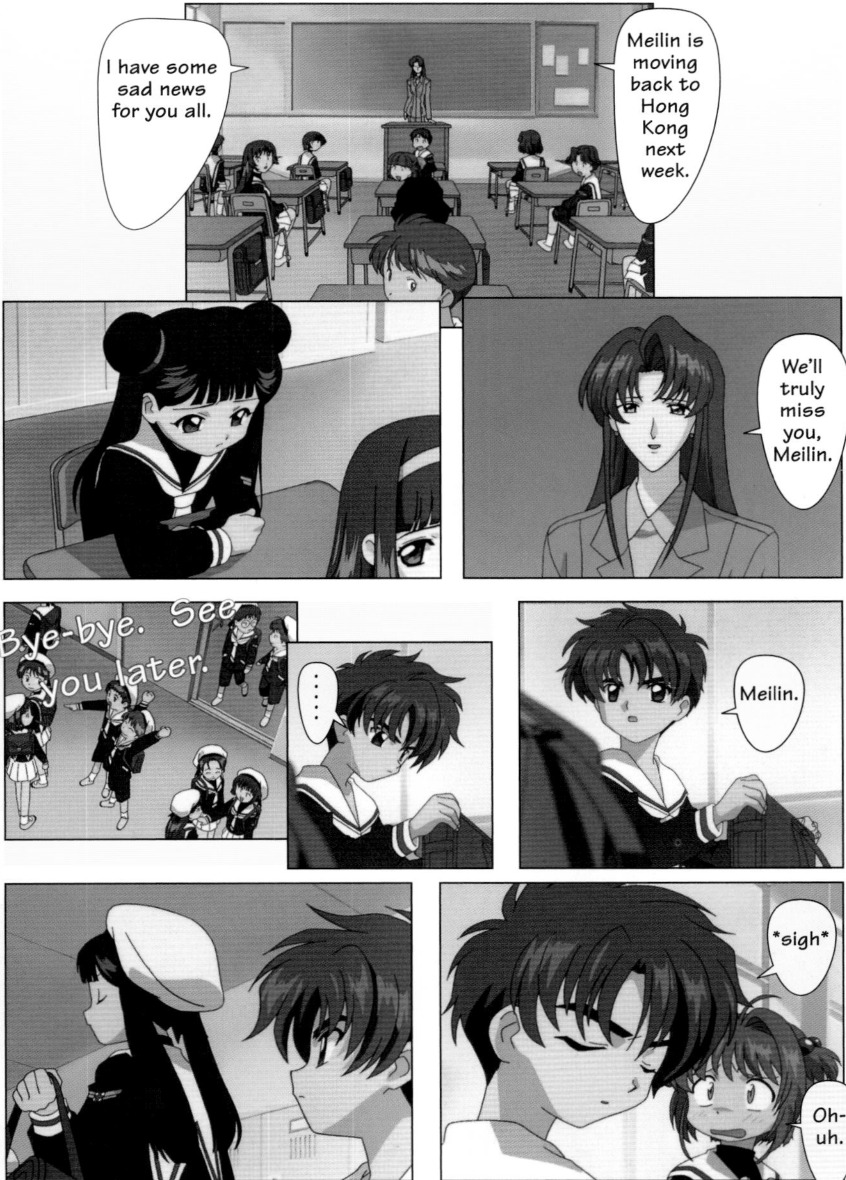
I have some sad news for you all.
Meilin is moving back to Hong Kong next week.
We'll truly miss you, Meilin.
Bye-bye. See you later.
......
Meilin.
sigh
Oh-uh.

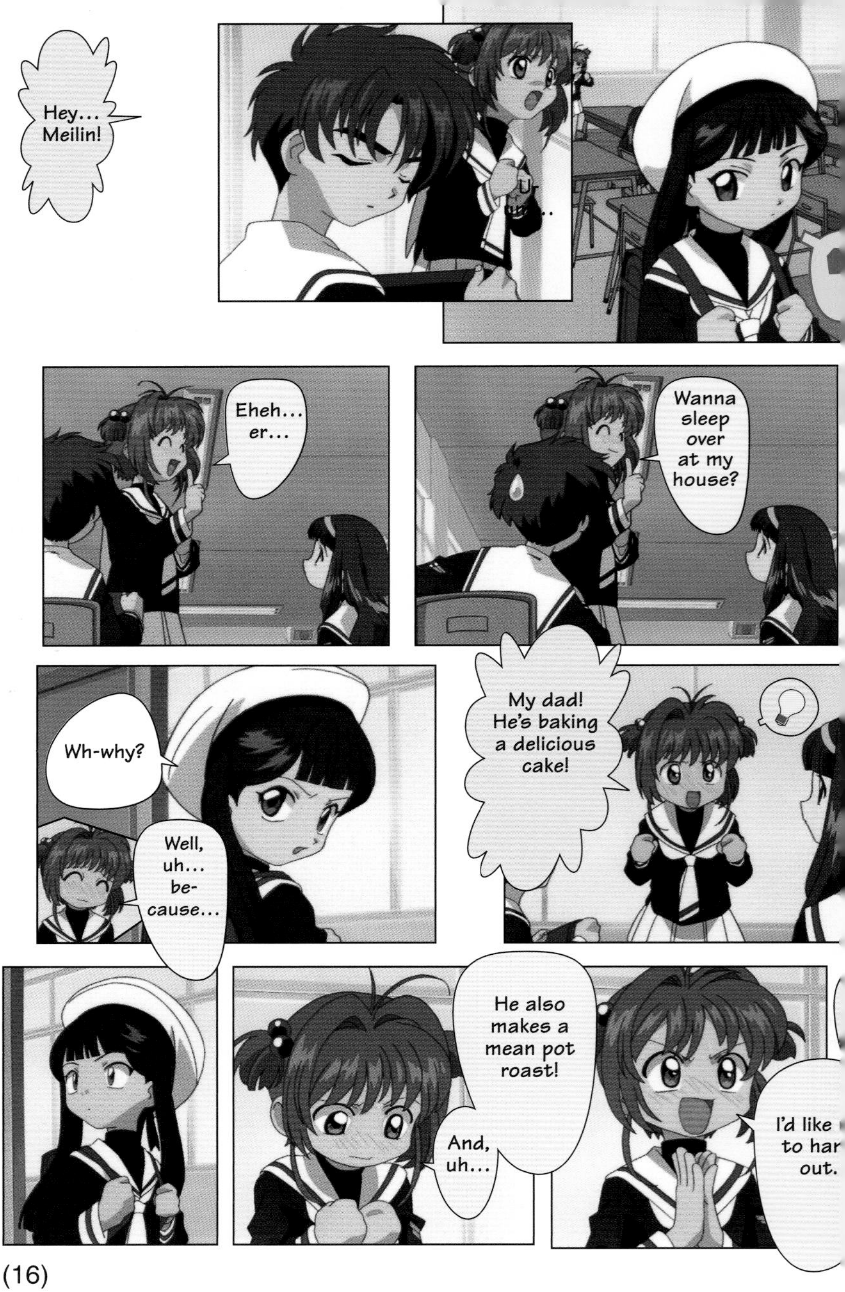
Hey... Meilin!
Eheh... er...
Wanna sleep over at my house?
Wh-why?
Well, uh... be-cause...
My dad! He's baking a delicious cake!
He also makes a mean pot roast!
And, uh...
I'd like to har out.

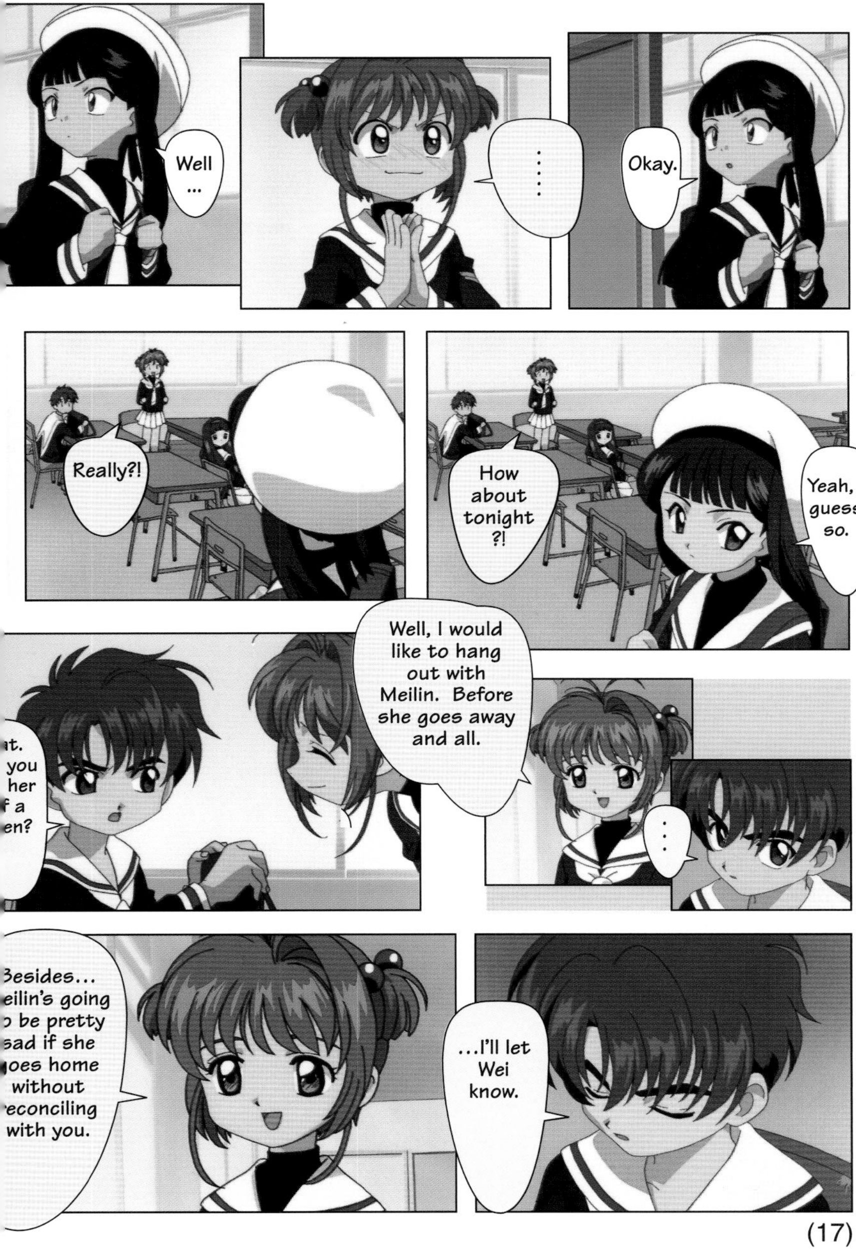
Well ...
.....
Okay.
Really?!
How about tonight ?!
Yeah, I guess so.
t. you her f a en?
Well, I would like to hang out with Meilin. Before she goes away and all.
...
esides... eilin's going o be pretty sad if she oes home without econciling with you.
...I'll let Wei know.

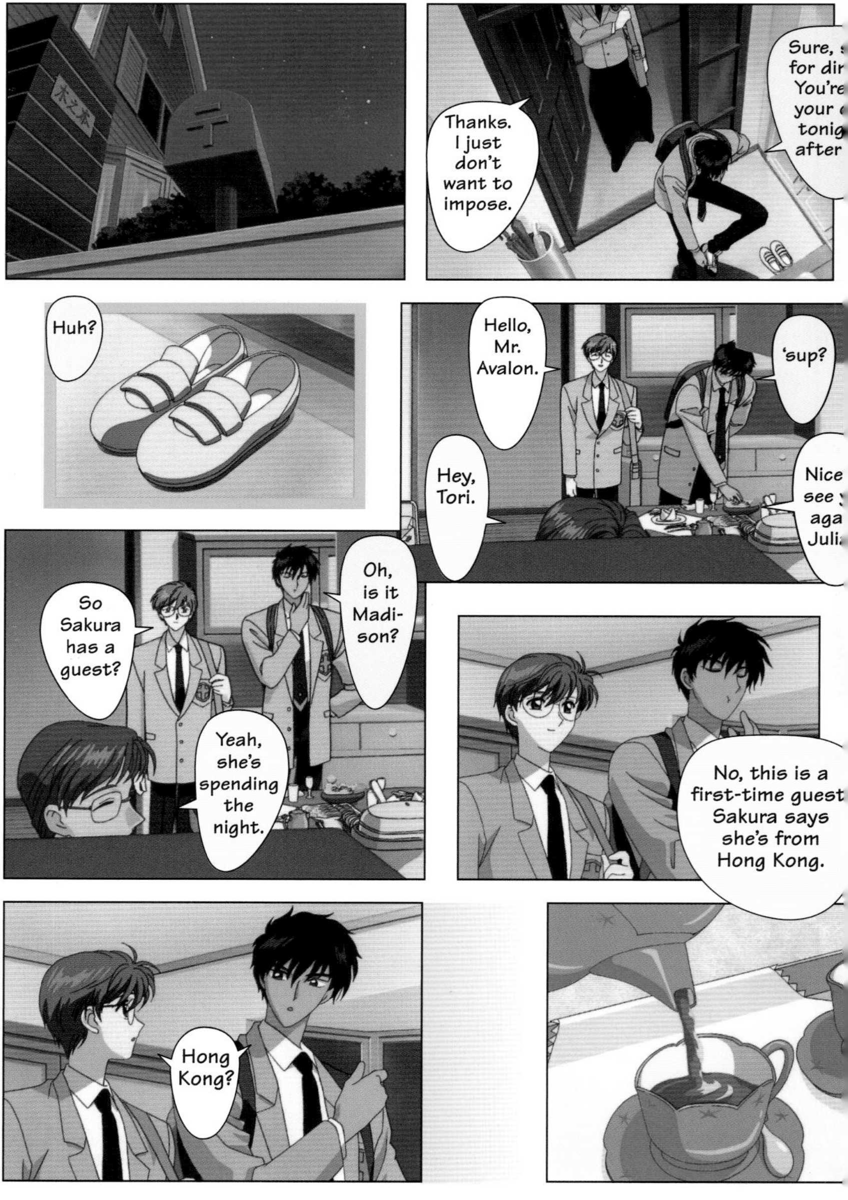
Sure, s
for dir
You're
your
tonig
after
Thanks. I just don't want to impose.
Huh?
Hello, Mr. Avalon.
'sup?
Hey, Tori.
Nice
see
aga
Juli
So Sakura has a guest?
Oh, is it Madison?
Yeah, she's spending the night.
No, this is a first-time guest Sakura says she's from Hong Kong.
Hong Kong?

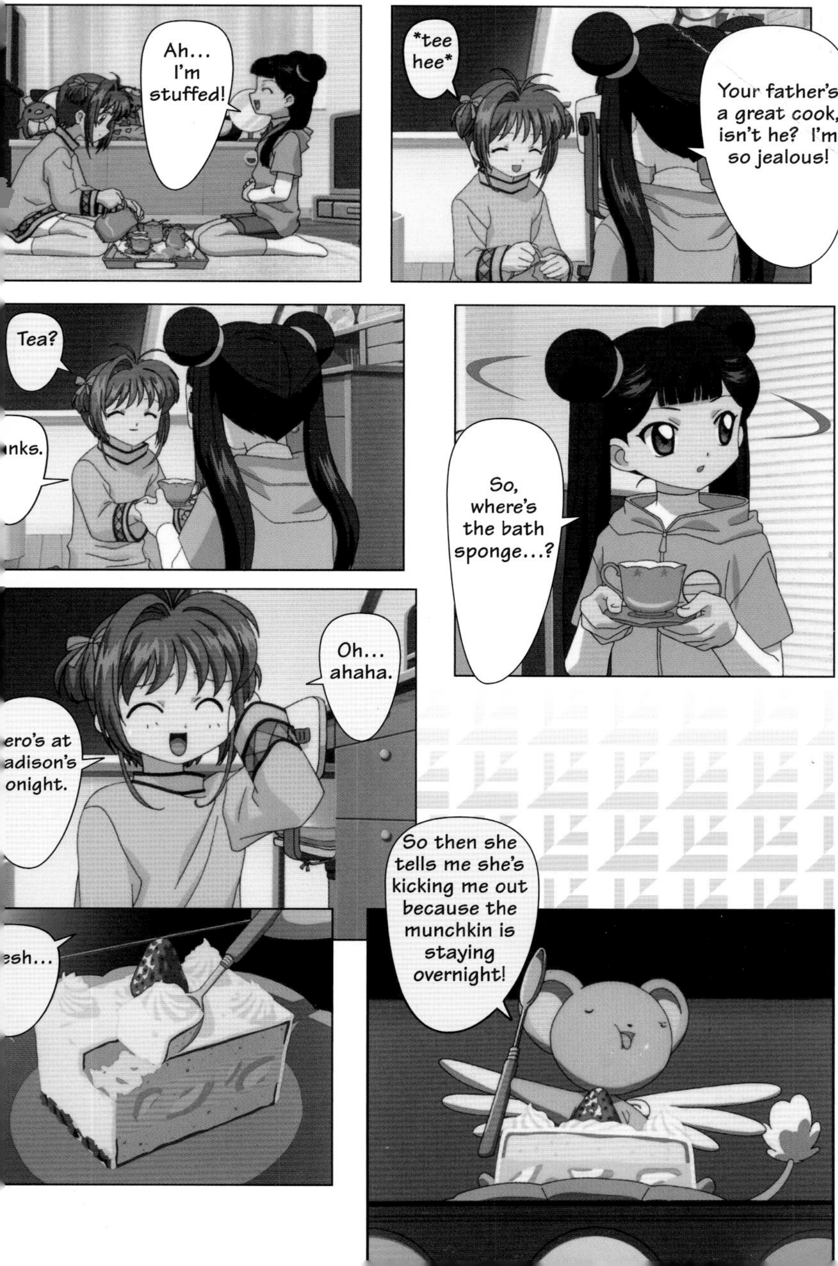
Ah... I'm stuffed!
tee hee
Your father's a great cook, isn't he? I'm so jealous!
Tea?
nks.
So, where's the bath sponge...?
Oh... ahaha.
ero's at adison's onight.
esh...
So then she tells me she's kicking me out because the munchkin is staying overnight!

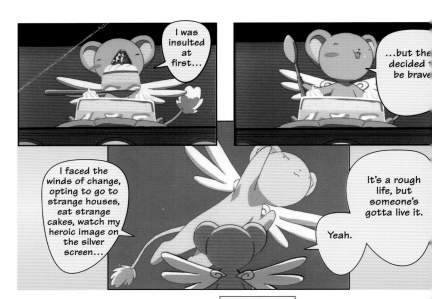

I was insulted at first...

...but the decided to be brave

I faced the winds of change, opting to go to strange houses, eat strange cakes, watch my heroic image on the silver screen...

It's a rough life, but someone's gotta live it.

Yeah.

giggle

I'm glad that Sakura's finally hanging out with Meilin... but I wish I could be there, too.

Oh! This is delicious, too!

So's this!

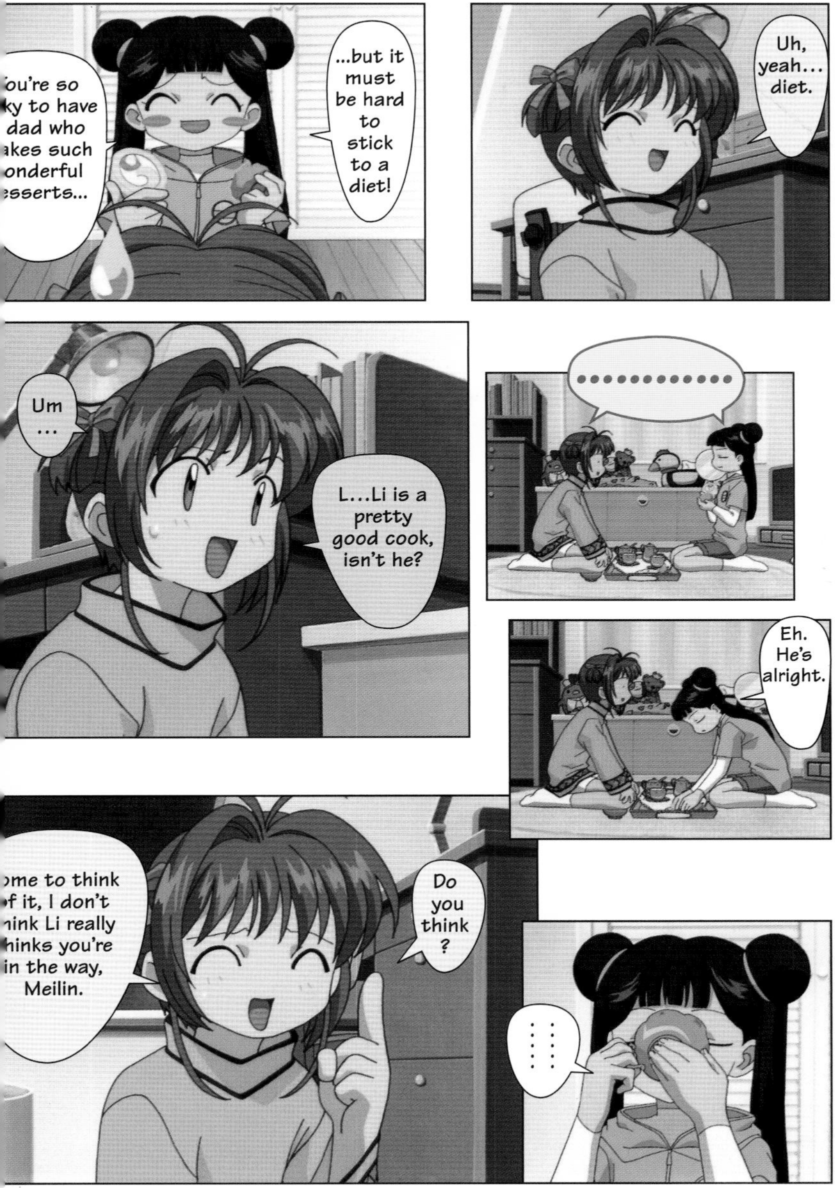
ou're so ky to have dad who akes such onderful esserts...
...but it must be hard to stick to a diet!
Uh, yeah... diet.
Um ...
L...Li is a pretty good cook, isn't he?
....
Eh. He's alright.
ome to think f it, I don't ink Li really hinks you're in the way, Meilin.
Do you think ?
....

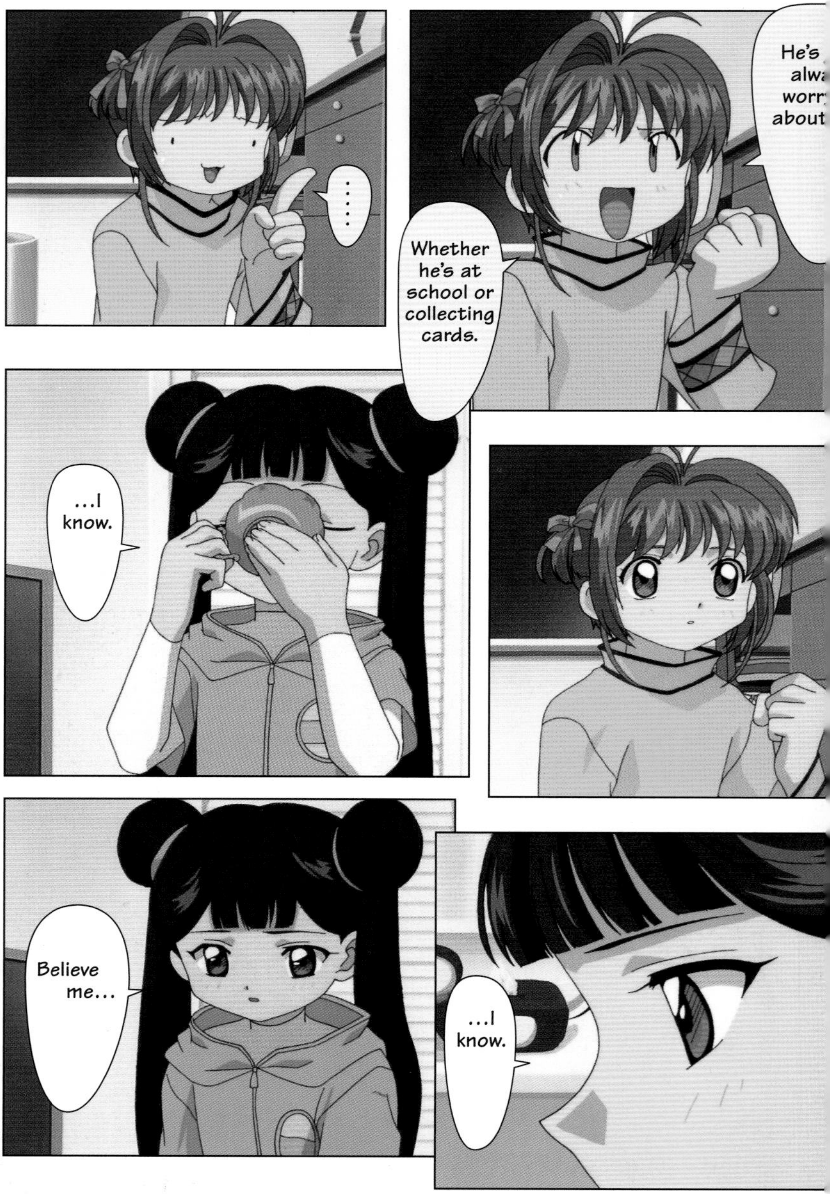
……
He's
Whether he's at school or collecting cards.
…I know.
Believe me…
…I know.

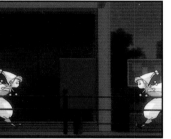

Hmm hmm hmmm...

Wha-- ?

I don't remember two mailboxes being here...

Of course he worries, but that's not how I want him to feel.

I see what you mean.

Let's talk about you, Sakura! When did you start to like that guy?

Uh, Julian? Well...

Was it love at first sight?

...he's in the same grade as my big brother... and... he visits a lot. So I just...

...Yea

(24)

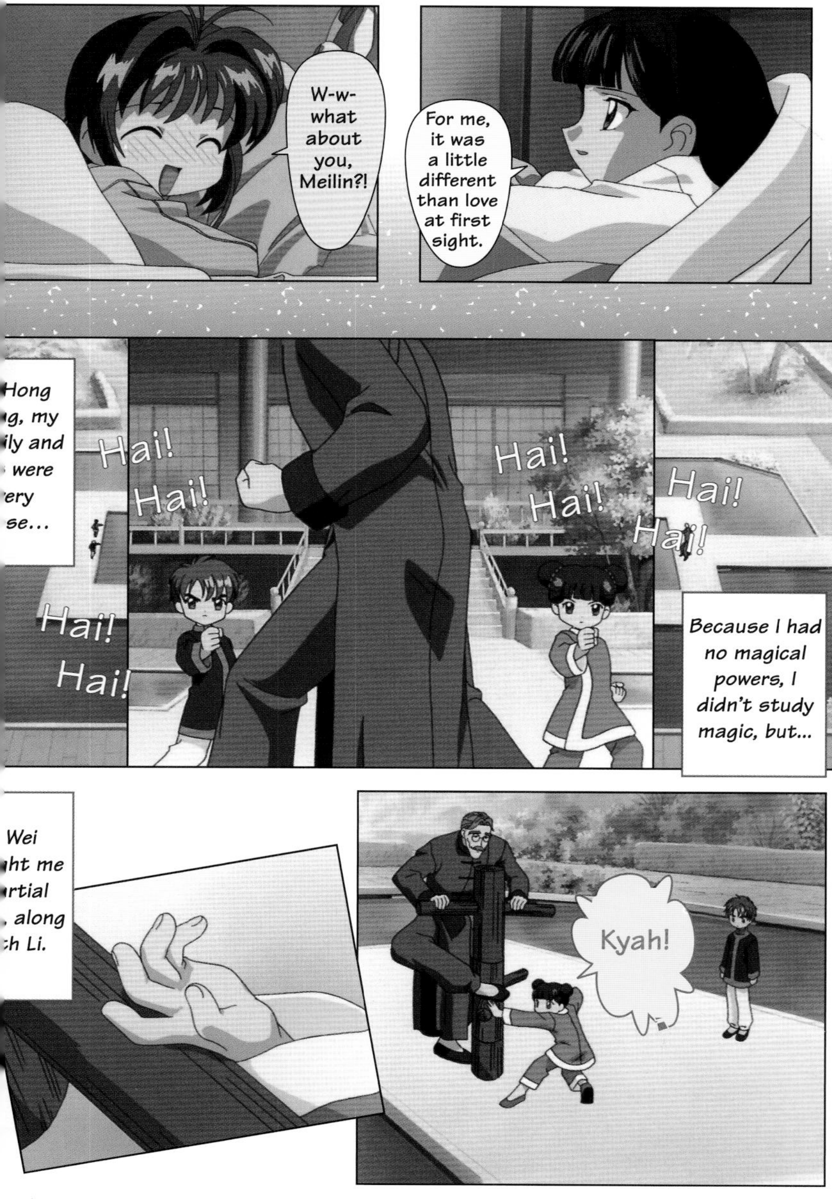
W-w-what about you, Meilin?!
For me, it was a little different than love at first sight.
Hong g, my ily and were ery se...
Hai! Hai!
Hai! Hai!
Hai! Hai!
Hai! Hai!
Because I had no magical powers, I didn't study magic, but...
Wei ht me rtial , along h Li.
Kyah!

Hai-yah!

Heh, heh, heh.

Eheh eheh...

N y

...

But...

Tah!

Li di smile a

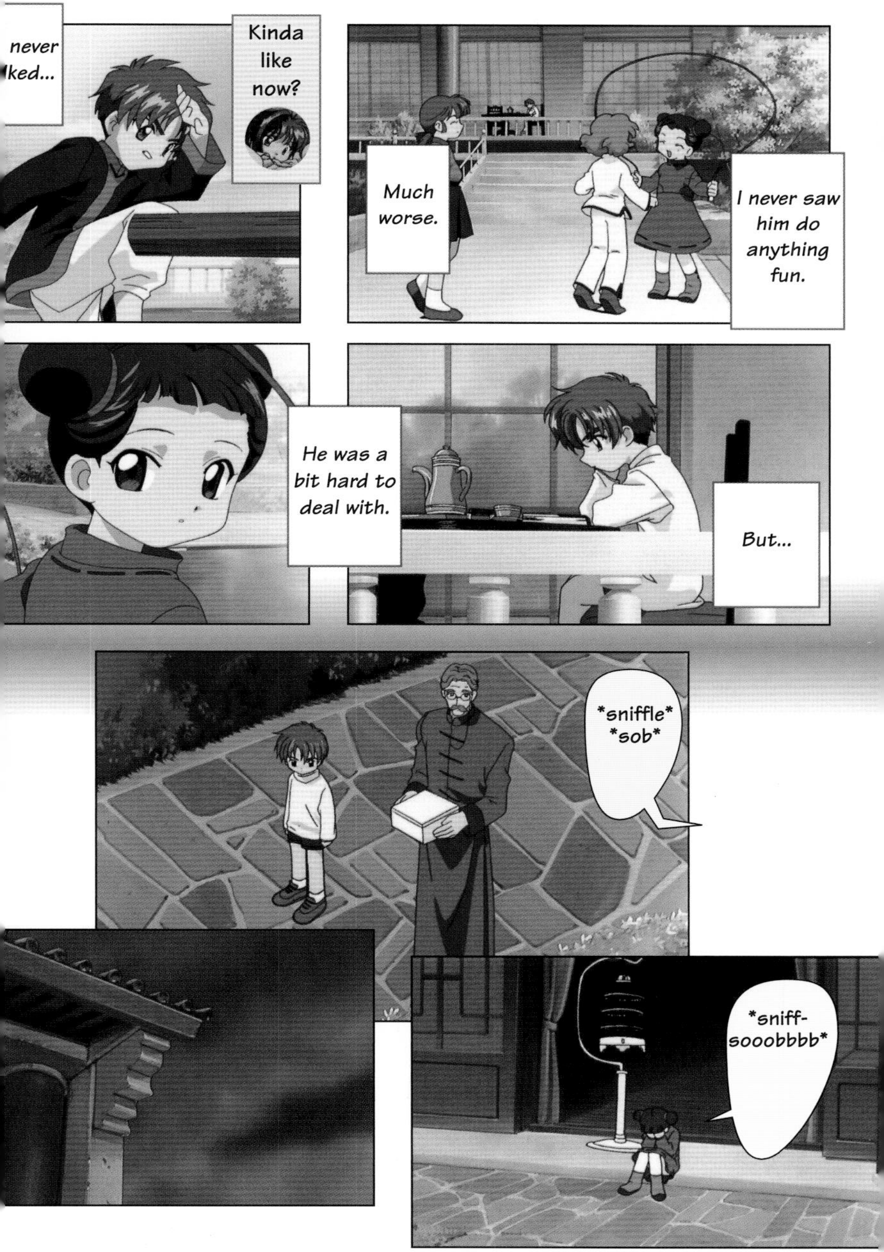
never
ked...
Kinda like now?
Much worse.
I never saw him do anything fun.
He was a bit hard to deal with.
But...
sniffle *sob*
sniff-sooobbbb

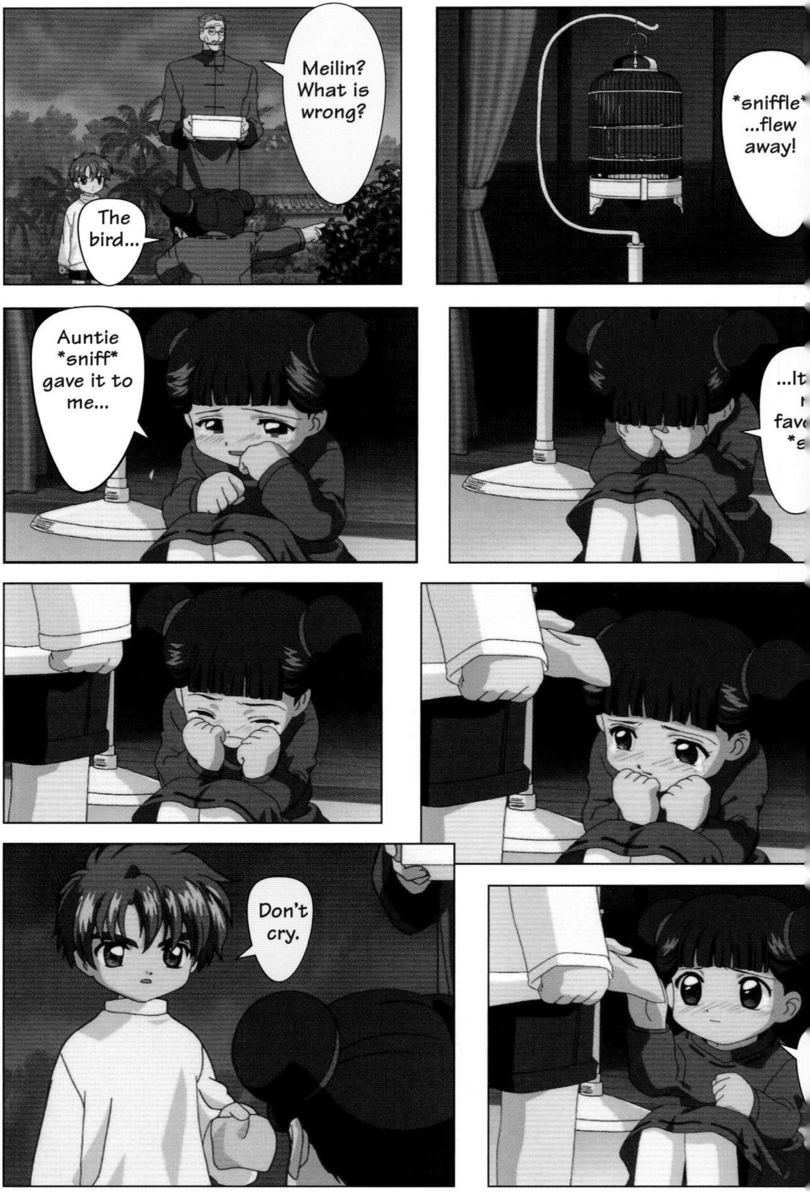
Meilin? What is wrong?
The bird...
sniffle ...flew away!
Auntie *sniff* gave it to me...
...It
Don't cry.

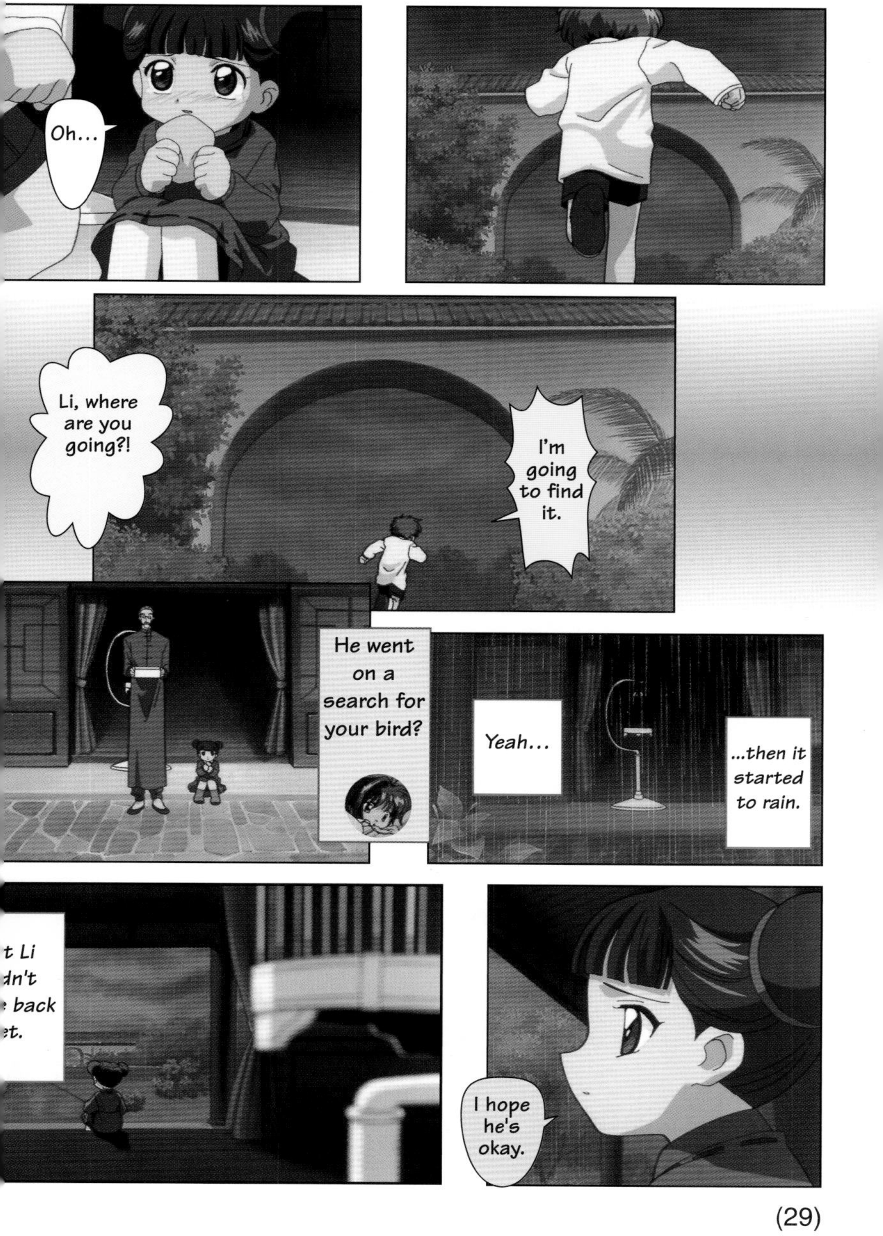

Oh...
Li, where are you going?!
I'm going to find it.
He went on a search for your bird?
Yeah...
...then it started to rain.
t Li dn't back et.
I hope he's okay.

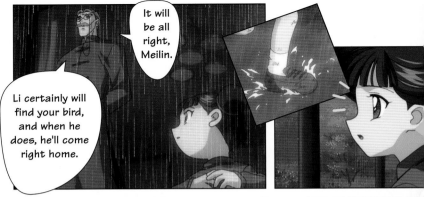

It will be all right, Meilin.

Li certainly will find your bird, and when he does, he'll come right home.

...Li?

Huff

*Huf

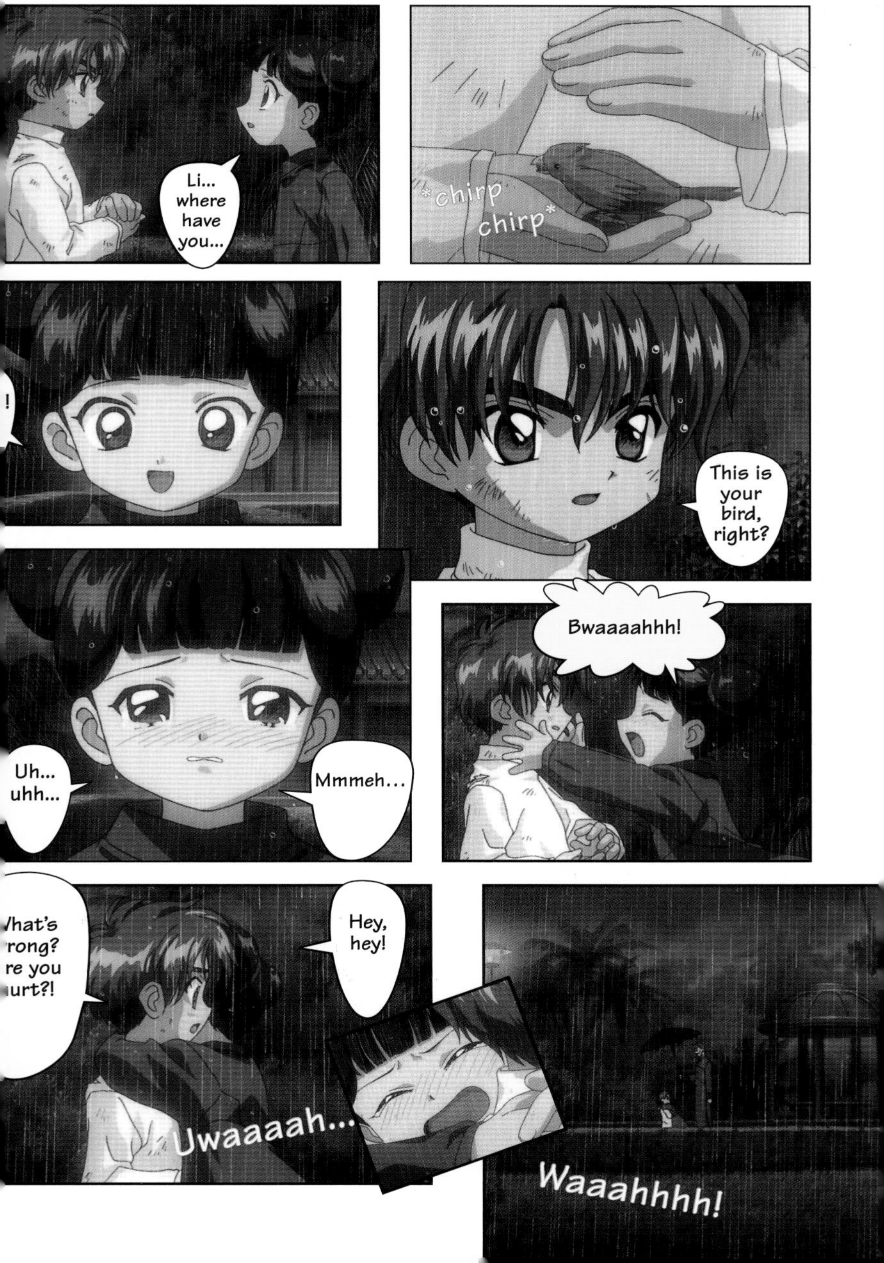

Li... where have you...
chirp chirp
!
This is your bird, right?
Uh... uhh...
Mmmeh...
Bwaaaahhh!
hat's rong? re you urt?!
Hey, hey!
Uwaaaah...
Waaahhhh!

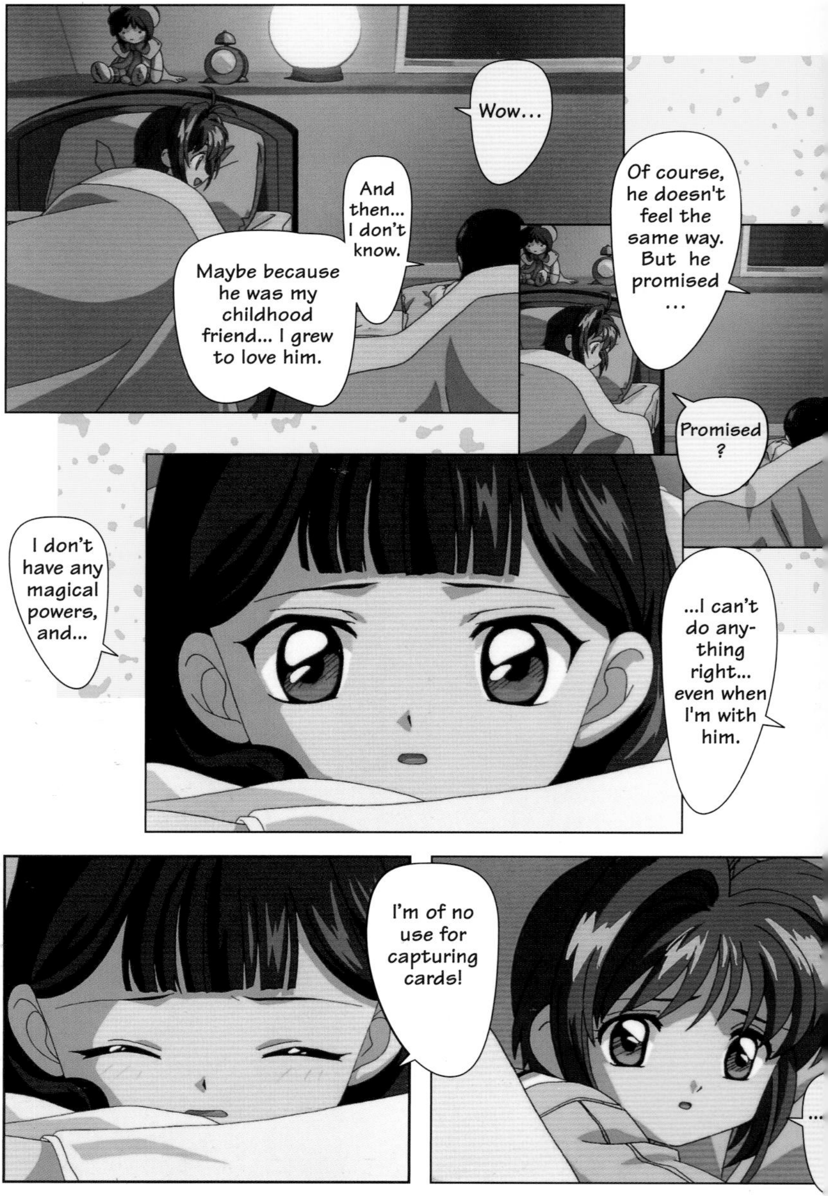
Wow...
And then... I don't know.
Maybe because he was my childhood friend... I grew to love him.
Of course, he doesn't feel the same way. But he promised ...
Promised ?
I don't have any magical powers, and...
...I can't do any-thing right... even when I'm with him.
I'm of no use for capturing cards!
...

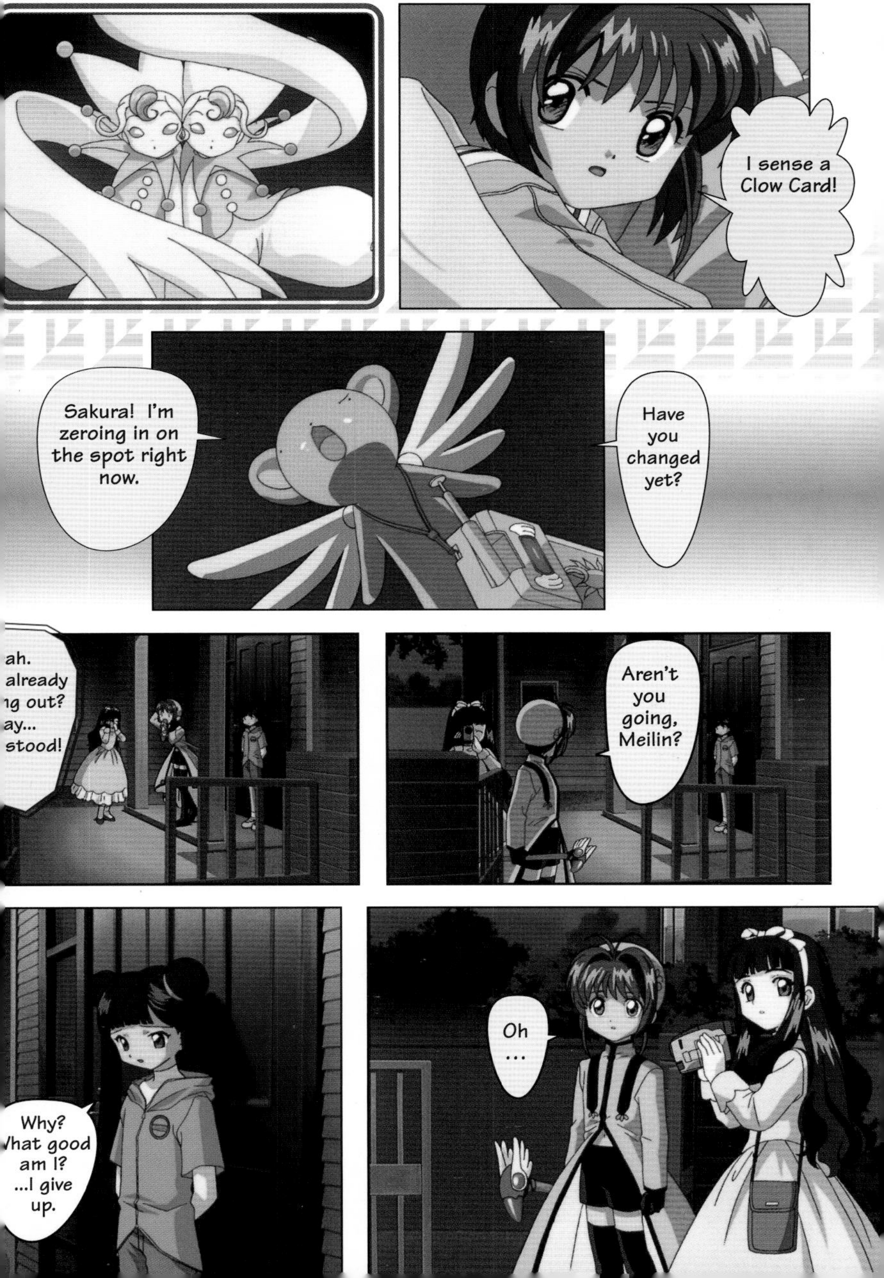

I sense a Clow Card!
Sakura! I'm zeroing in on the spot right now.
Have you changed yet?
ah. already ng out? ay... stood!
Aren't you going, Meilin?
Why? hat good am I? ...I give up.
Oh ...

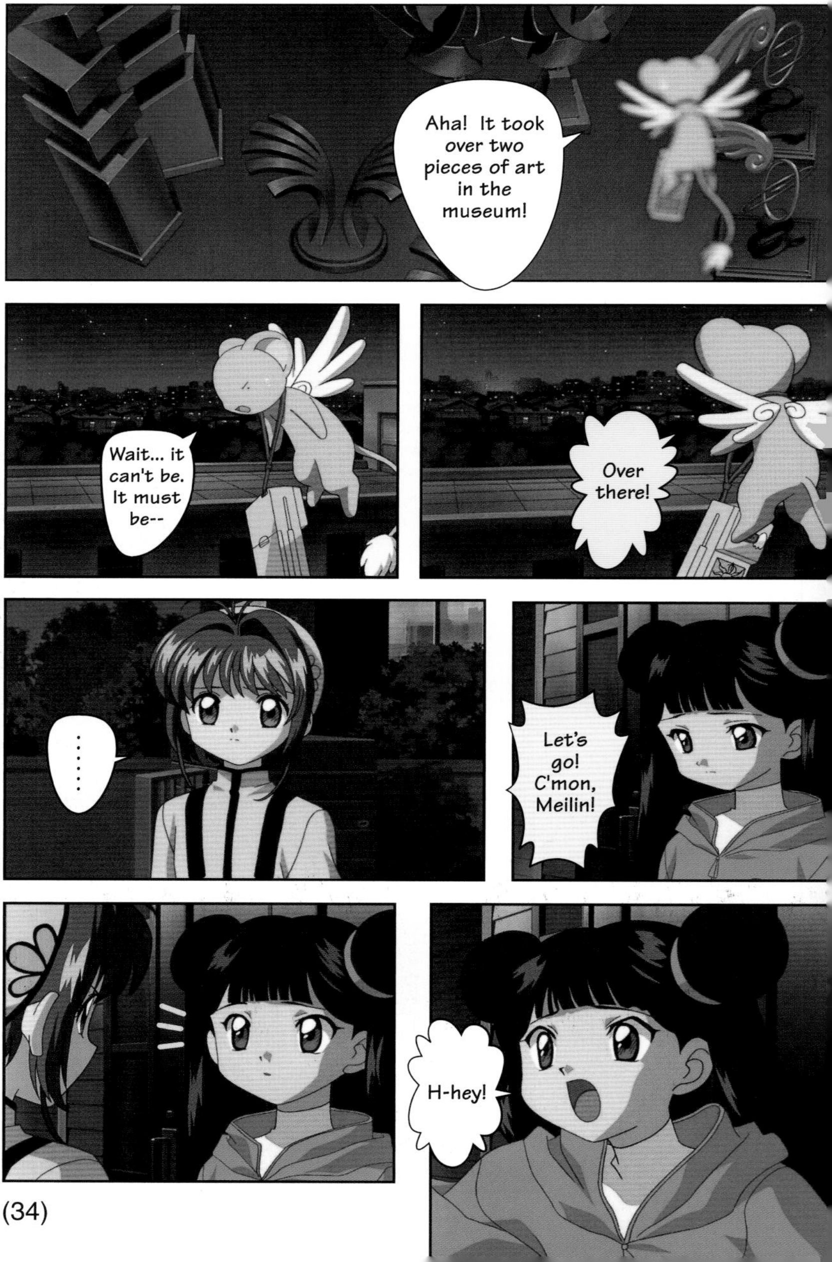

Aha! It took over two pieces of art in the museum!
Wait... it can't be. It must be--
Over there!
......
Let's go! C'mon, Meilin!
H-hey!

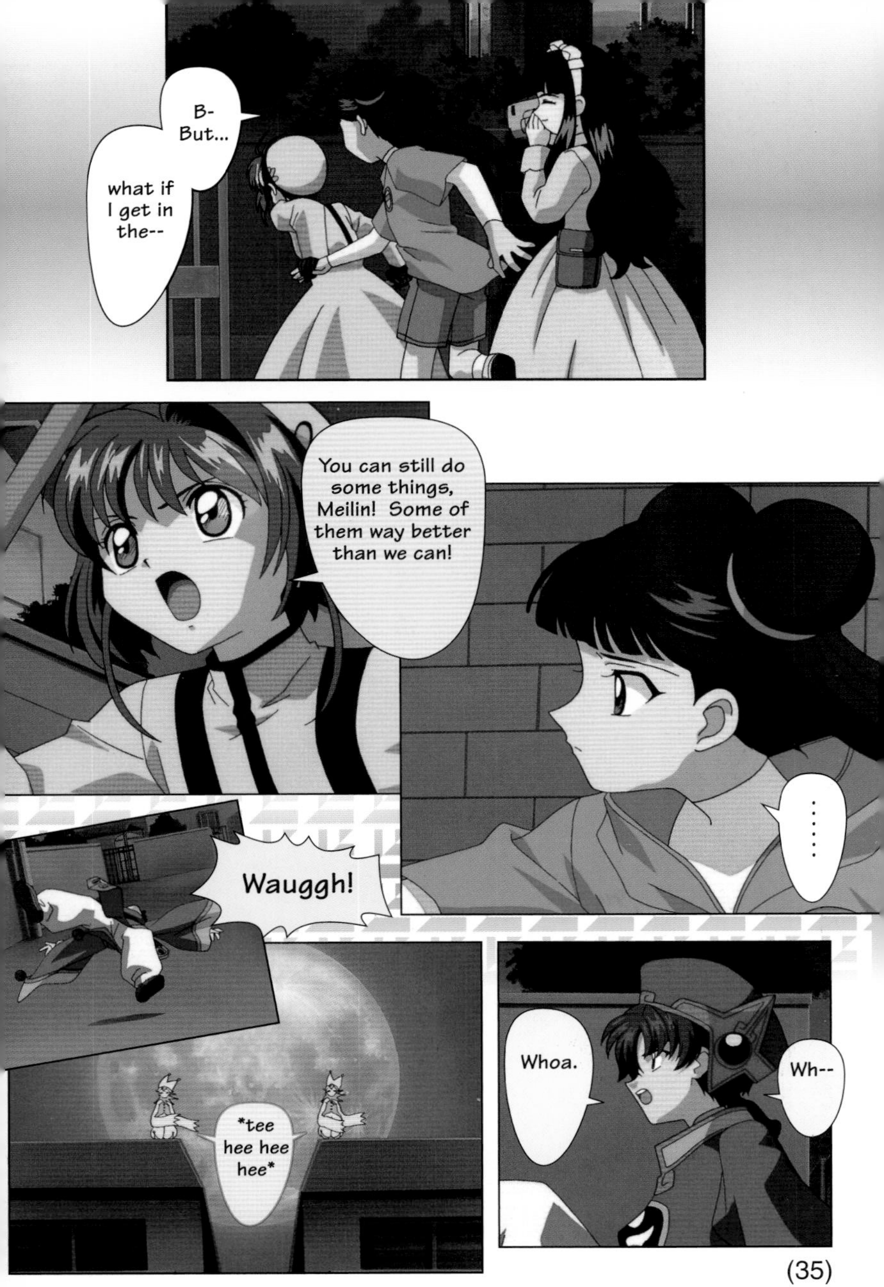
B- But...
what if I get in the--
You can still do some things, Meilin! Some of them way better than we can!
......
Waugghh!
tee hee hee hee
Whoa.
Wh--

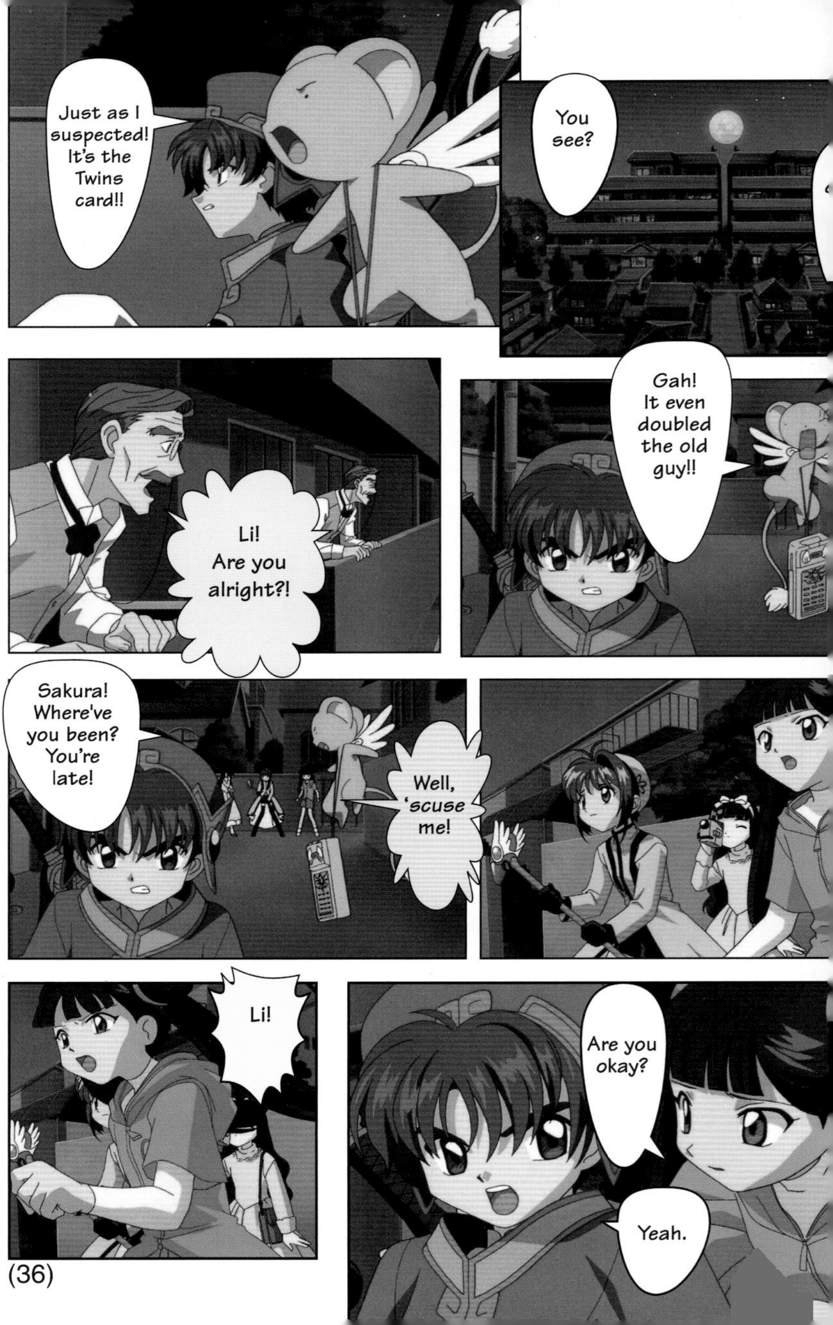
Just as I suspected! It's the Twins card!!
You see?
Li! Are you alright?!
Gah! It even doubled the old guy!!
Sakura! Where've you been? You're late!
Well, 'scuse me!
Li!
Are you okay?
Yeah.

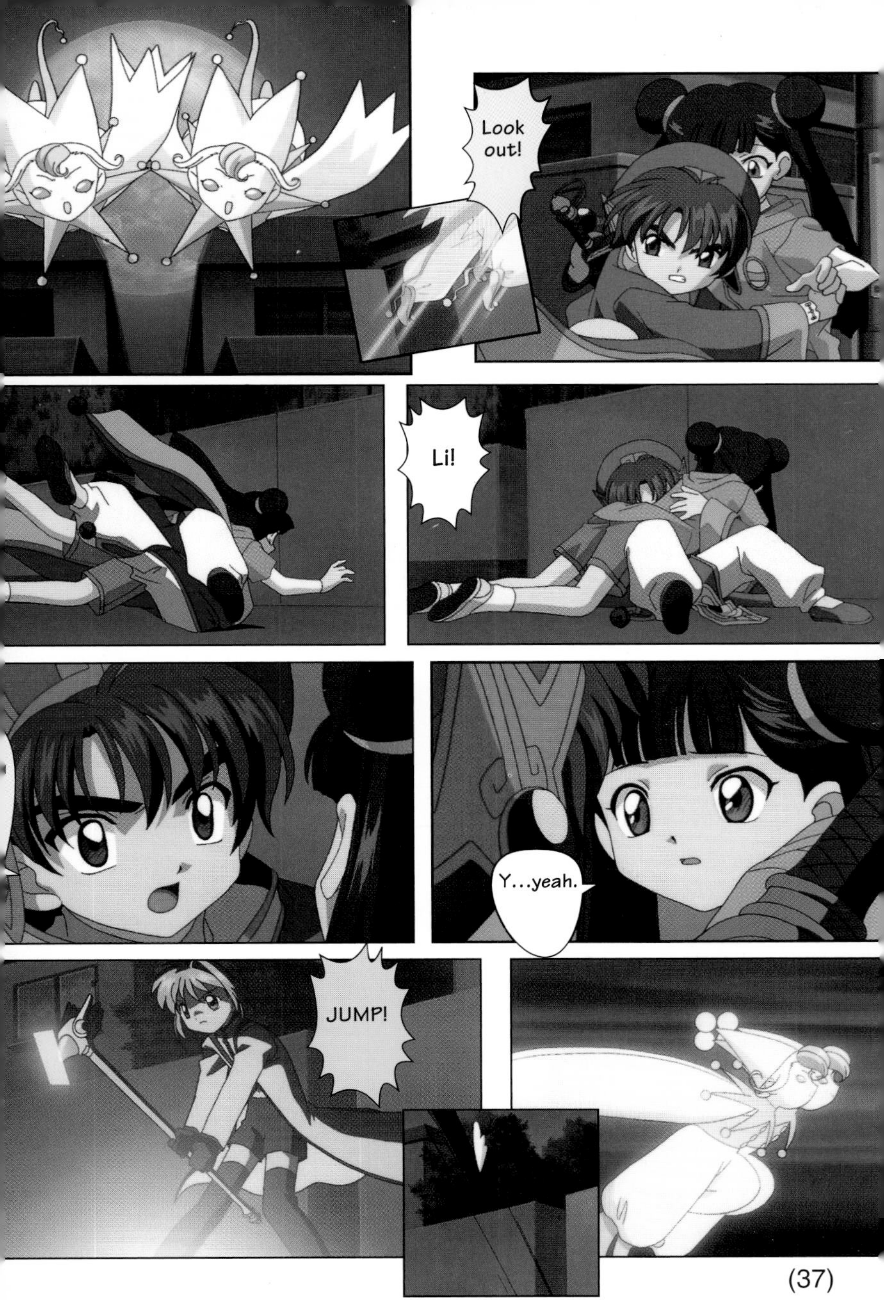
Look out!
Li!
Y...yeah.
JUMP!

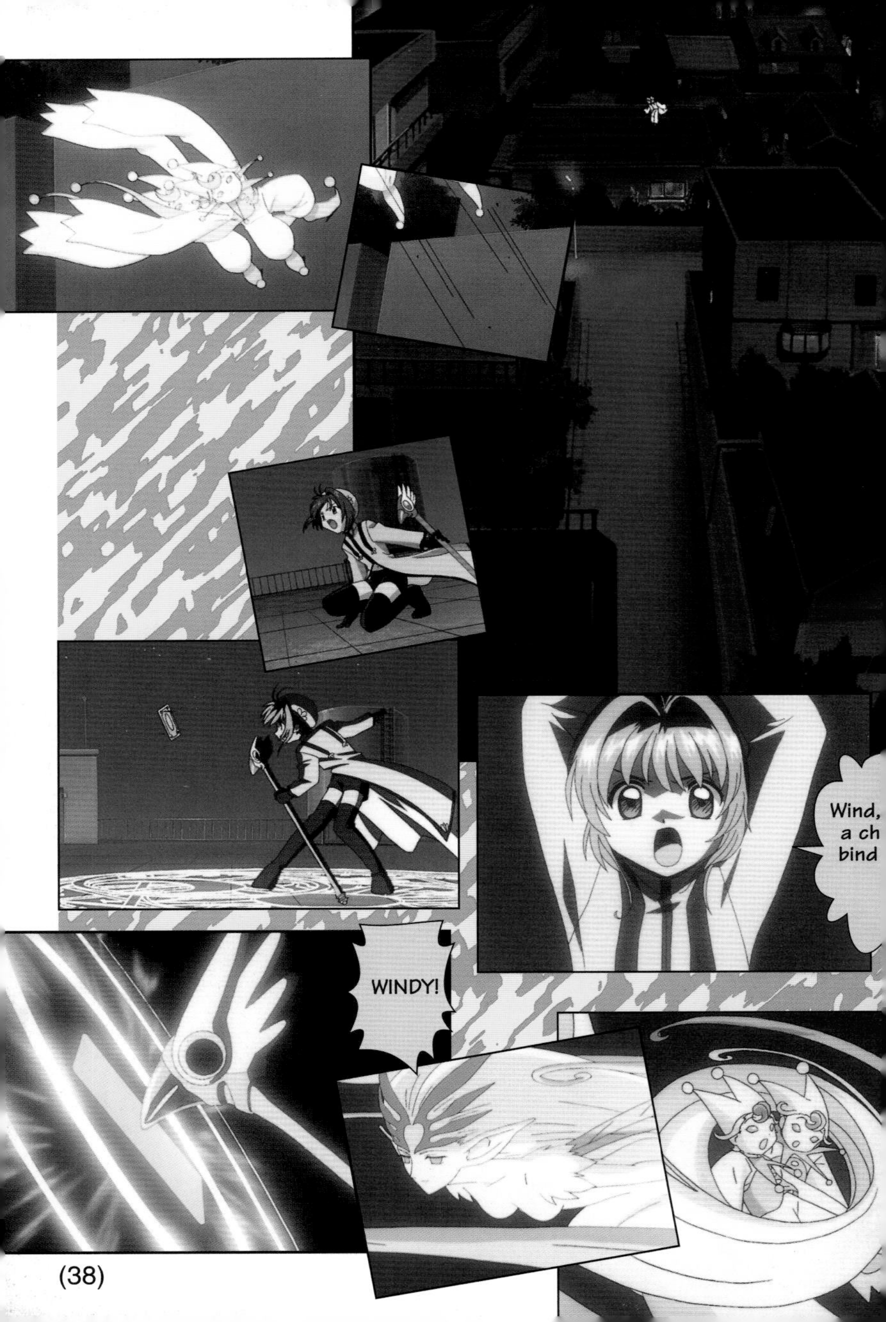
Wind, a ch bind
WINDY!

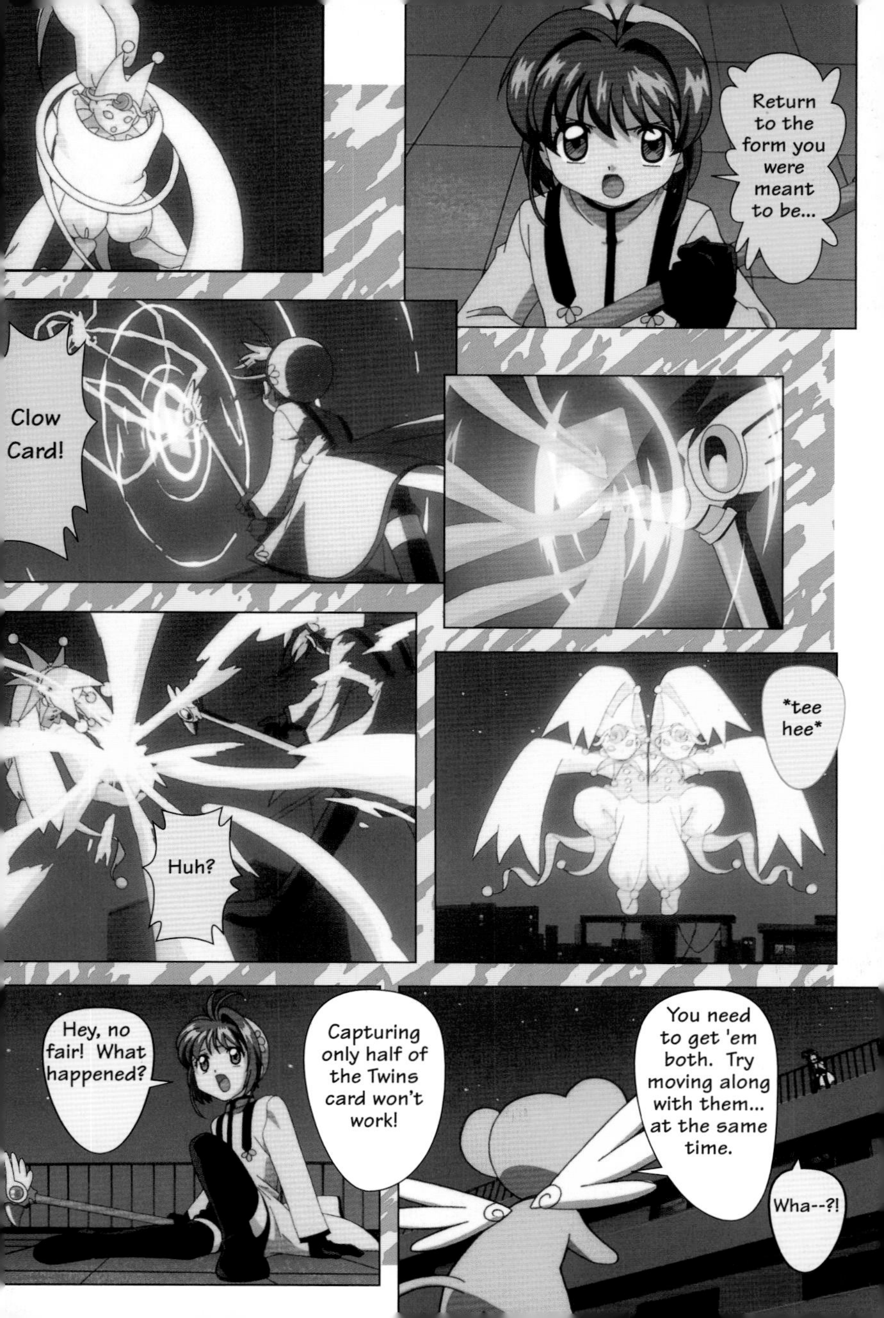
Return to the form you were meant to be...
Clow Card!
Huh?
tee hee
Hey, no fair! What happened?
Capturing only half of the Twins card won't work!
You need to get 'em both. Try moving along with them... at the same time.
Wha--?!

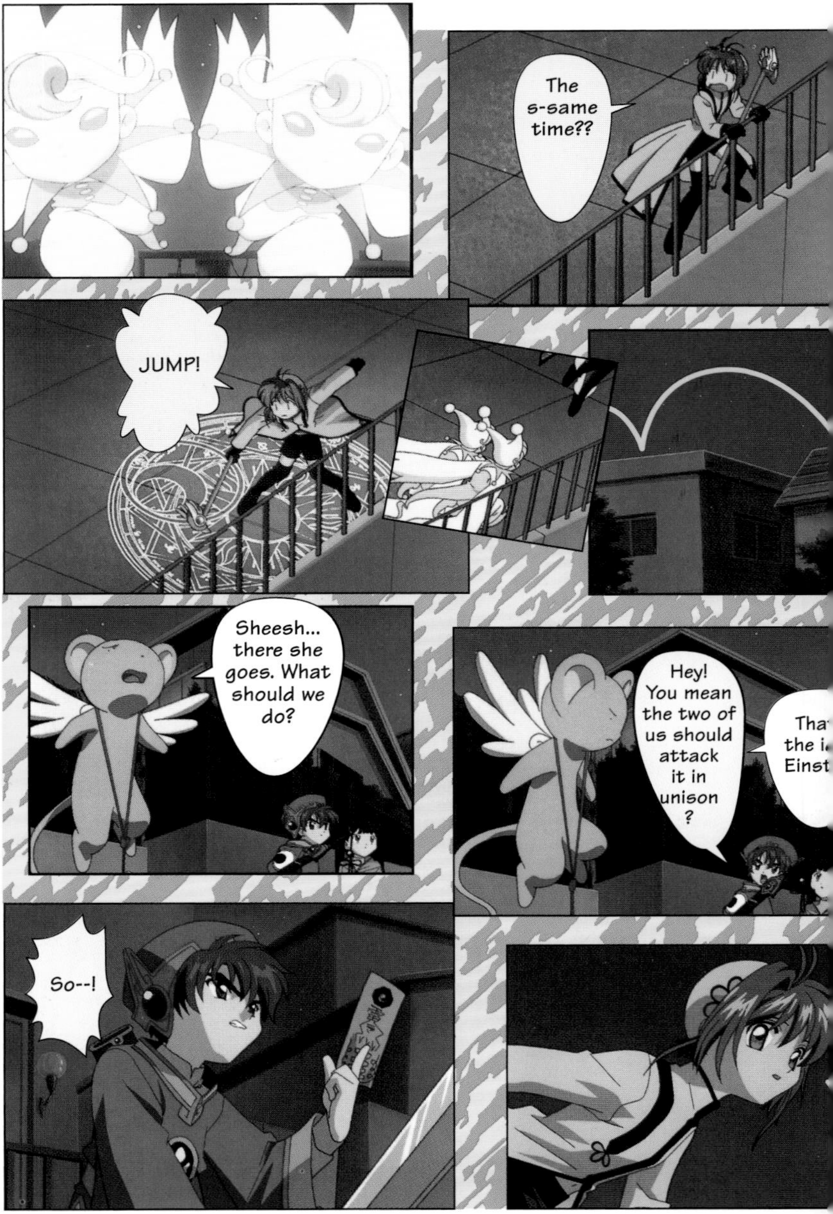
The s-same time??
JUMP!
Sheesh... there she goes. What should we do?
Hey! You mean the two of us should attack it in unison ?
Tha the i Einst
So--!

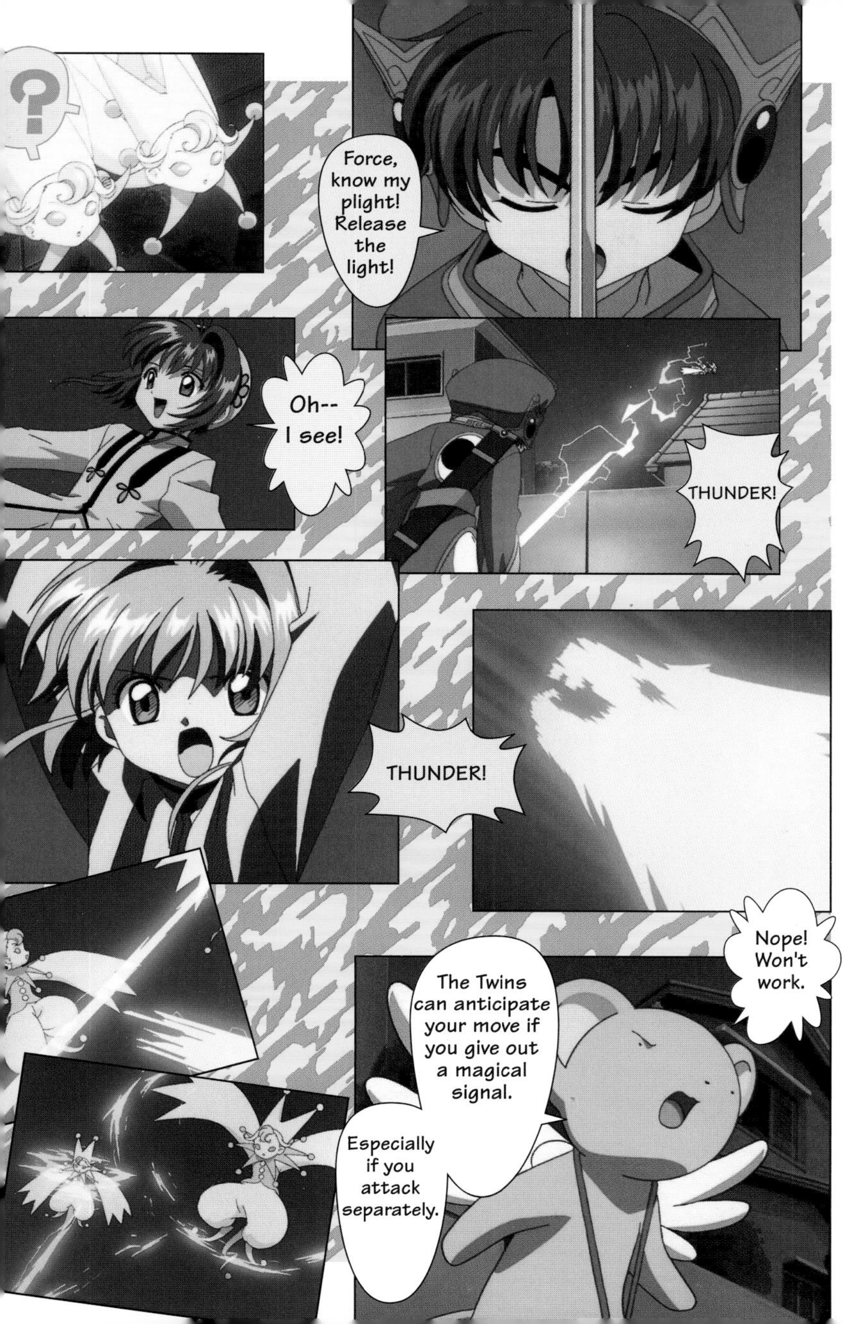
?
Force, know my plight! Release the light!
Oh-- I see!
THUNDER!
THUNDER!
Nope! Won't work.
The Twins can anticipate your move if you give out a magical signal.
Especially if you attack separately.

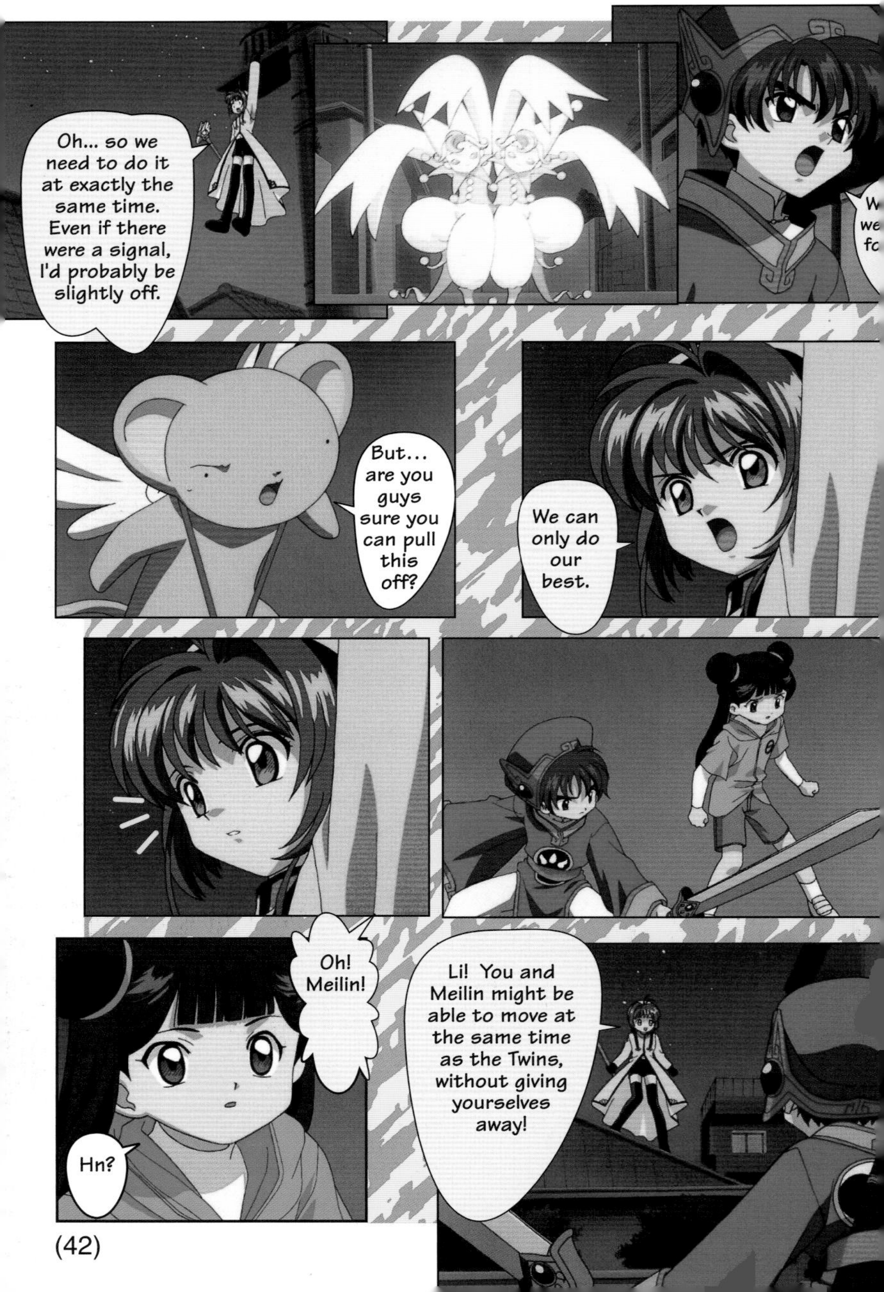
Oh... so we need to do it at exactly the same time. Even if there were a signal, I'd probably be slightly off.
But... are you guys sure you can pull this off?
We can only do our best.
Oh! Meilin!
Hn?
Li! You and Meilin might be able to move at the same time as the Twins, without giving yourselves away!

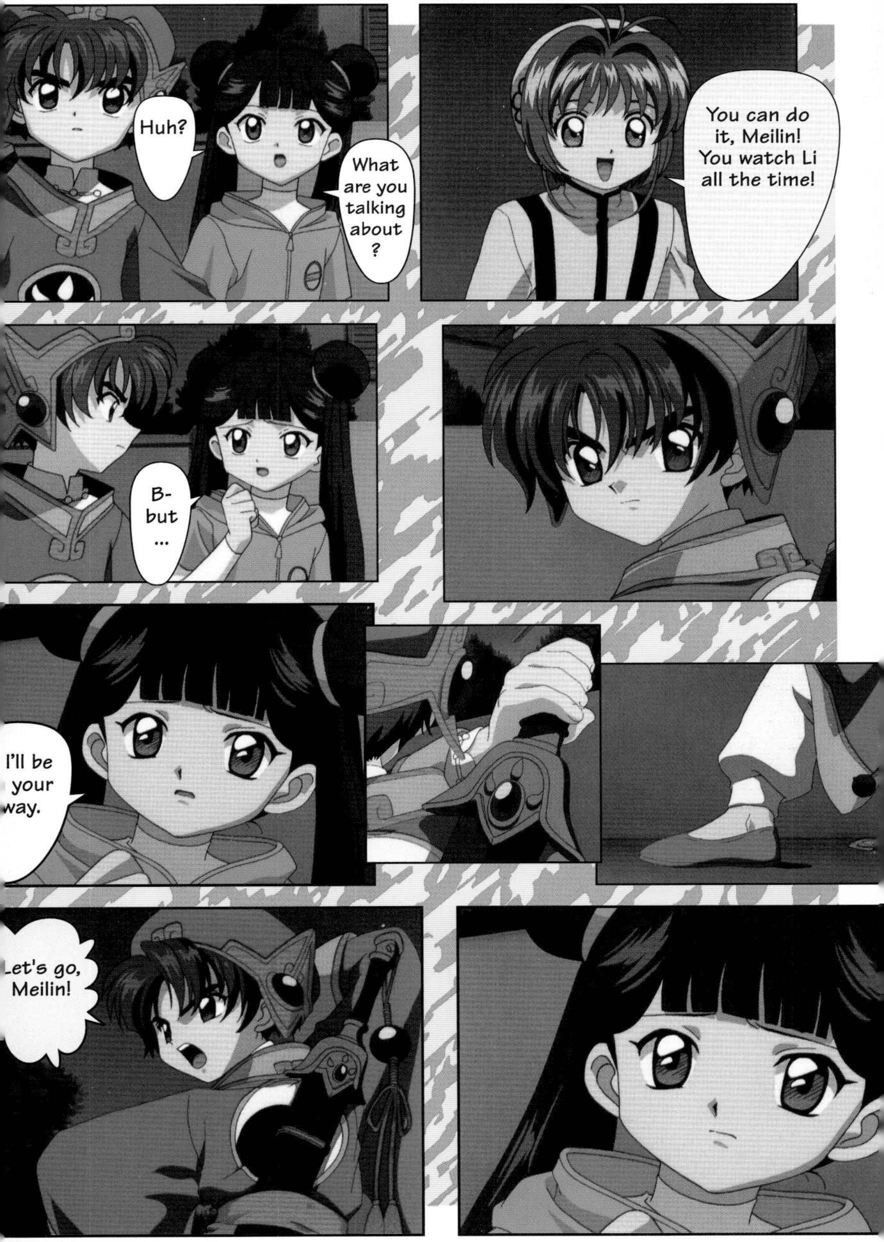
Huh?
What are you talking about?
You can do it, Meilin! You watch Li all the time!
B-but ...
I'll be your way.
Let's go, Meilin!

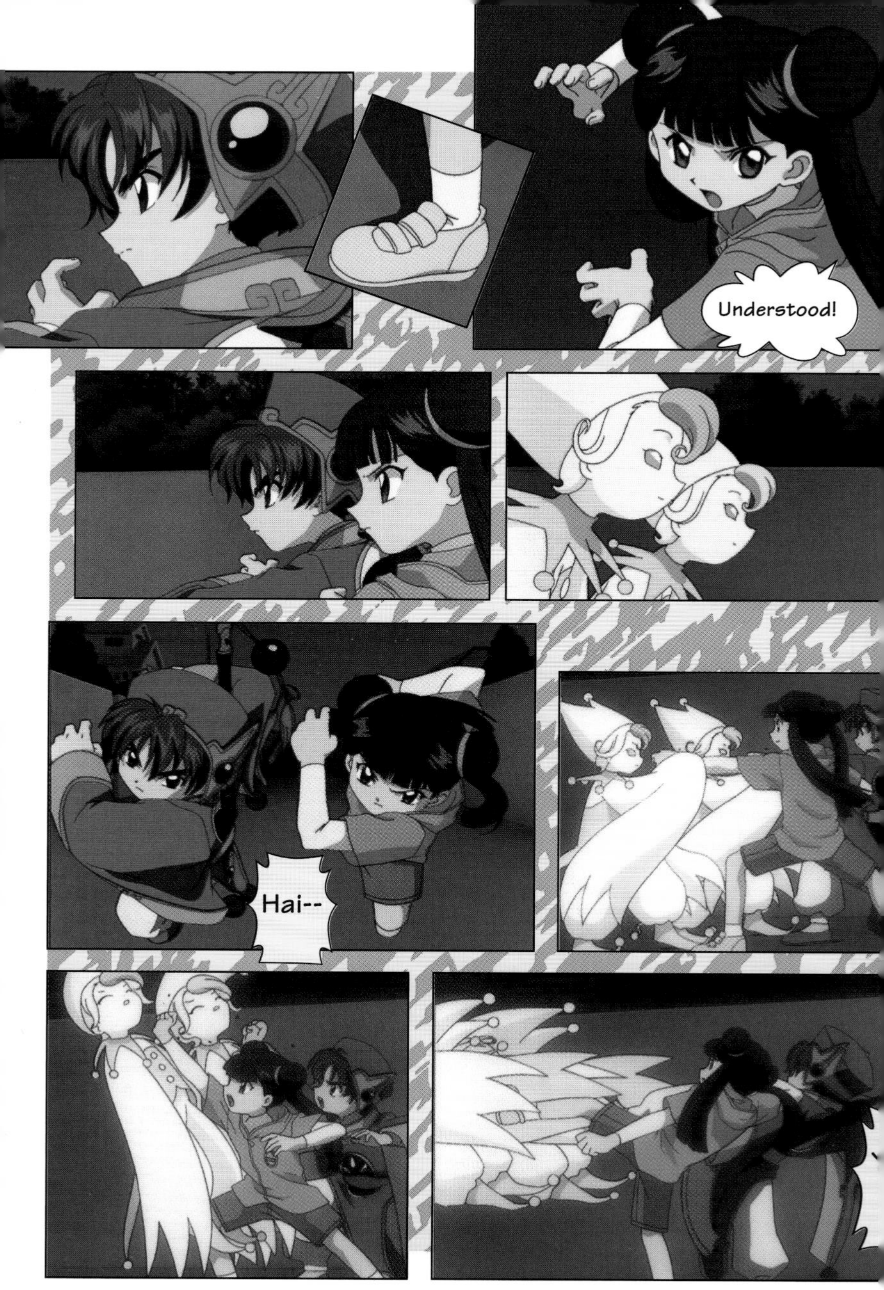
Understood!
Hai--

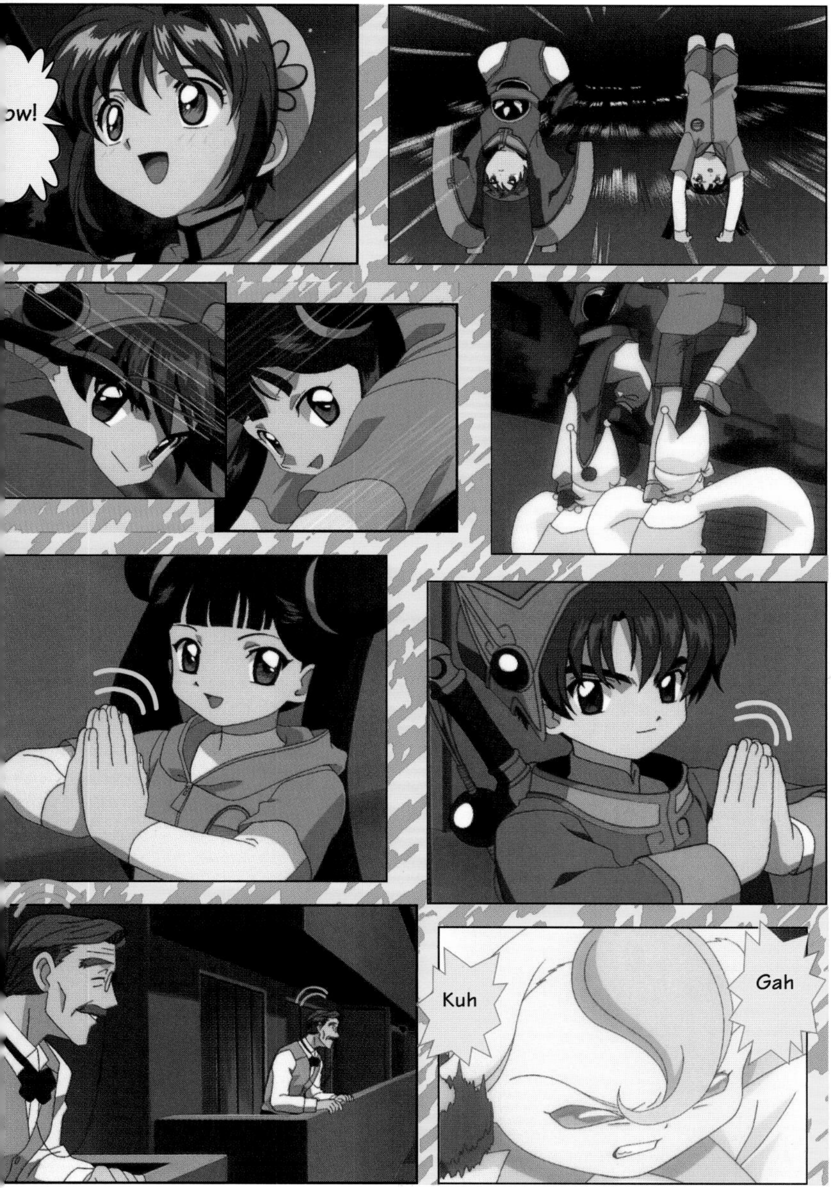
ow!
Kuh
Gah

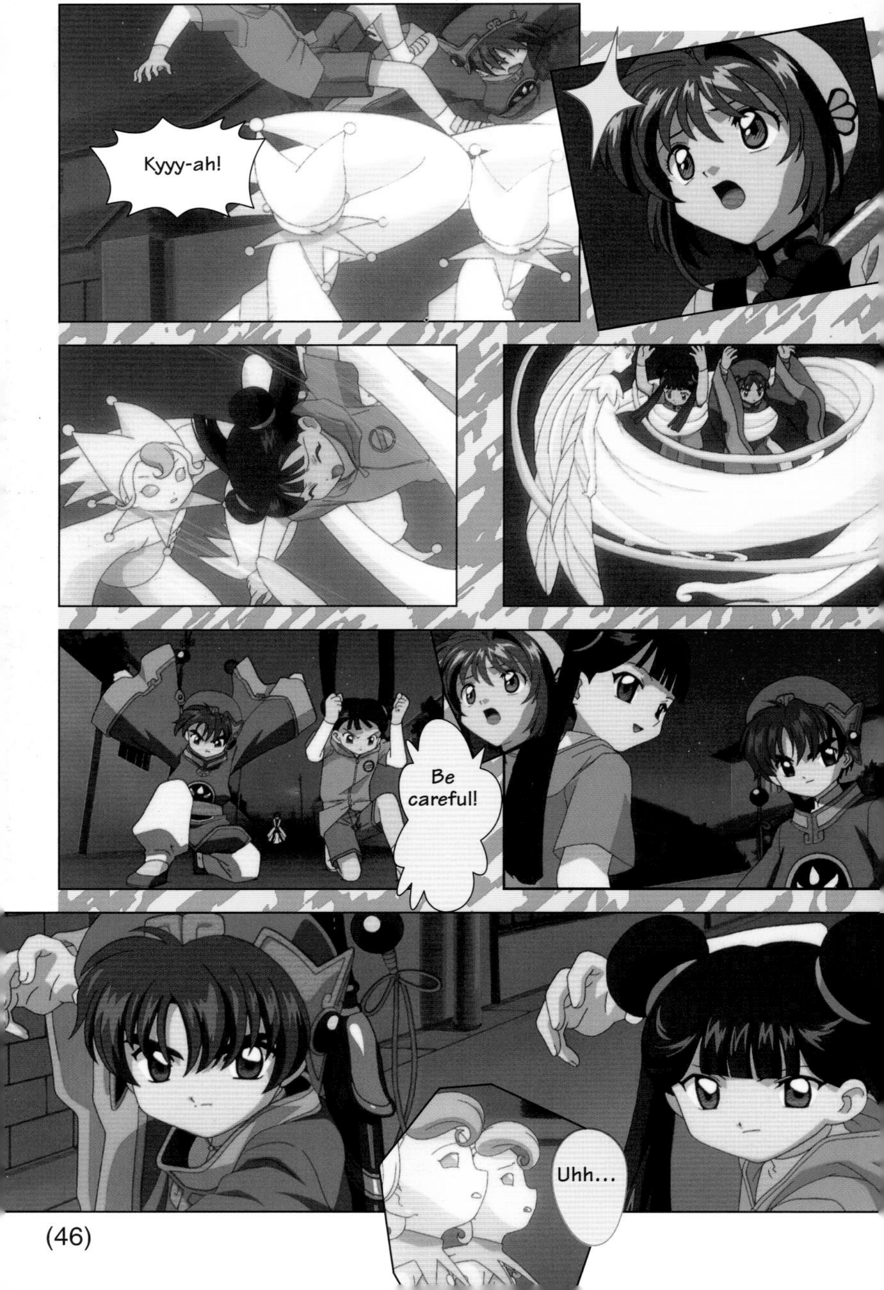

Kyyy-ah!
Be careful!
Uhh...

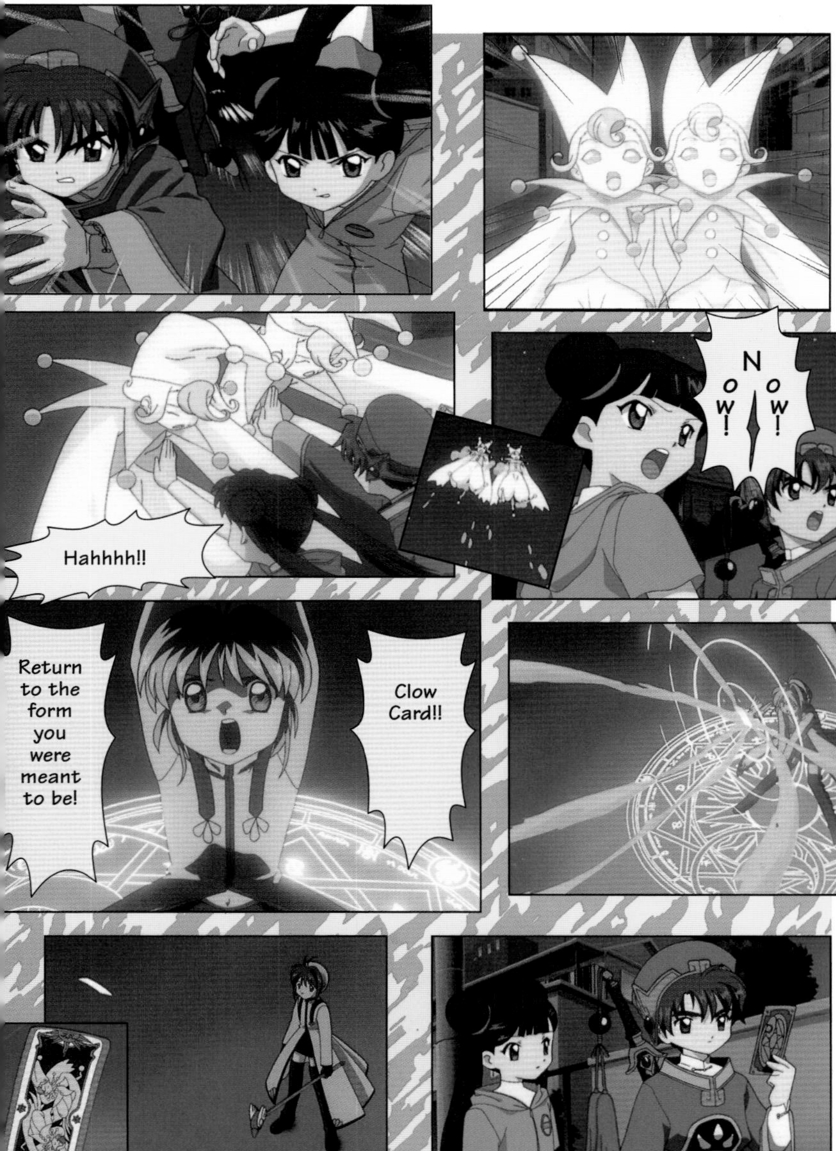
Hahhhh!!
NOW! NOW!
Return to the form you were meant to be!
Clow Card!!

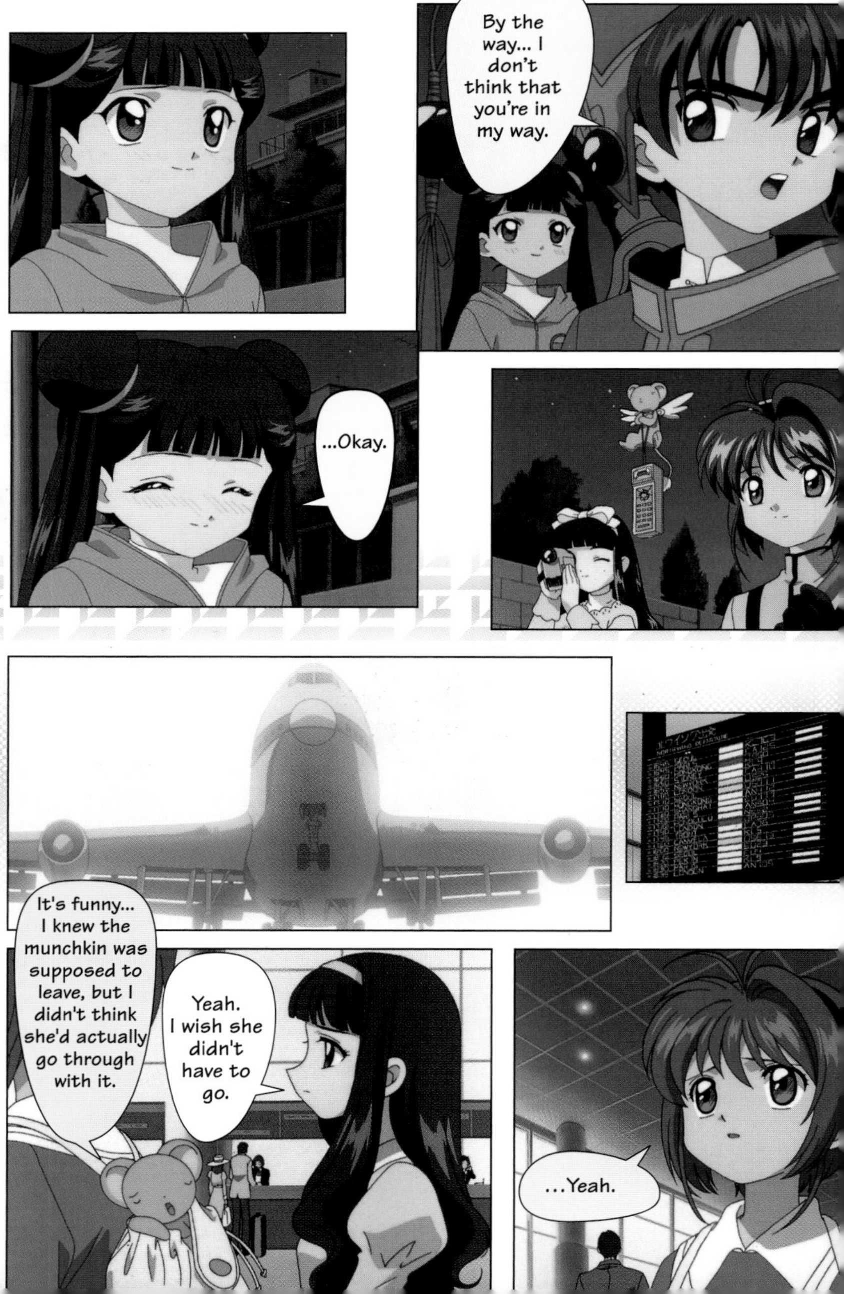

By the way... I don't think that you're in my way.
...Okay.
It's funny... I knew the munchkin was supposed to leave, but I didn't think she'd actually go through with it.
Yeah. I wish she didn't have to go.
...Yeah.

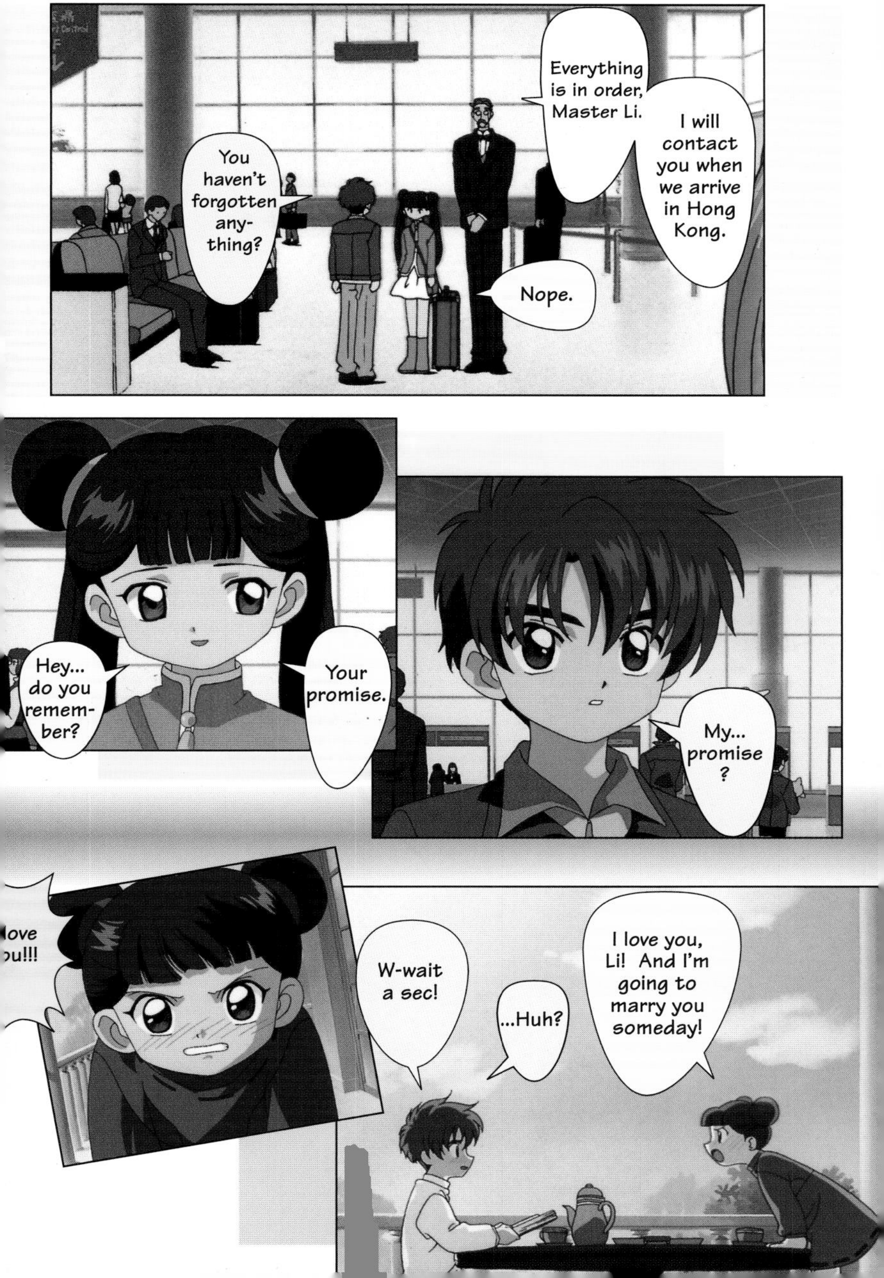
You haven't forgotten anything?
Nope.
Everything is in order, Master Li.
I will contact you when we arrive in Hong Kong.
Hey... do you remember?
Your promise.
My... promise?
love
u!!!
W-wait a sec!
...Huh?
I love you, Li! And I'm going to marry you someday!

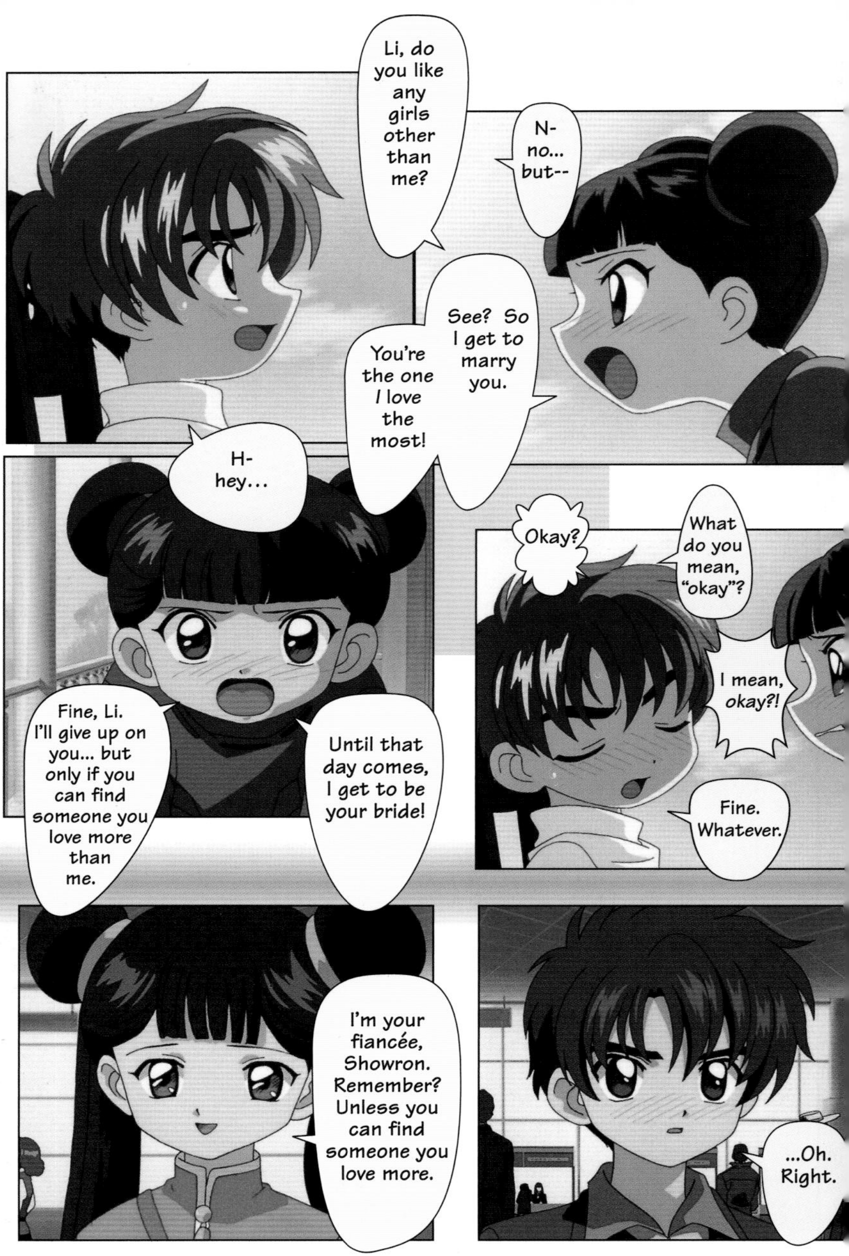

Li, do you like any girls other than me?
N- no... but--
See? So I get to marry you.
You're the one I love the most!
H- hey...
Fine, Li. I'll give up on you... but only if you can find someone you love more than me.
Until that day comes, I get to be your bride!
Okay?
What do you mean, "okay"?
I mean, okay?!
Fine. Whatever.
I'm your fiancée, Showron. Remember? Unless you can find someone you love more.
...Oh. Right.

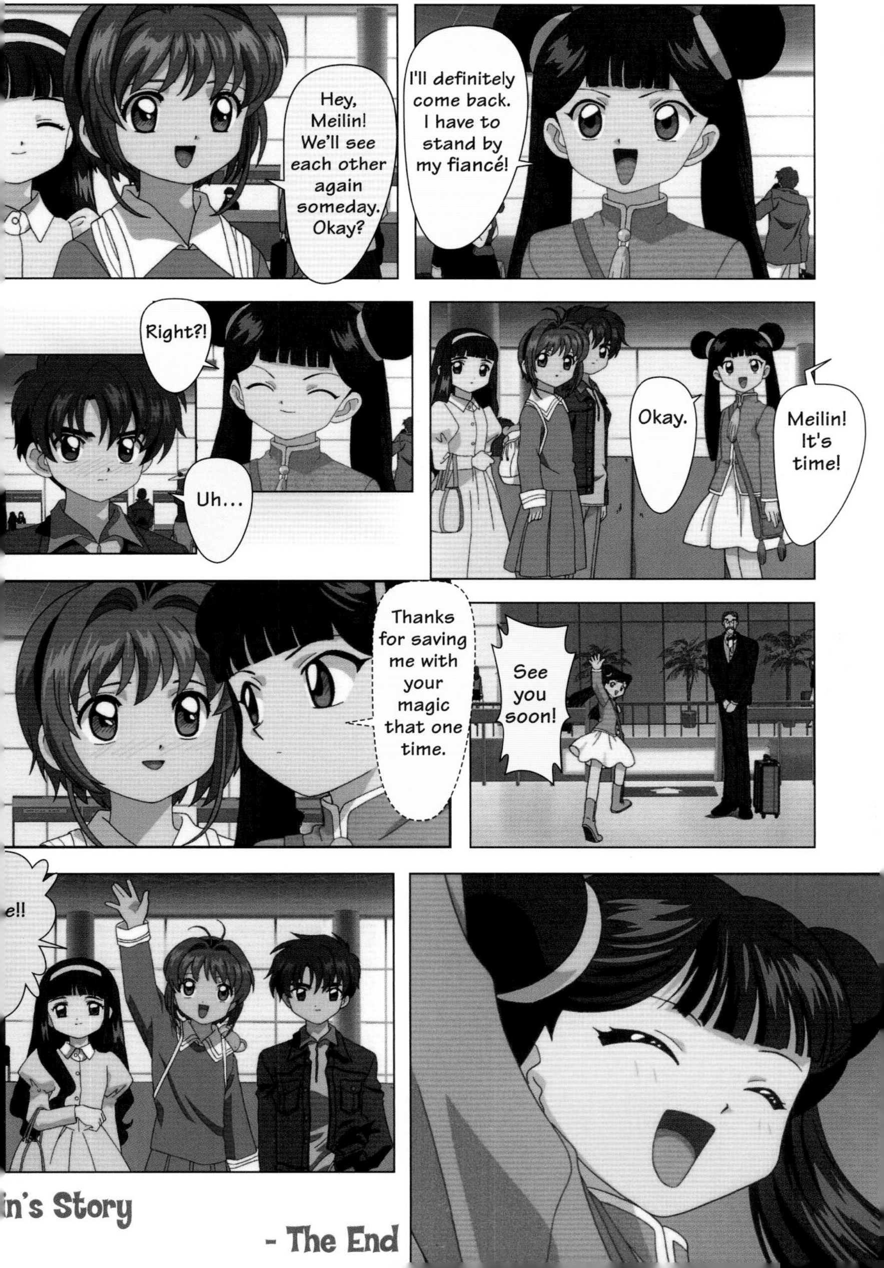
Hey, Meilin! We'll see each other again someday. Okay?
I'll definitely come back. I have to stand by my fiancé!
Right?!
Uh...
Meilin! It's time!
Okay.
Thanks for saving me with your magic that one time.
See you soon!
e!!
in's Story
- The End

Howdy, kids! Kero here, once again reporting on important events that didn't make it into these books. Sakura still has a few Clow Cards to collect. As for the final card, Earthy... where on Earth is it?!

CARDCAPTORS

FUTURE EPISODE!

Episode 44 - "The Last Card, Pt. 1"

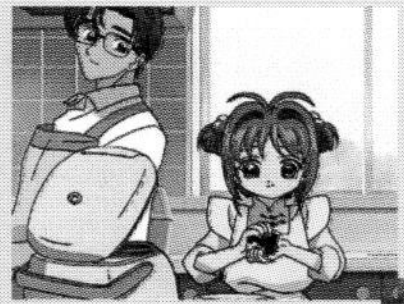

Sakura gets up early and makes lunch for Julian. She's making a lot... but Julian likes to eat a lot, so that should go over well.

Julian can do anything, can't he! He sure is good at archery. Nice outfit, too.

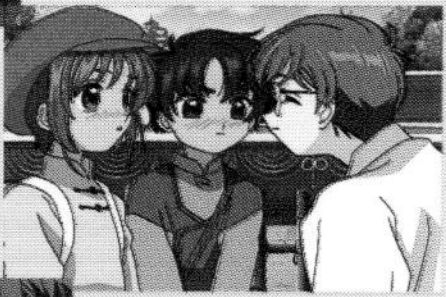

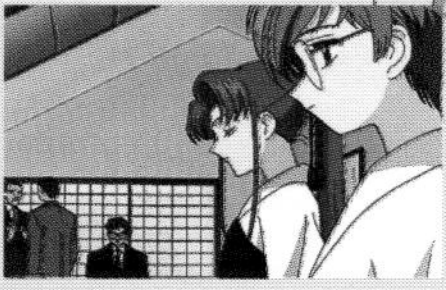

Julian's opponent in the final game is... Ms. MacKenzie?! Who should we root for? This is too confusing!

Kero is awfully suspicious about Ms. MacKenzie... he senses in her the magical power of the moon. Could she be the one he's waited for?

So Julian decided to participate in an arc tournament! Of course, Sakura helped— made lunch for Julian! Anyway, Julian did p weli, and before we knew it, he was in the match of the contest...where his opponent Ms. MacKenzie! It was a close match, but J won the championship. Then everyone ate lun but little did they know how special this l would be. For I, Kero, had met up with MacKenzie secretly beforehand. Turns out Layla (we're on a first name basis now) holds magical power of the moon. She told me she n't Yue, the Judge, as I had suspected. But I there was something special about her...

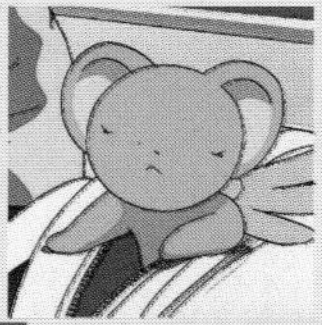

Ms. MacKenzie suddenly senses Kero's magic. Concentration is important in archery, Ms. MacKenzie!

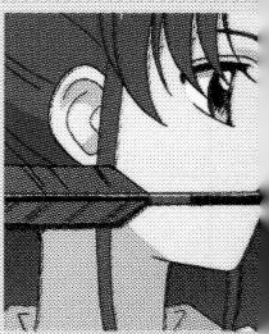

"Yue"

"Keroberos"

Kero's "CLOW CARD" EXPLANATION

There are two guardians of the "Clow Cards". The first person is me, Keroberos—the one who Chooses. The other is the Judge—Yue. All I can say about him is that he is the real master of the Clow Cards. Yue will carry out the final judgment on whether Sakura is a worthy master, too...

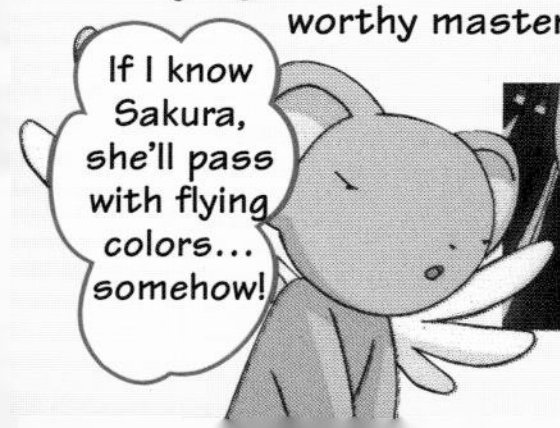
If I know Sakura, she'll pass with flying colors... somehow!

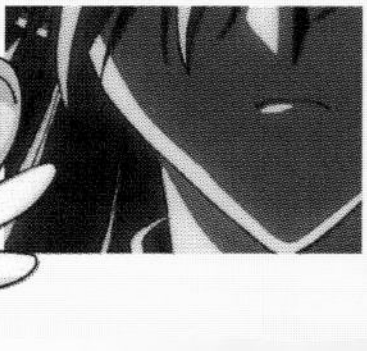

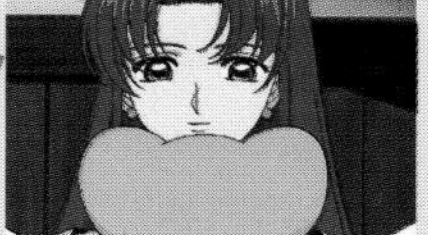

Kero meets in secret wi Ms. MacKenzie. The two them have been sensing each other's presence f while now... it's about t they were acquainted!

Sakura comes looking for Kero, only to catch him and Ms. MacKenzie in mid-conversation. Needless to say, she's a bit surprised!

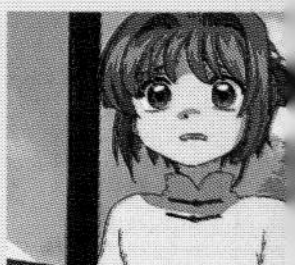

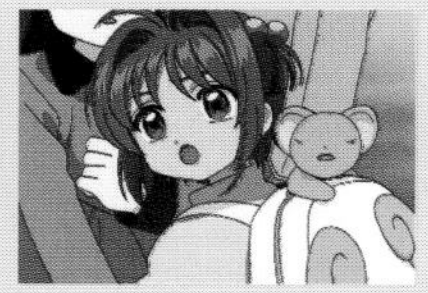

The match over, every heads home. But all c sudden, there's a hug earthquake! What's going on?!

Episode 45

The Last Card

CARDCAPTORS™

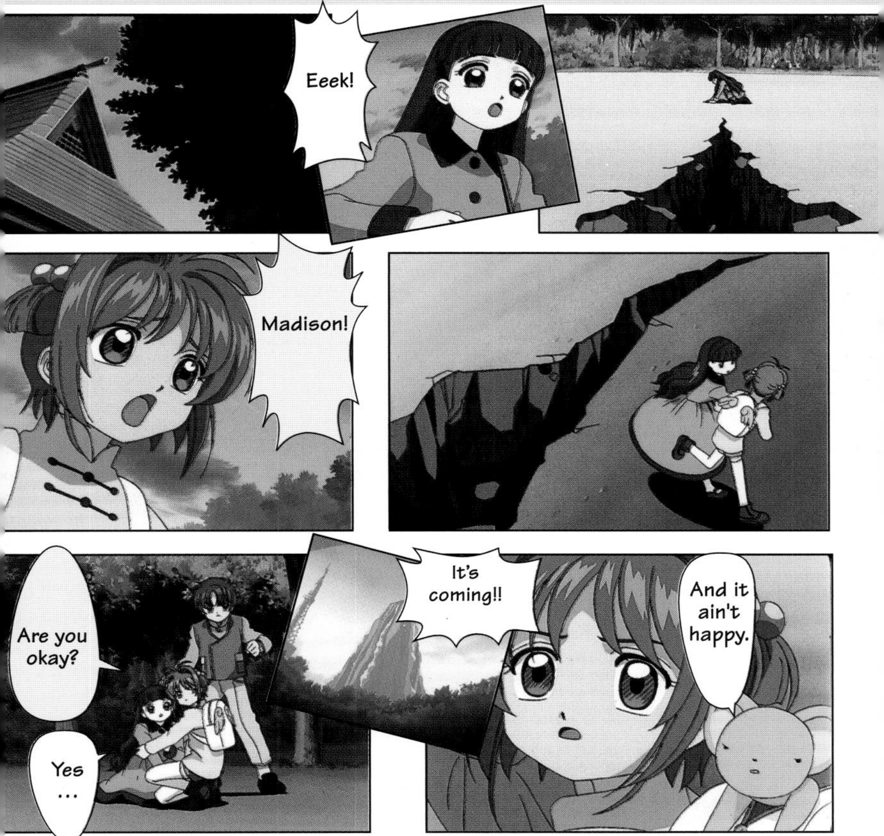

Eeek!
Madison!
Are you okay?
Yes …
It's coming!!
And it ain't happy.

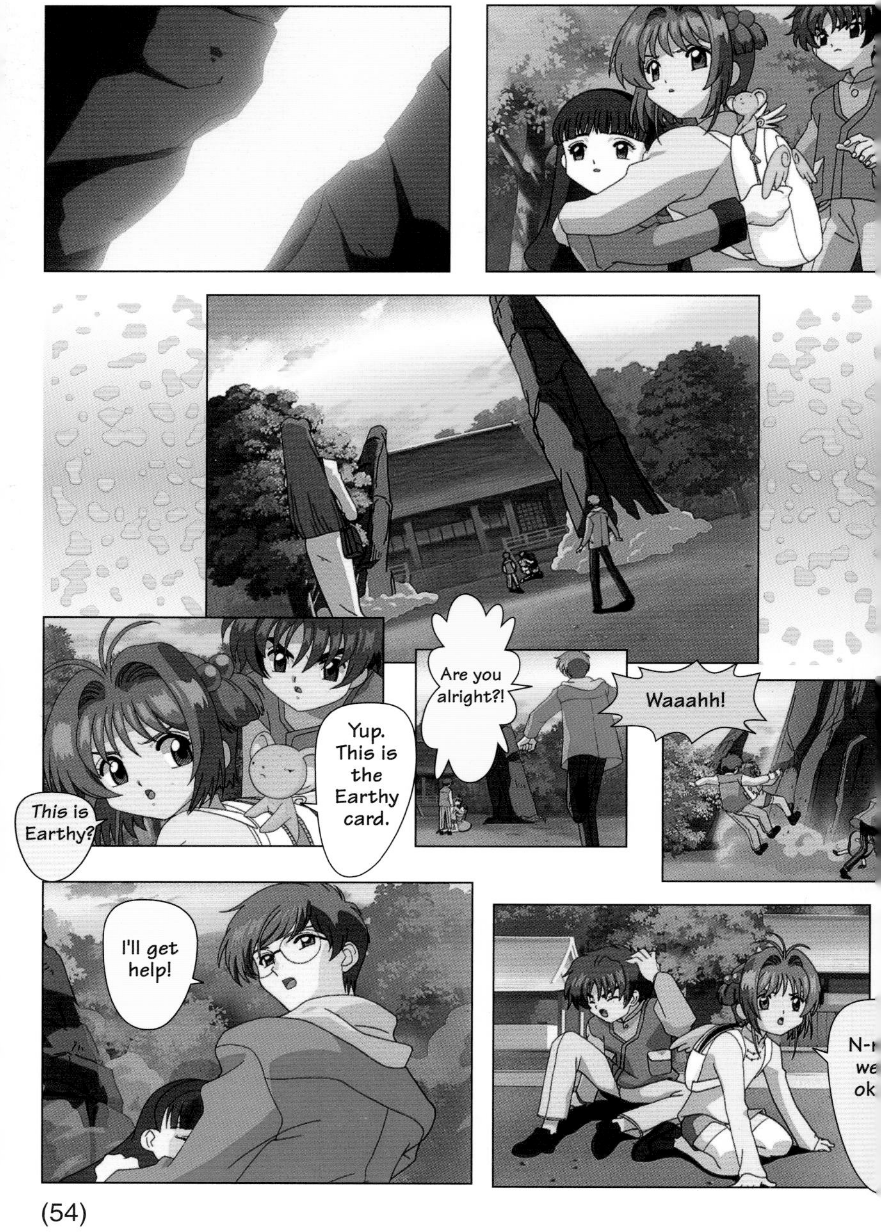
This is Earthy?
Yup. This is the Earthy card.
Are you alright?!
Waaahh!
I'll get help!

h...

Ow!

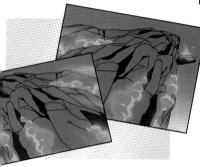

Ms. MacKenzie!

That's weird... nothing's happening around her.

like she's tected or nething...

Use your magic!

But... y'mean, here?

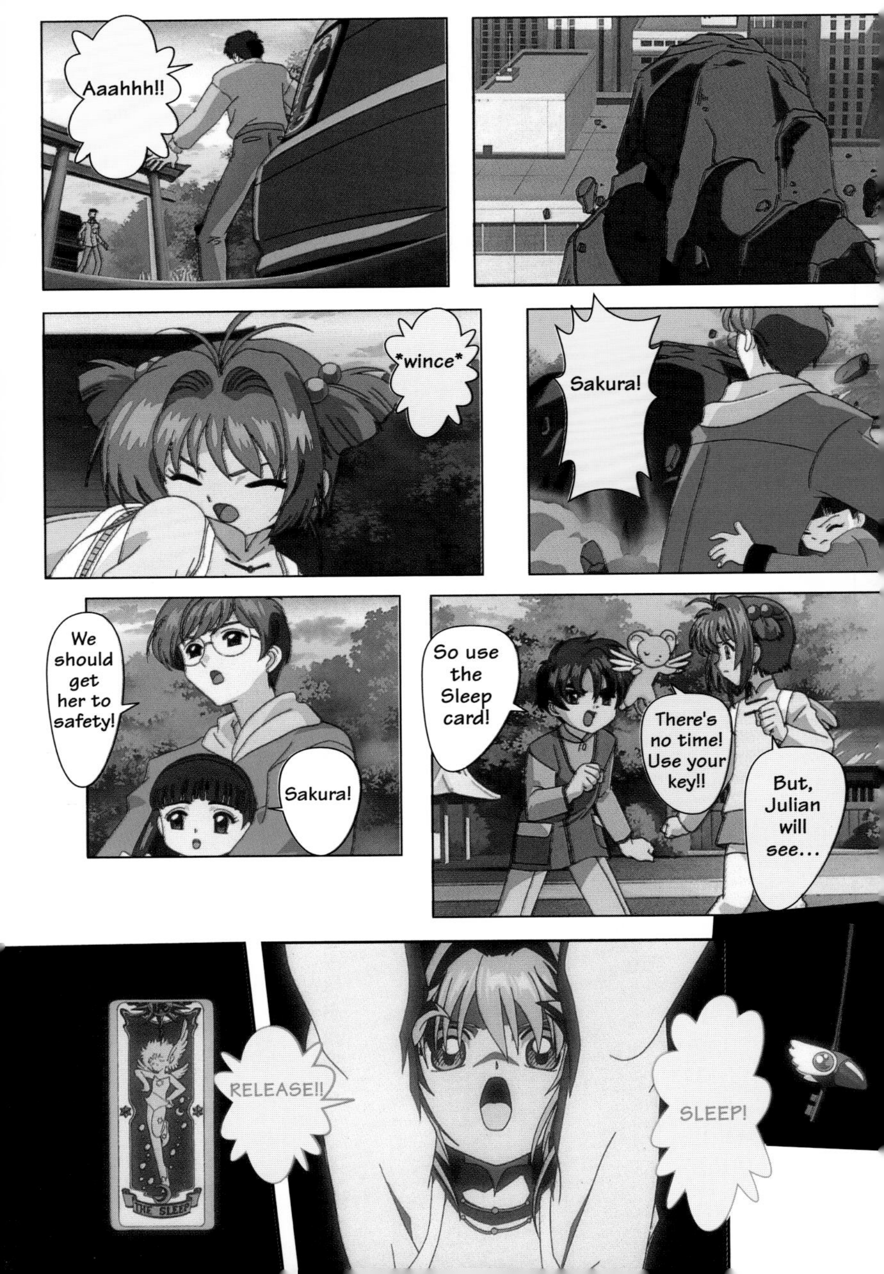
Aaahhh!!
wince
Sakura!
We should get her to safety!
Sakura!
So use the Sleep card!
There's no time! Use your key!!
But, Julian will see...
THE SLEEP
RELEASE!!
SLEEP!

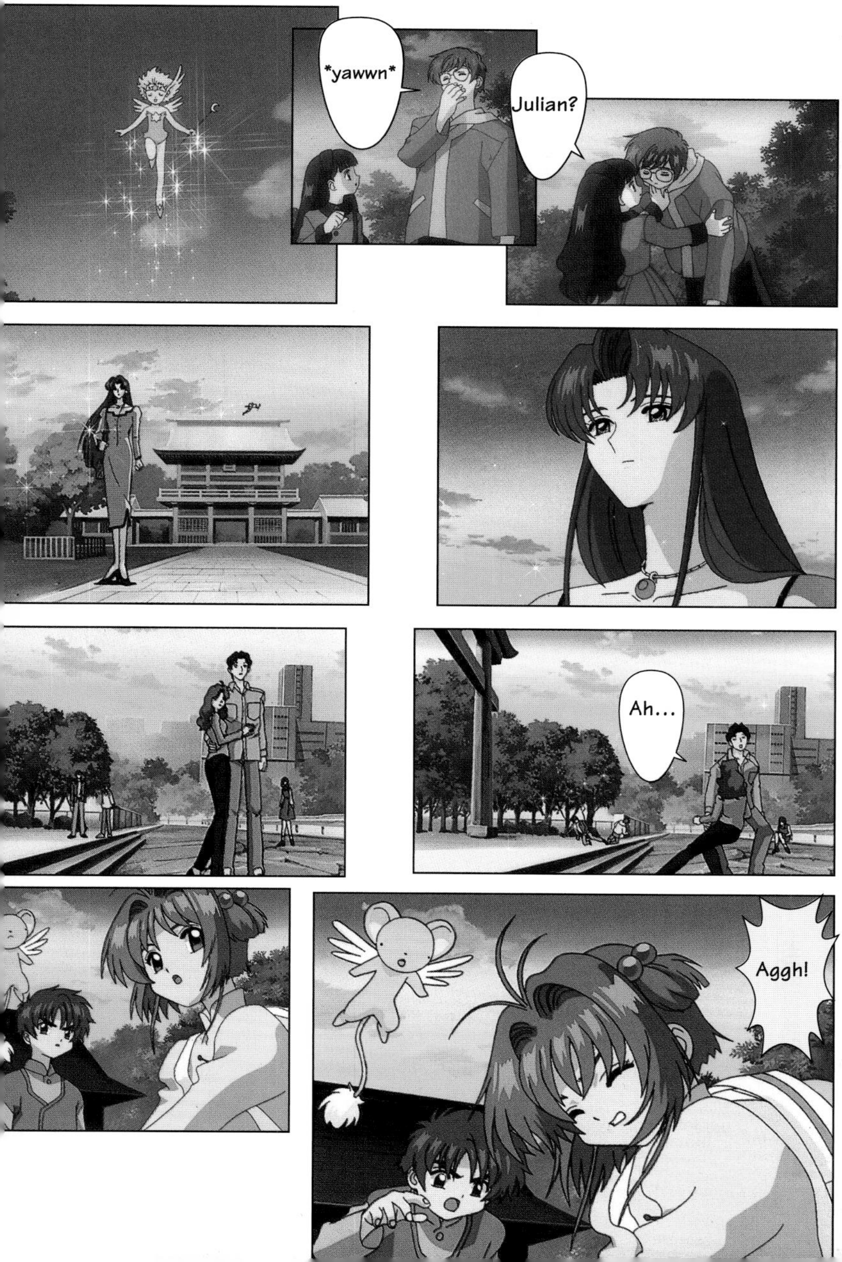
yawwn
Julian?
Ah...
Aggh!

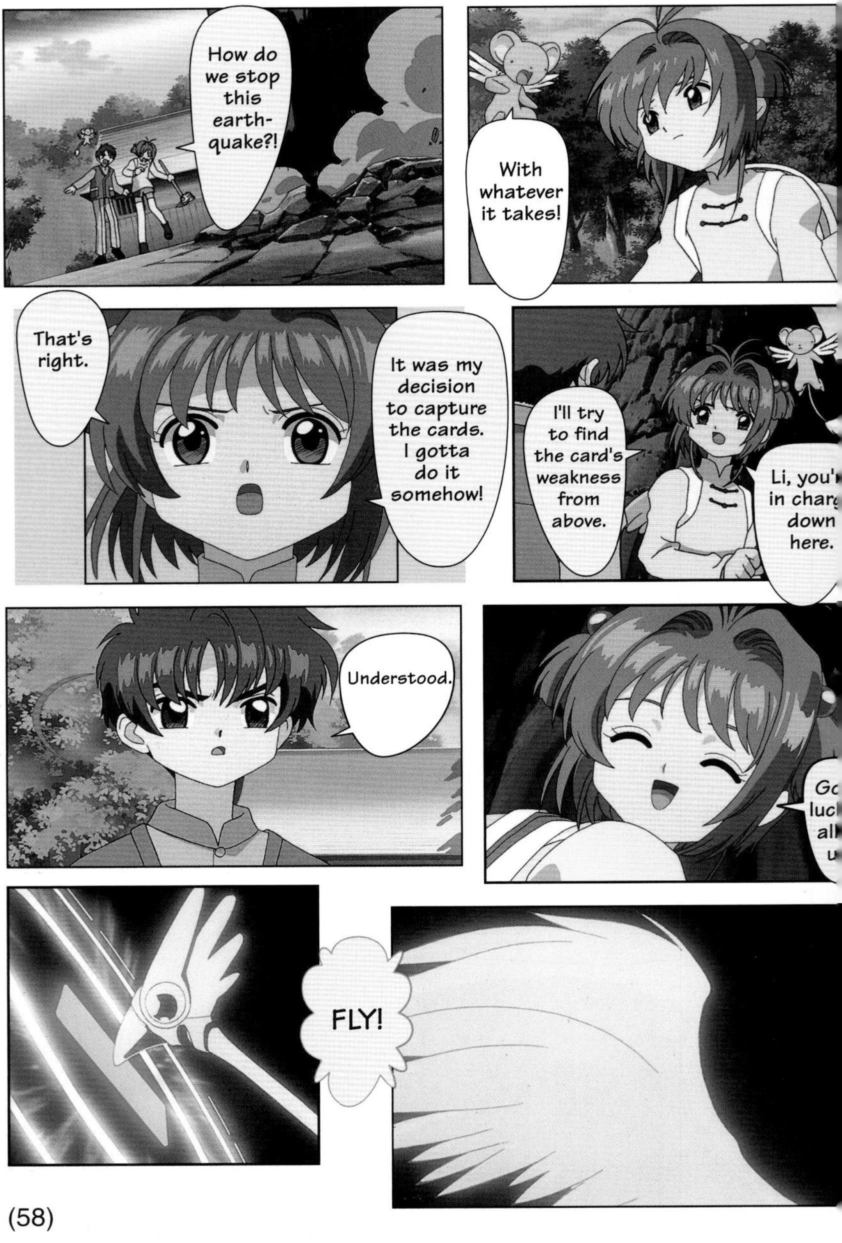
How do we stop this earth-quake?!
With whatever it takes!
That's right.
It was my decision to capture the cards. I gotta do it somehow!
I'll try to find the card's weakness from above.
Li, you' in char down here.
Understood.
FLY!

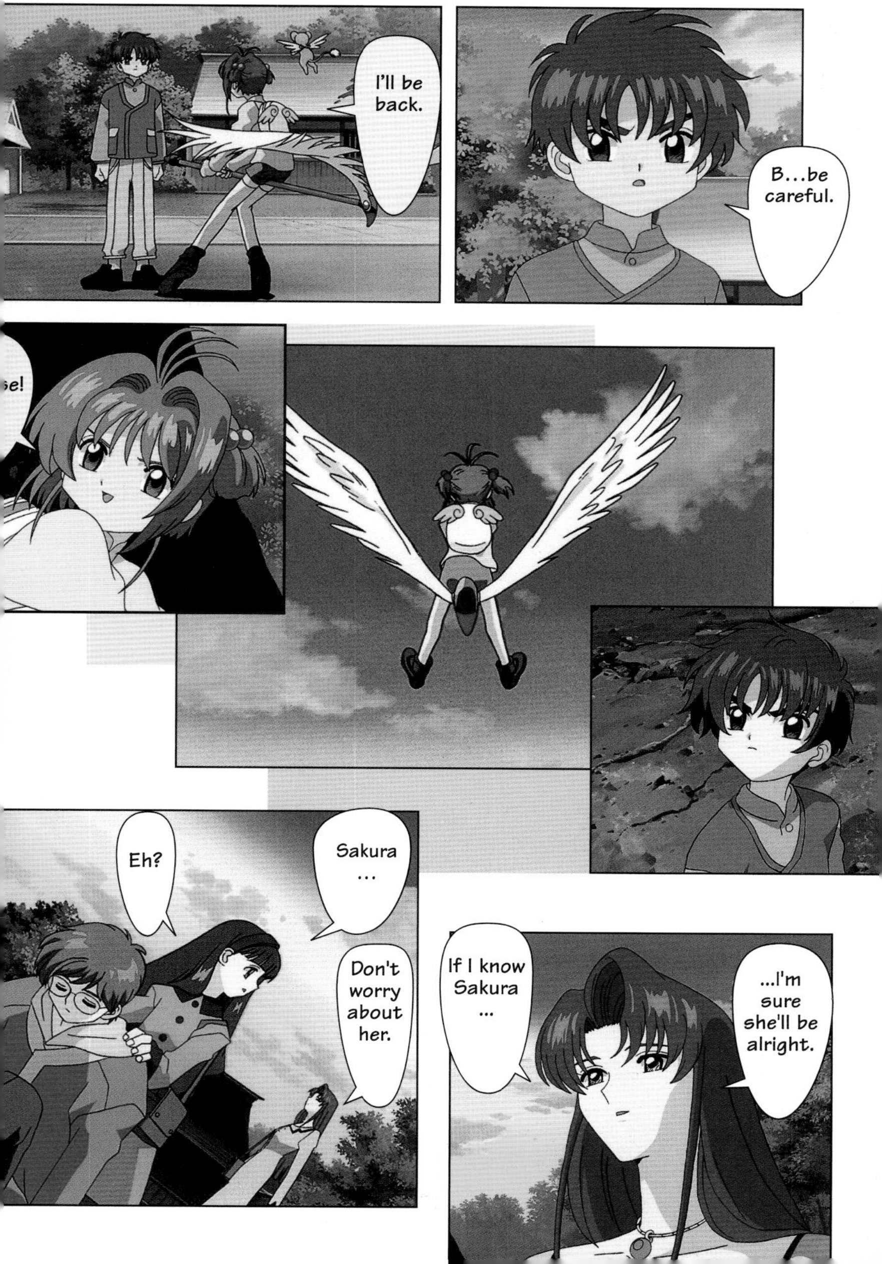

I'll be back.
B...be careful.
se!
Eh?
Sakura ...
Don't worry about her.
If I know Sakura ...
...I'm sure she'll be alright.

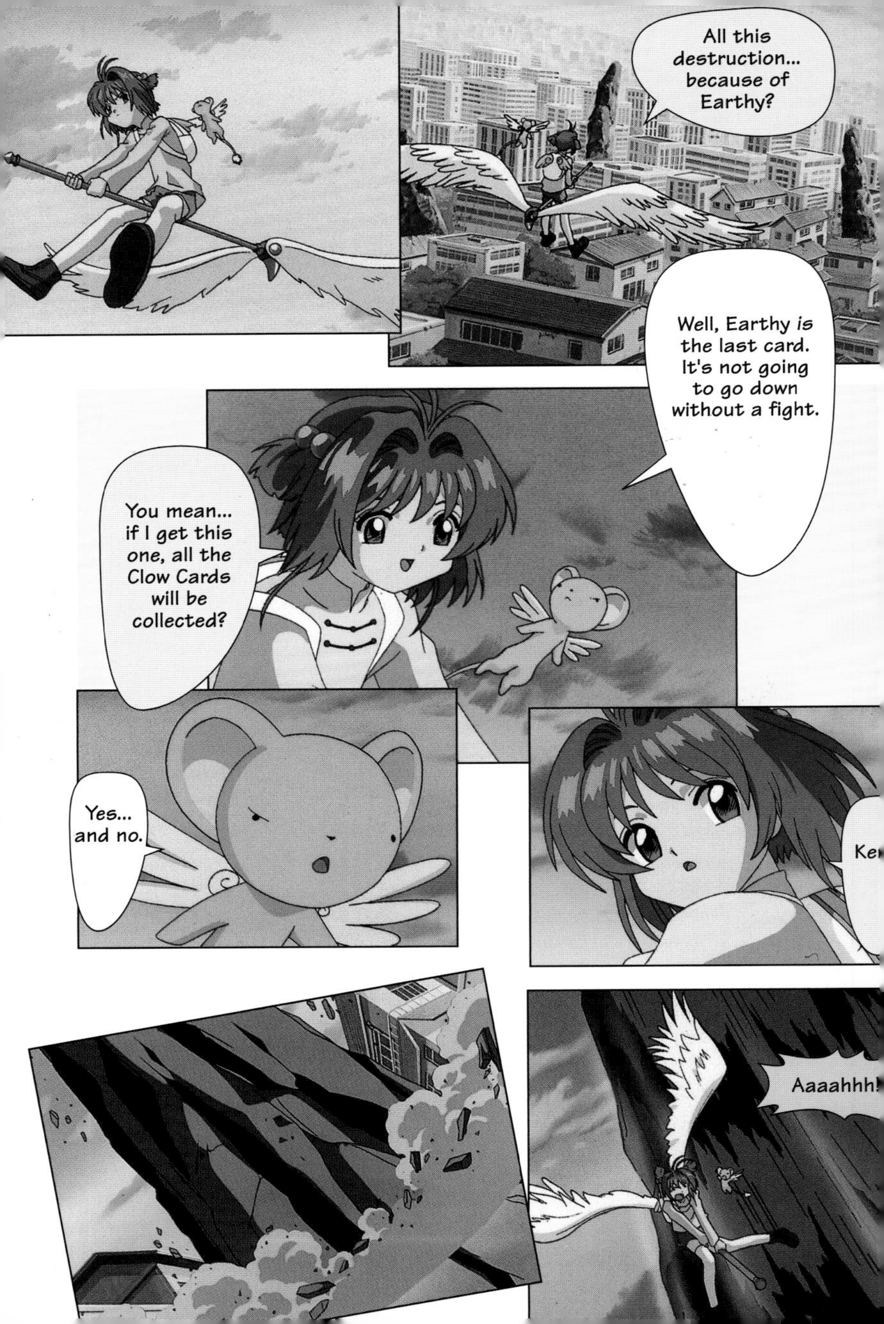
All this destruction... because of Earthy?
Well, Earthy is the last card. It's not going to go down without a fight.
You mean... if I get this one, all the Clow Cards will be collected?
Yes... and no.
Ke
Aaaahhh!

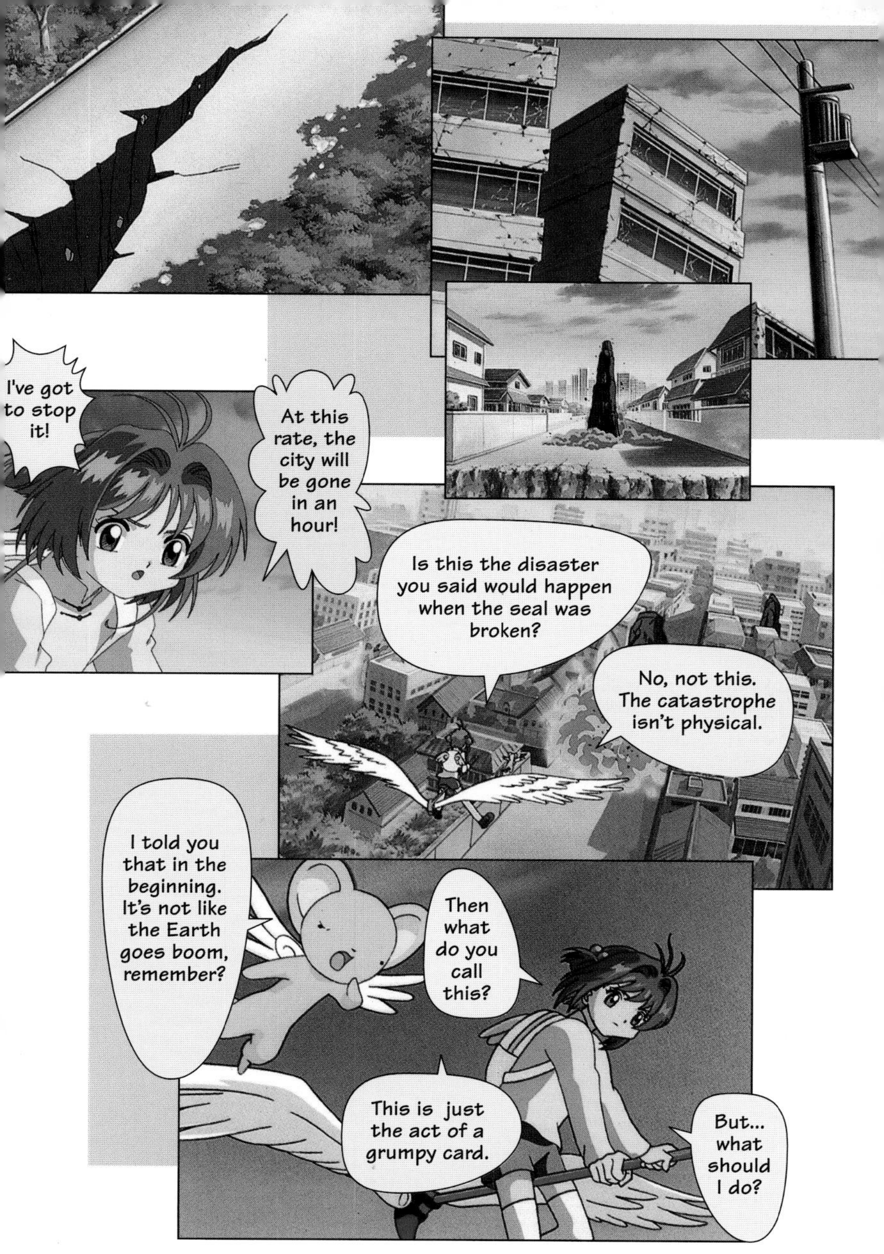
I've got to stop it!
At this rate, the city will be gone in an hour!
Is this the disaster you said would happen when the seal was broken?
No, not this. The catastrophe isn't physical.
I told you that in the beginning. It's not like the Earth goes boom, remember?
Then what do you call this?
This is just the act of a grumpy card.
But... what should I do?

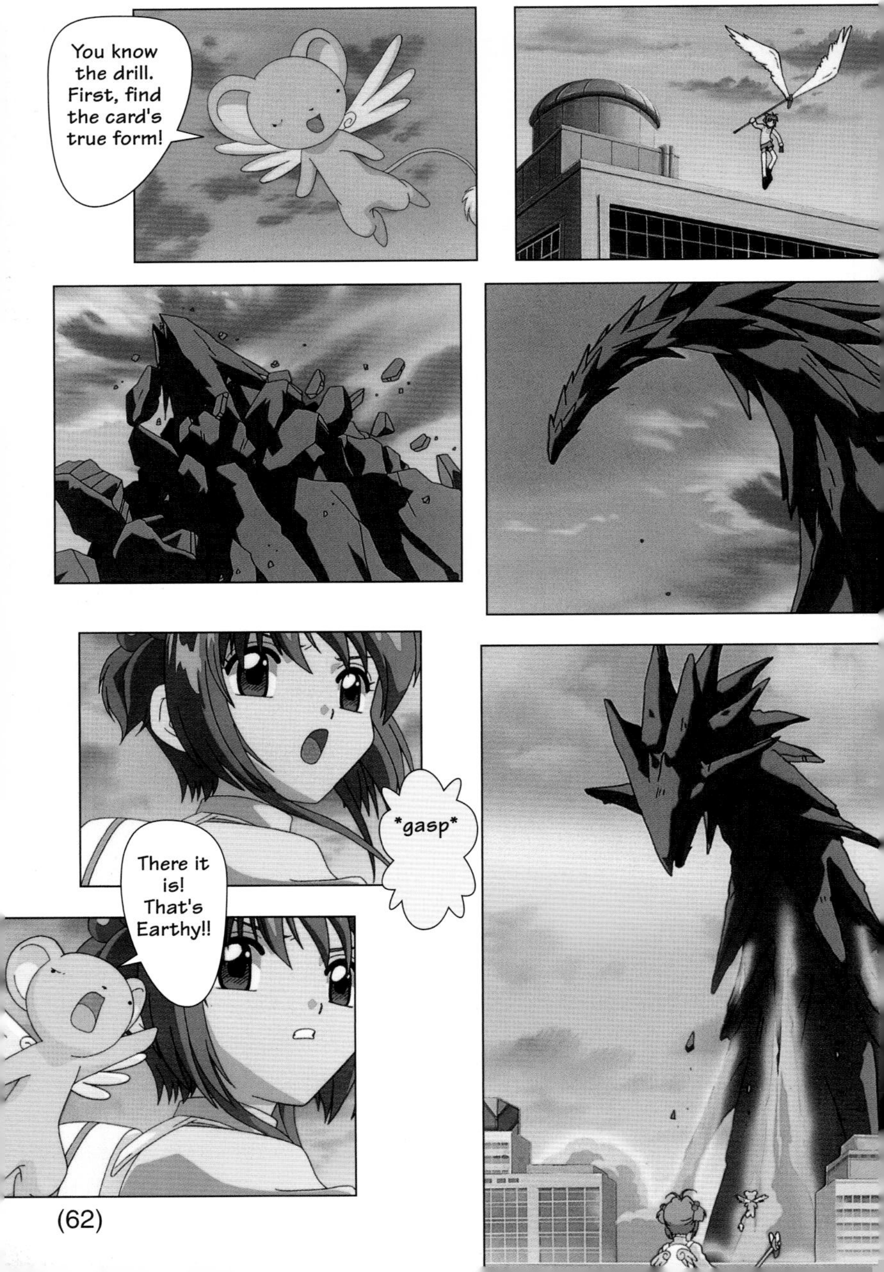

You know the drill. First, find the card's true form!
gasp
There it is! That's Earthy!!

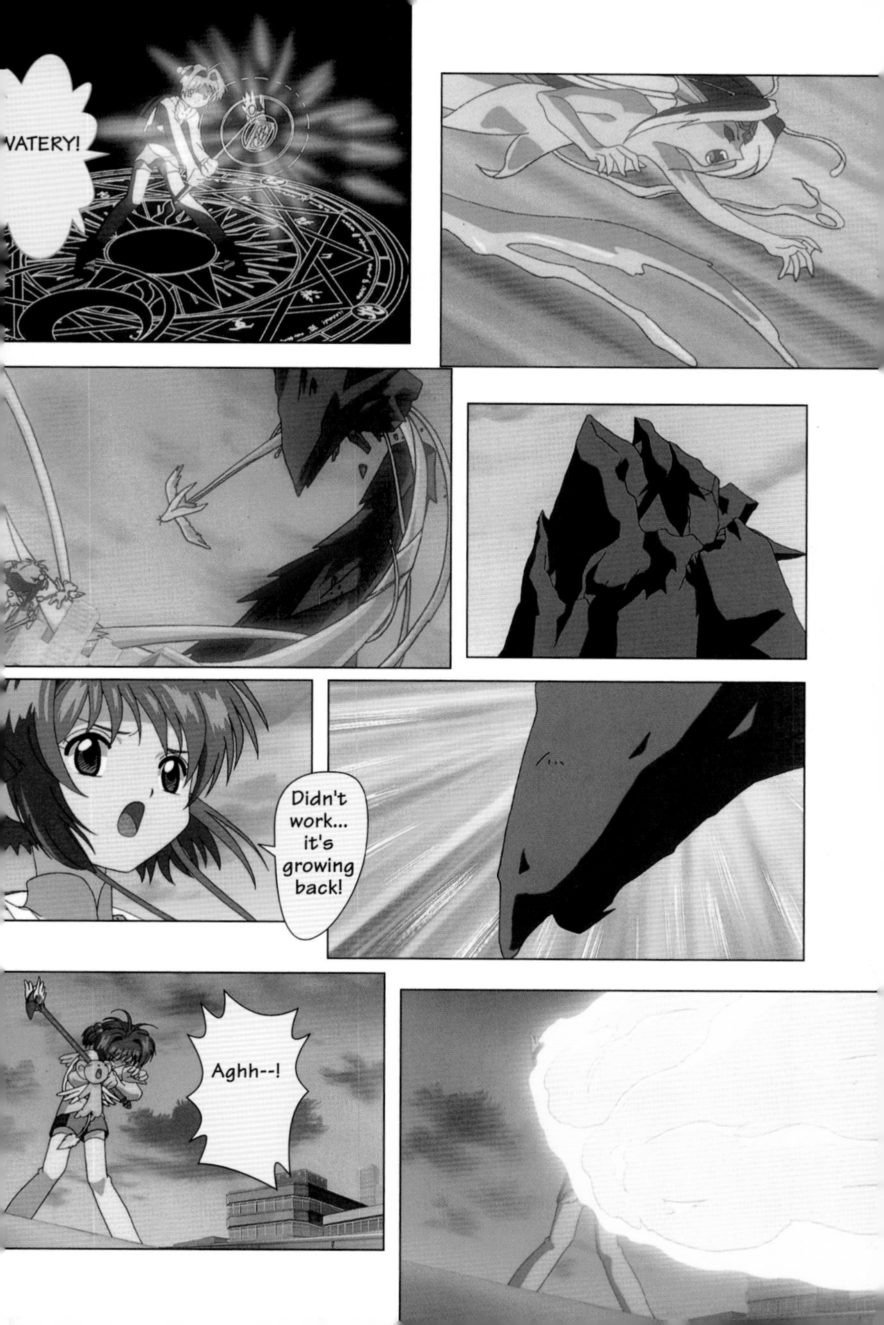
WATERY!
Didn't work... it's growing back!
Aghh--!

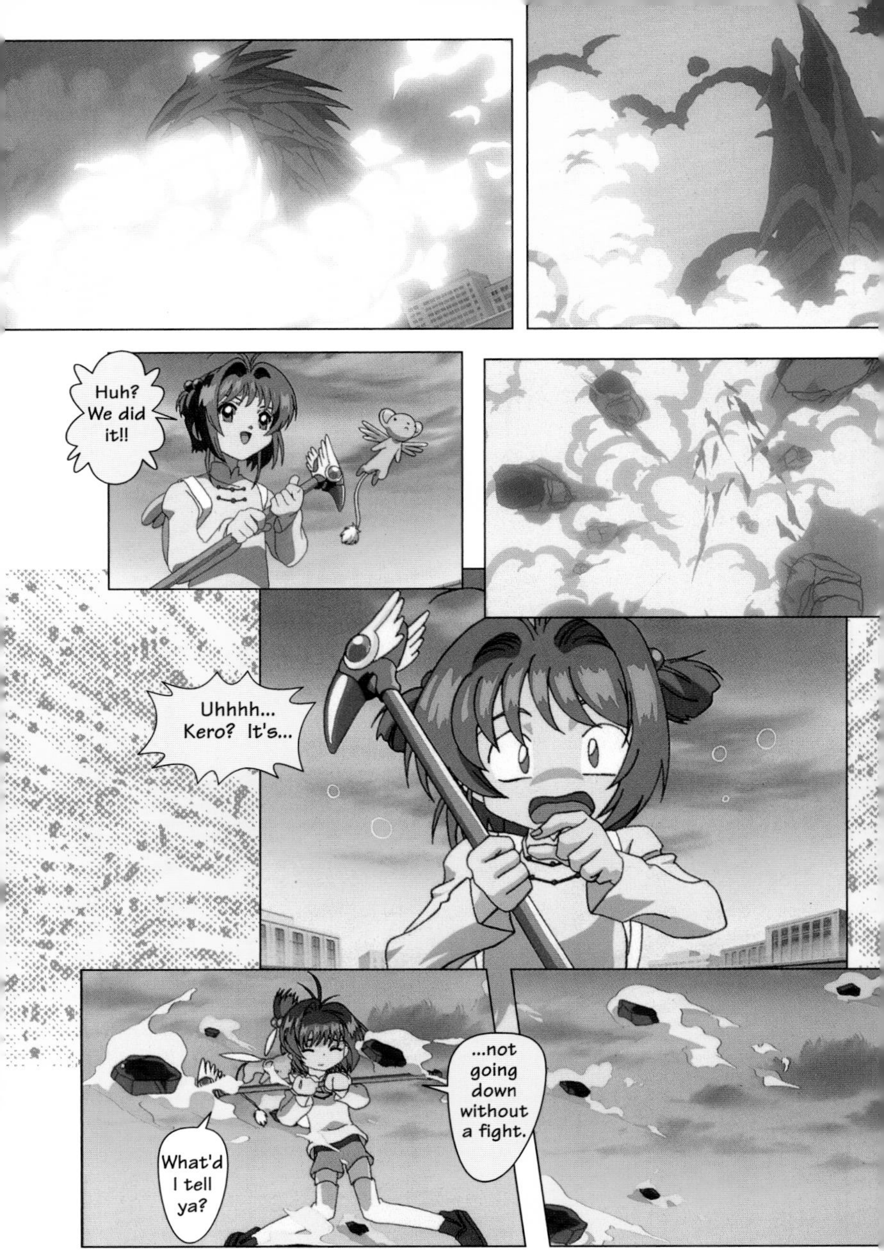
Huh? We did it!!
Uhhhh... Kero? It's...
...not going down without a fight.
What'd I tell ya?

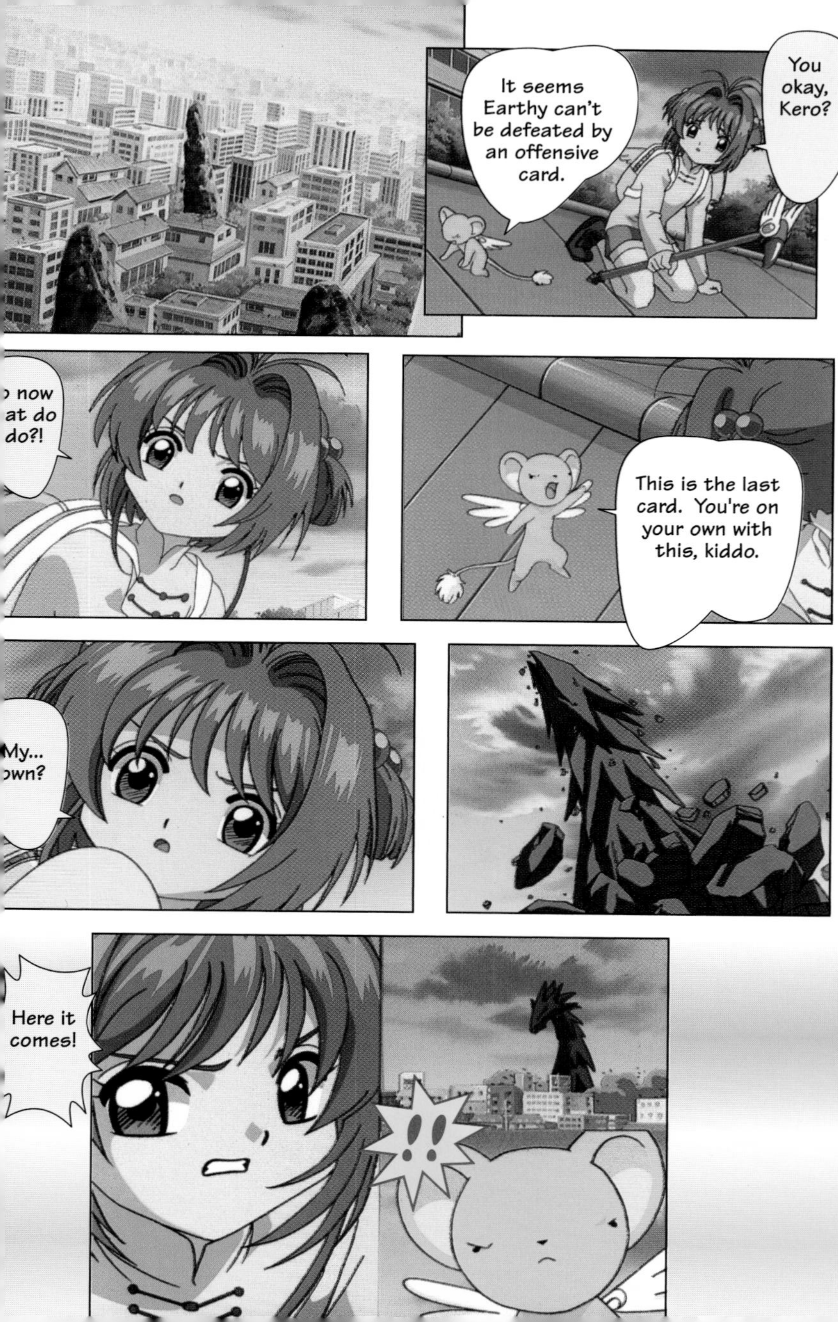
You okay, Kero?
It seems Earthy can't be defeated by an offensive card.
o now at do do?!
This is the last card. You're on your own with this, kiddo.
My... wn?
Here it comes!
!!

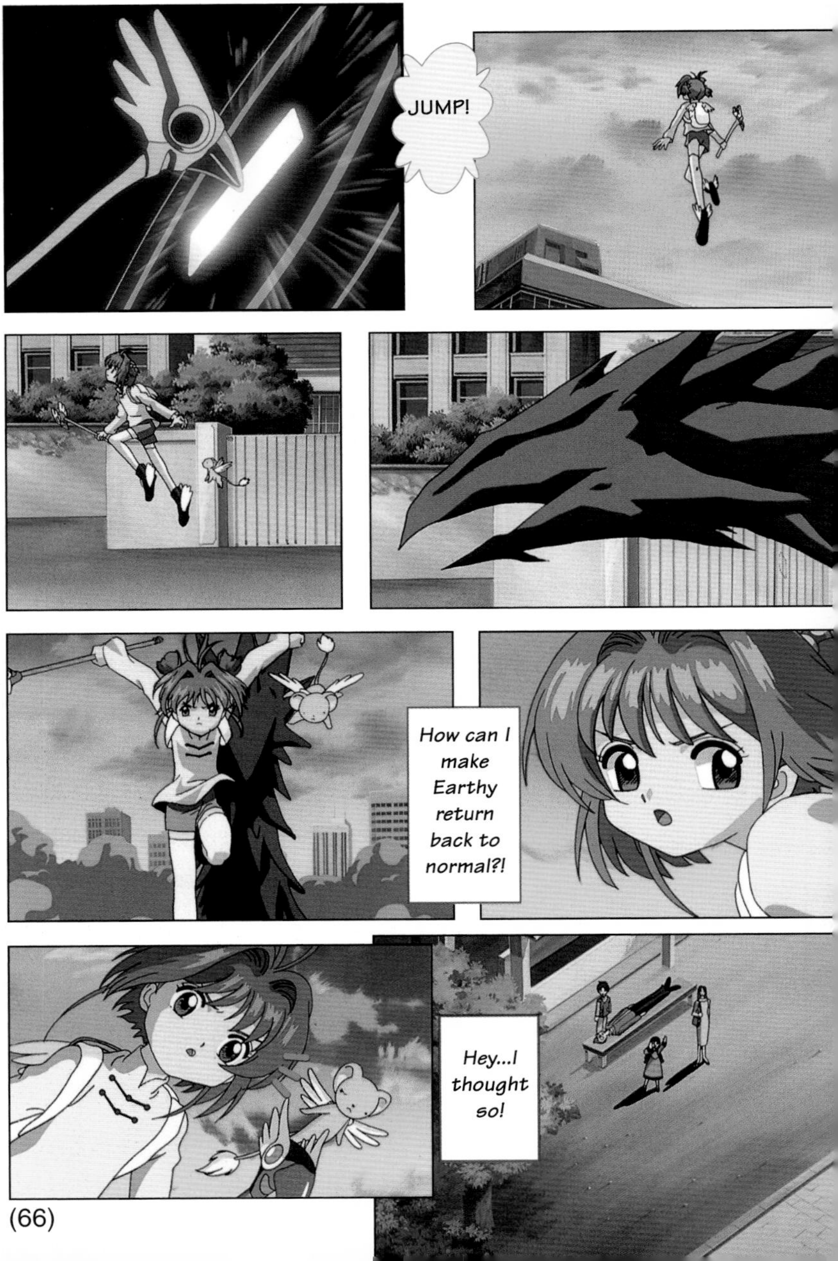
JUMP!
How can I make Earthy return back to normal?!
Hey...I thought so!

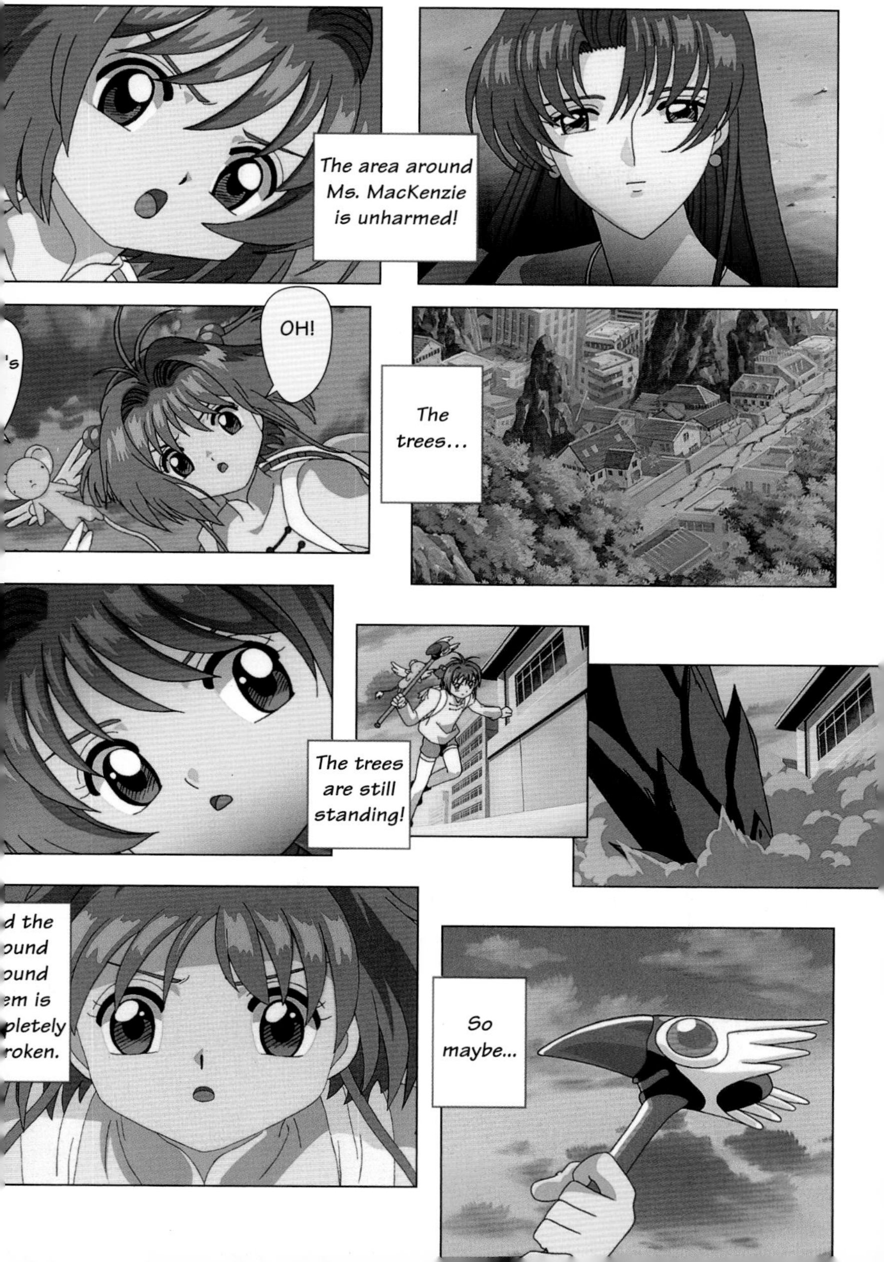
The area around Ms. MacKenzie is unharmed!
's
OH!
The trees...
The trees are still standing!
d the
ound
ound
em is
pletely
roken.
So maybe...

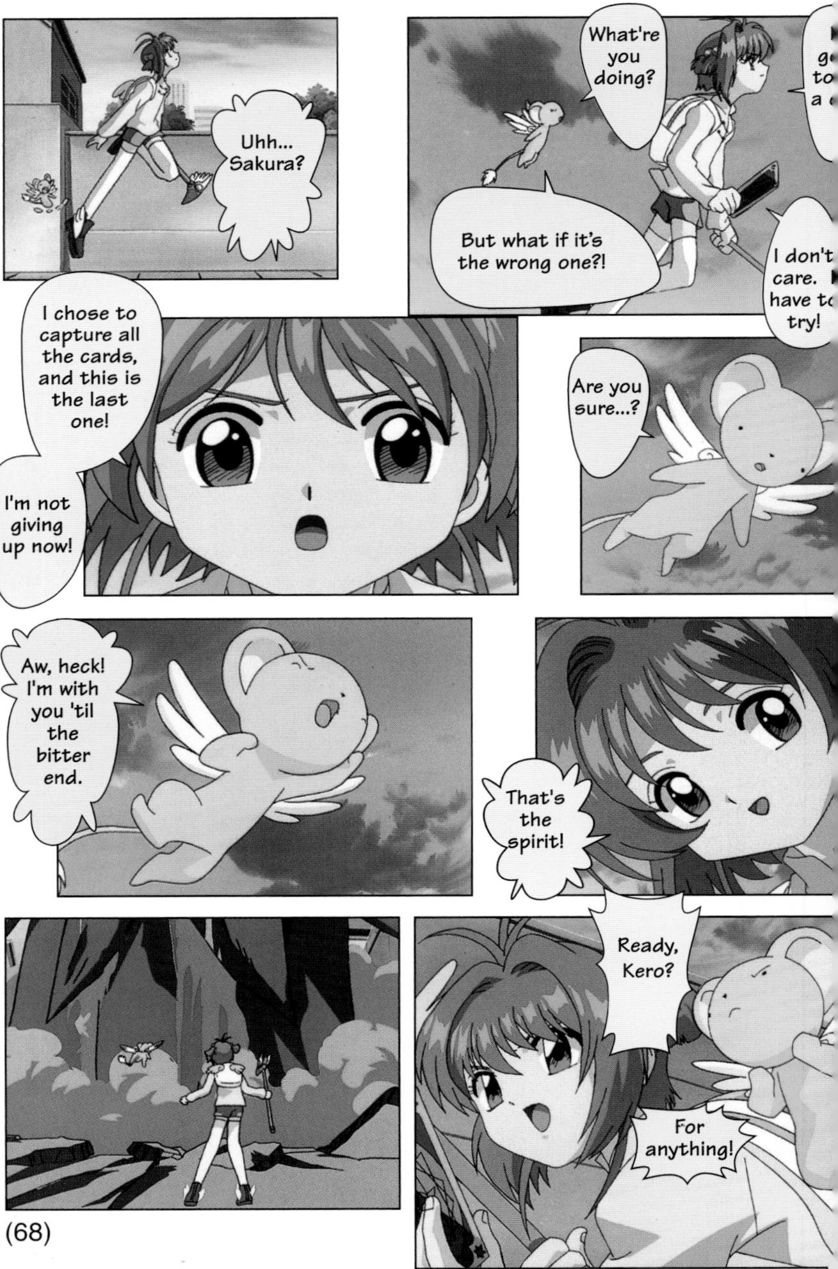

Uhh... Sakura?
What're you doing?
But what if it's the wrong one?!
I don't care. have to try!
I chose to capture all the cards, and this is the last one!
I'm not giving up now!
Are you sure...?
Aw, heck! I'm with you 'til the bitter end.
That's the spirit!
Ready, Kero?
For anything!

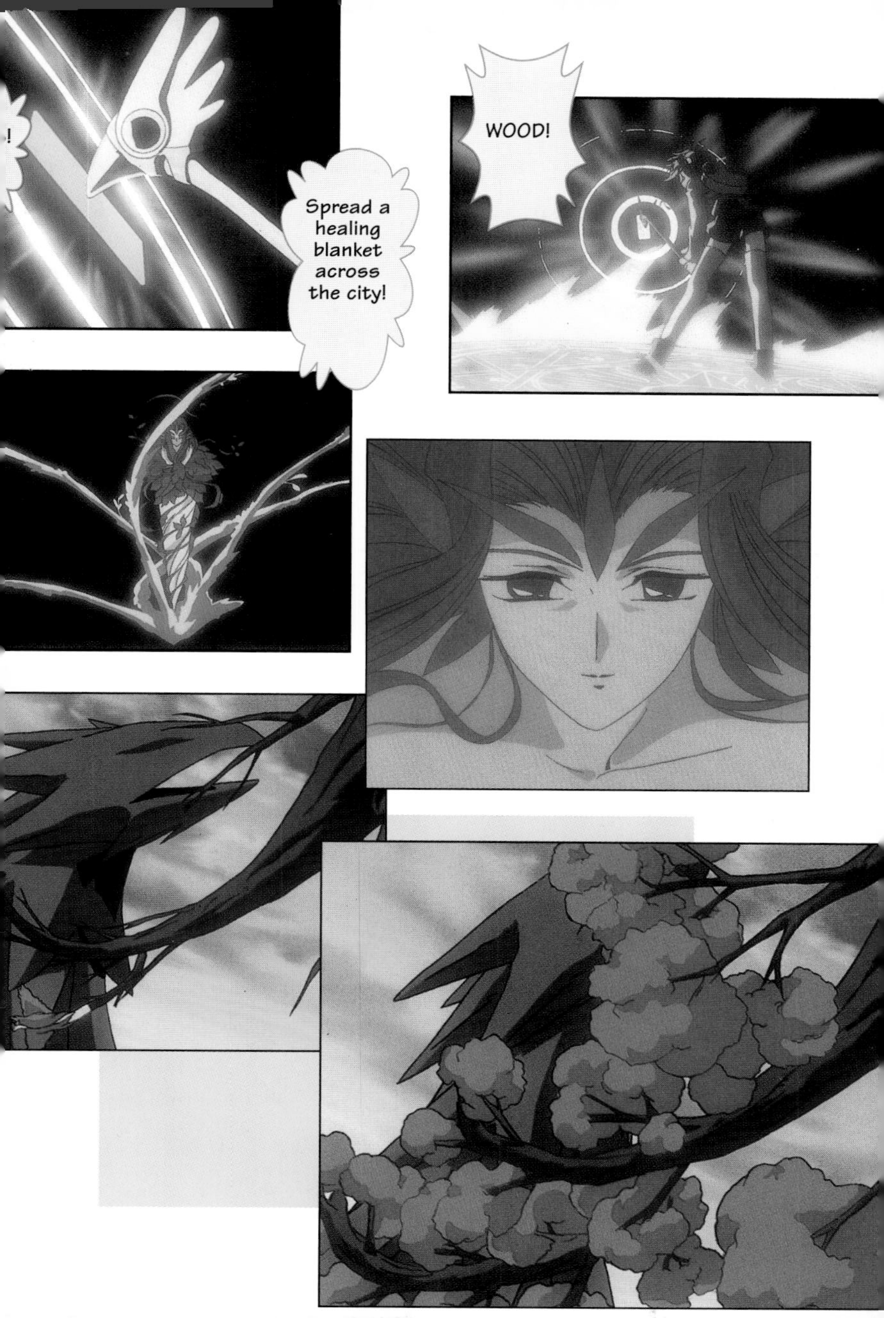
!
Spread a healing blanket across the city!
WOOD!

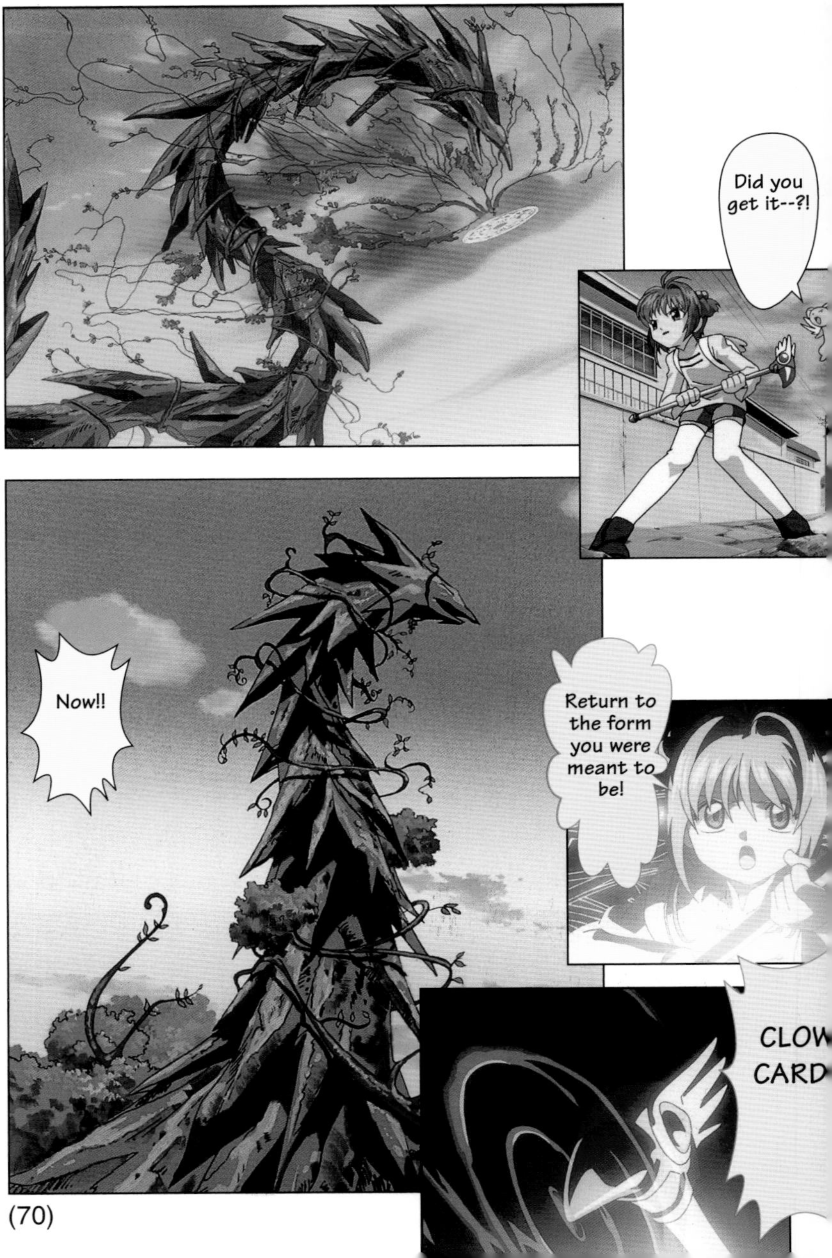

Did you get it--?!
Now!!
Return to the form you were meant to be!
CLOW CARD

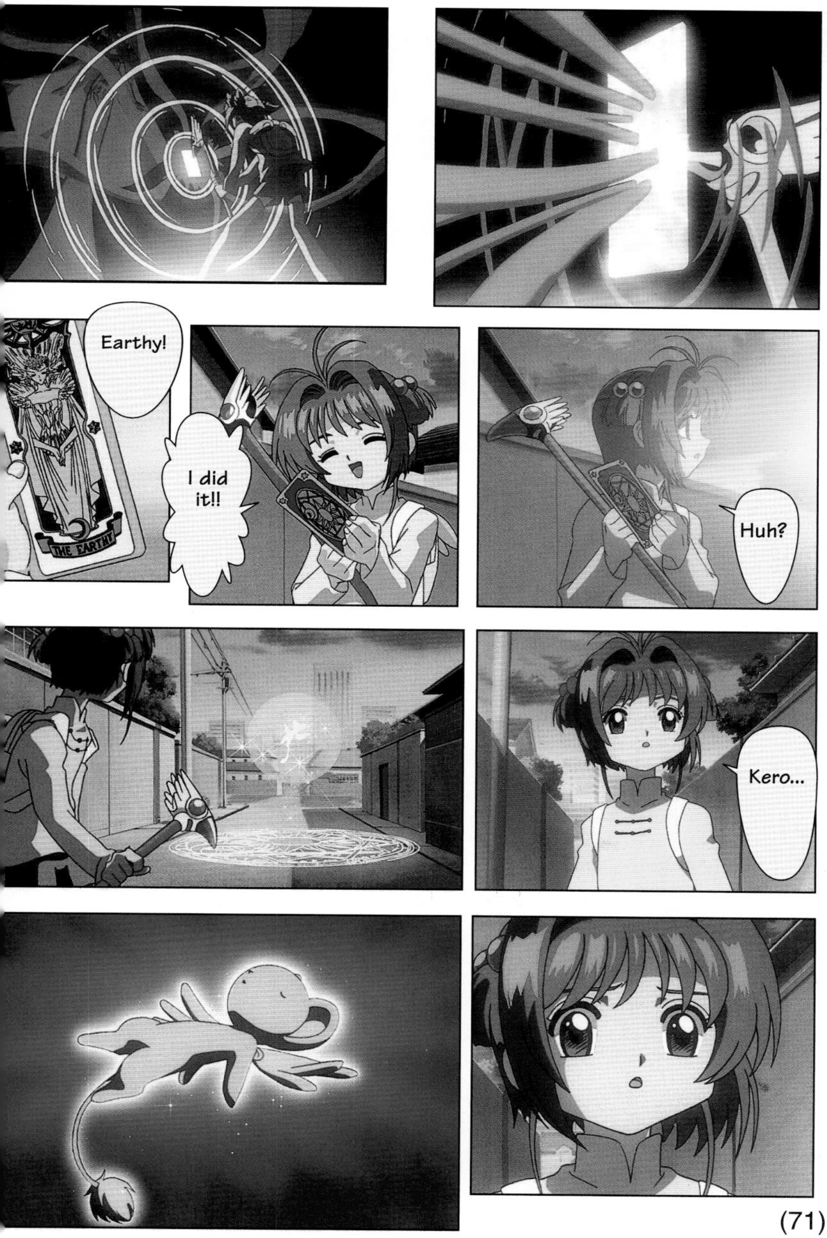
Earthy!
THE EARTHY
I did it!!
Huh?
Kero...

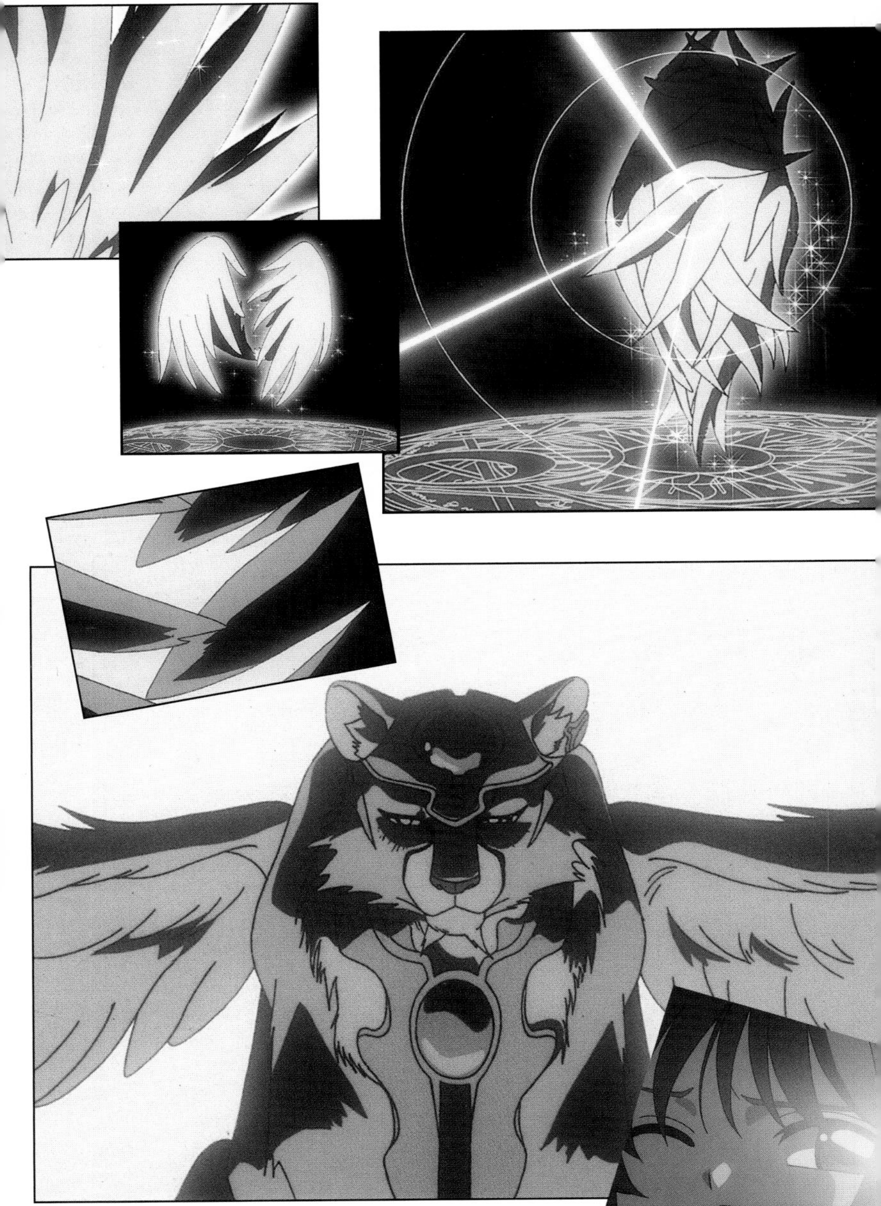

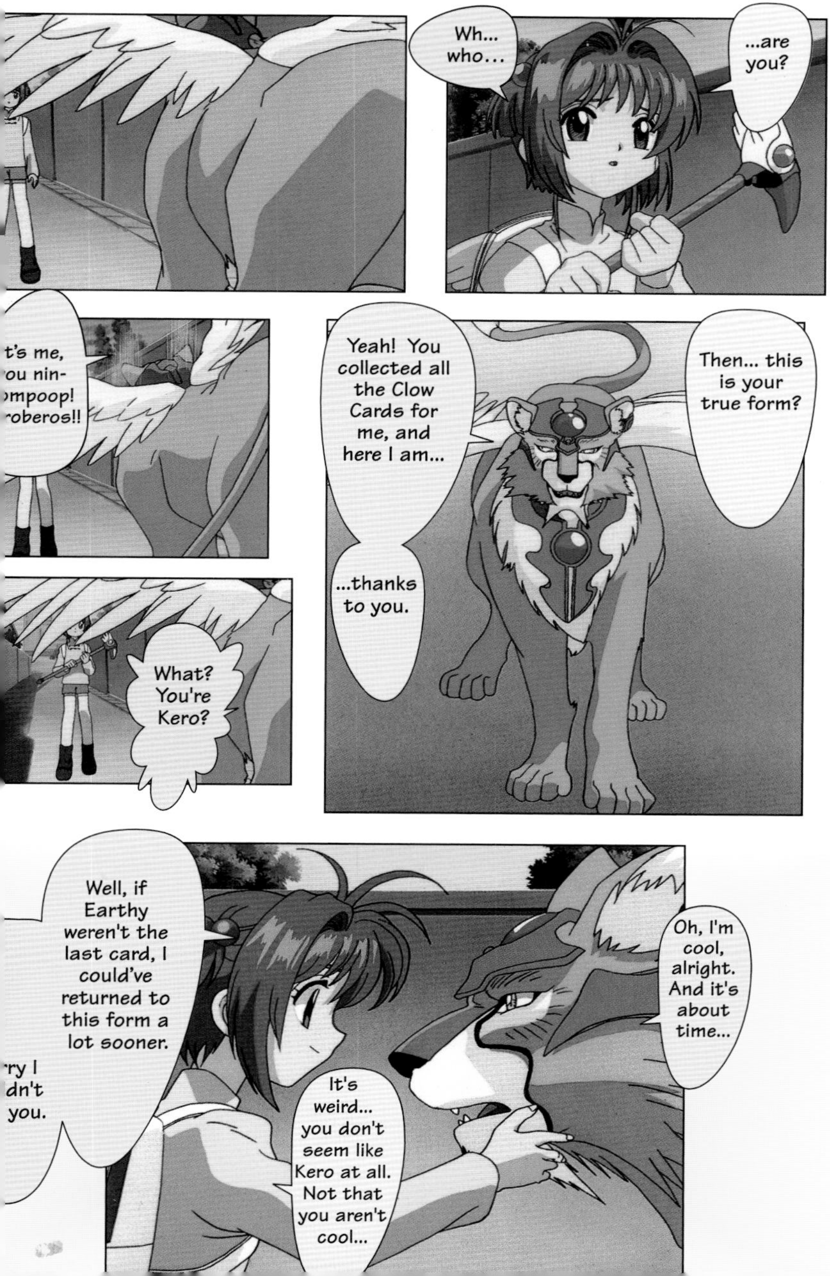
Wh... who...
...are you?
t's me, ou nin- mpoop! roberos!!
What? You're Kero?
Yeah! You collected all the Clow Cards for me, and here I am...
...thanks to you.
Then... this is your true form?
Well, if Earthy weren't the last card, I could've returned to this form a lot sooner.
rry I dn't you.
It's weird... you don't seem like Kero at all. Not that you aren't cool...
Oh, I'm cool, alright. And it's about time...

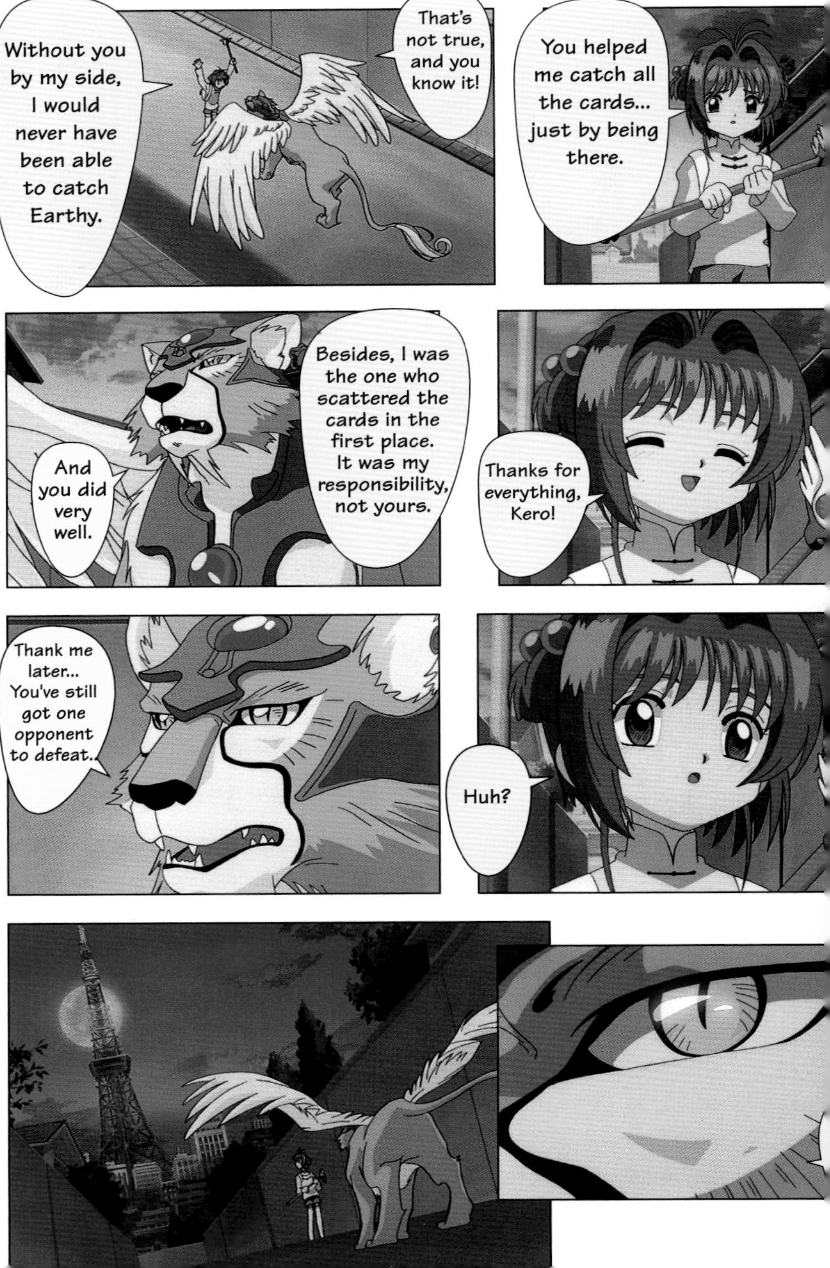
Without you by my side, I would never have been able to catch Earthy.
That's not true, and you know it!
You helped me catch all the cards... just by being there.
Besides, I was the one who scattered the cards in the first place. It was my responsibility, not yours.
And you did very well.
Thanks for everything, Kero!
Thank me later... You've still got one opponent to defeat...
Huh?

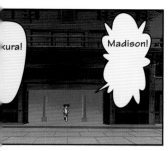

Madison!

...kura!

Are you okay?!

Yeah! Look, the final card! I've got 'em all!

Now that you've captured the final Clow Card, Sakura, what are you going to do?

CAM 1:47:12

Eheh heh... going home?

...oh my.

1:47:15

Um... who are you?

Not this again.

CAM 1:48:3

How cute! It really suits you, Sakura.

B-but... how come I have to dress up?

(75)

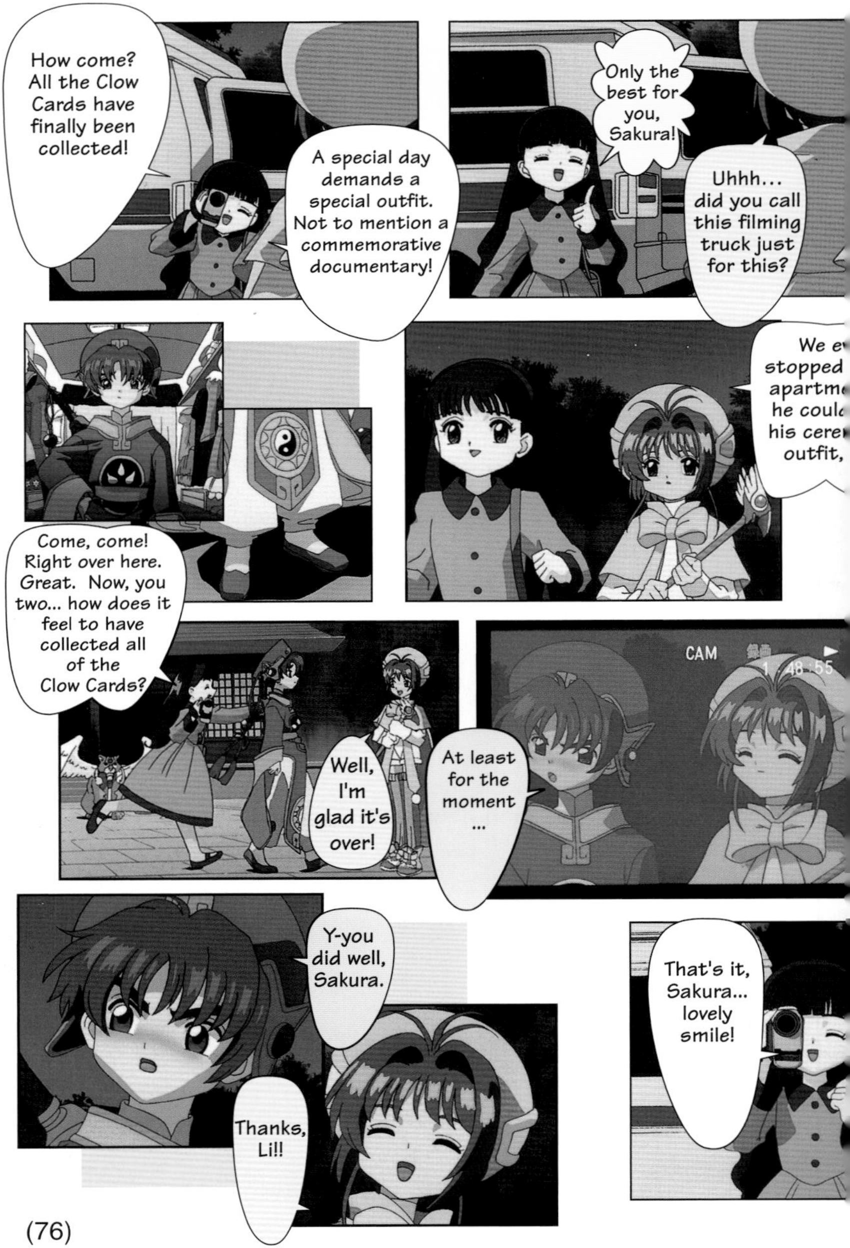
How come? All the Clow Cards have finally been collected!
A special day demands a special outfit. Not to mention a commemorative documentary!
Only the best for you, Sakura!
Uhhh... did you call this filming truck just for this?
We e stopped apartm he coul his cere outfit,
Come, come! Right over here. Great. Now, you two... how does it feel to have collected all of the Clow Cards?
Well, I'm glad it's over!
At least for the moment ...
CAM
48:55
Y-you did well, Sakura.
Thanks, Li!!
That's it, Sakura... lovely smile!

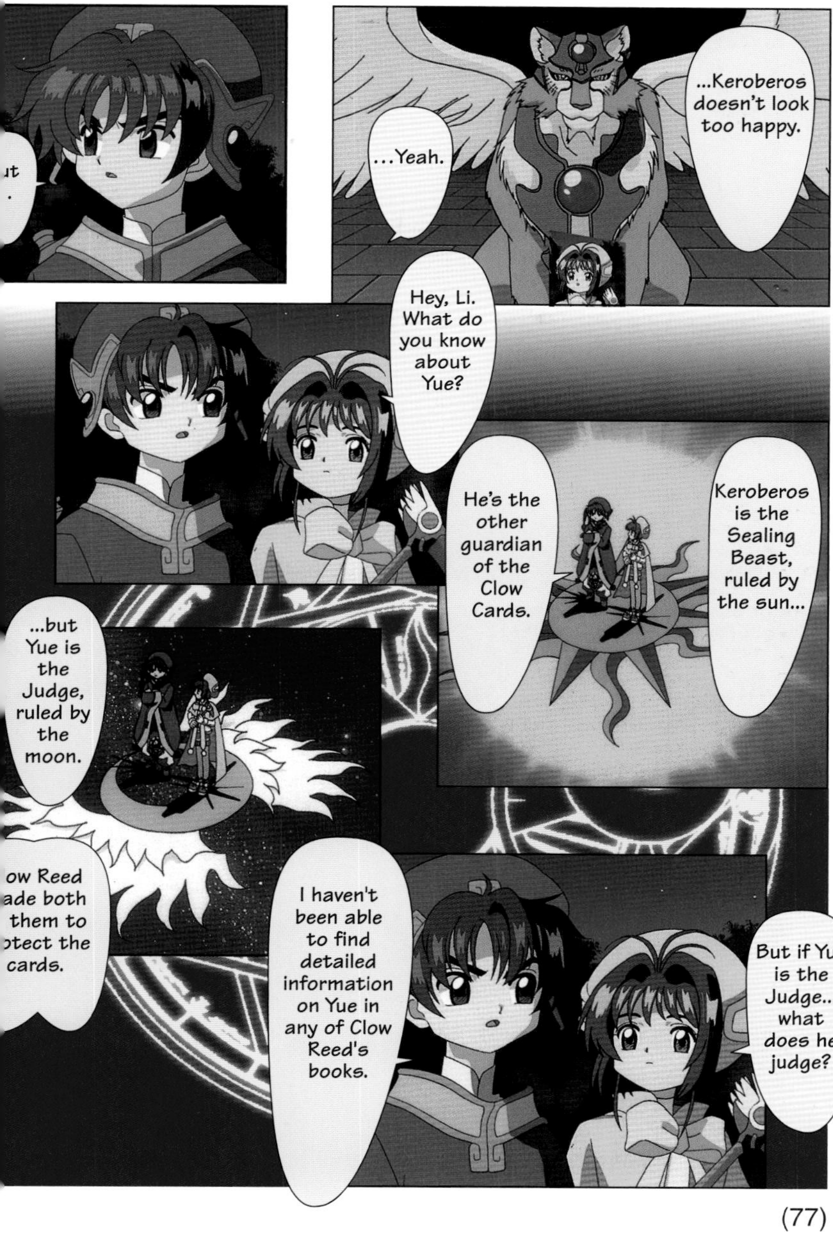

...Keroberos doesn't look too happy.
...Yeah.
Hey, Li. What do you know about Yue?
He's the other guardian of the Clow Cards.
Keroberos is the Sealing Beast, ruled by the sun...
...but Yue is the Judge, ruled by the moon.
ow Reed ade both them to otect the cards.
I haven't been able to find detailed information on Yue in any of Clow Reed's books.
But if Yue is the Judge... what does he judge?

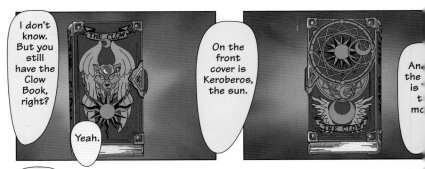

I don't know. But you still have the Clow Book, right?

Yeah.

On the front cover is Keroberos, the sun.

An... the... is "... t... mo...

I don't remember a moon on the back of the book.

WHAT?! Then...Yue must have taken a temporary form, just like Keroberos.

Have you written your name on the card, Sakura?

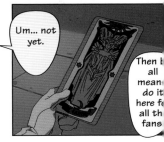

Um... not yet.

Then b... all mean... do it... here f... all th... fans...

(78)

When you write your name, Sakura, all of the cards will be sealed.

Yeah!

...ve ...re ...or ...ng, ...a.

Kero?

What's wrong?

Uh... nothing. I'll write it now.

Phew! Okay...

- Don't ...th have ? Some ...akura's, ...ome are ...i's.

So who's going to be the official owner of the Clow Cards?

You'll find out soon enough.

(79)

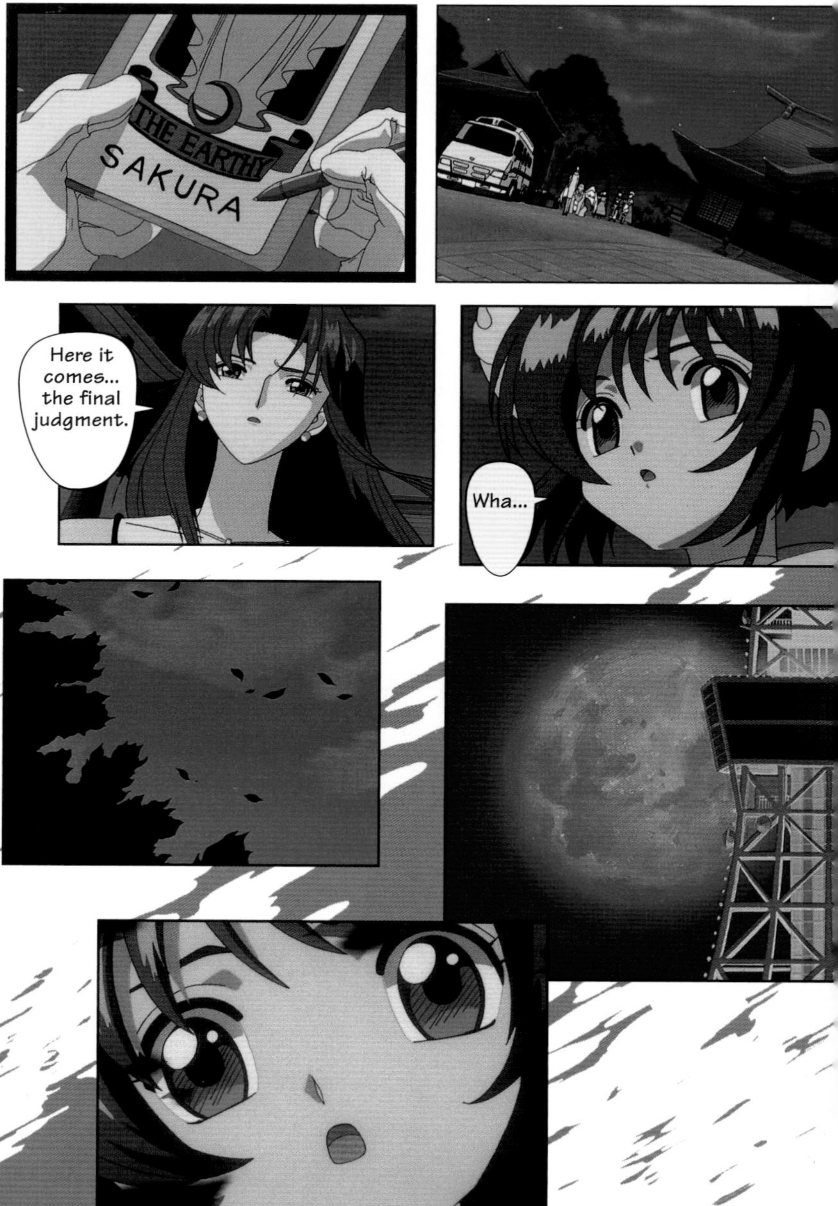
THE EARTHY
SAKURA
Here it comes... the final judgment.
Wha...

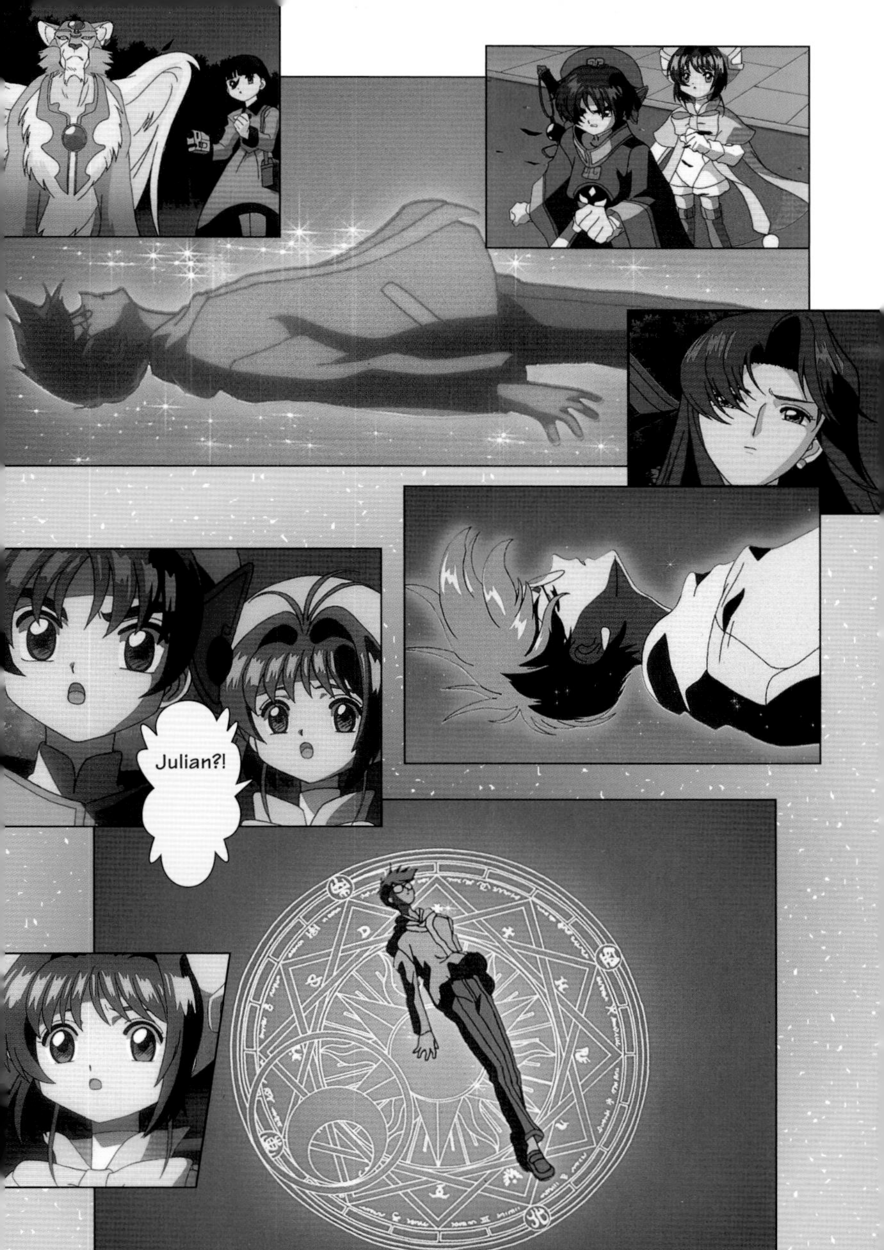
Julian?!

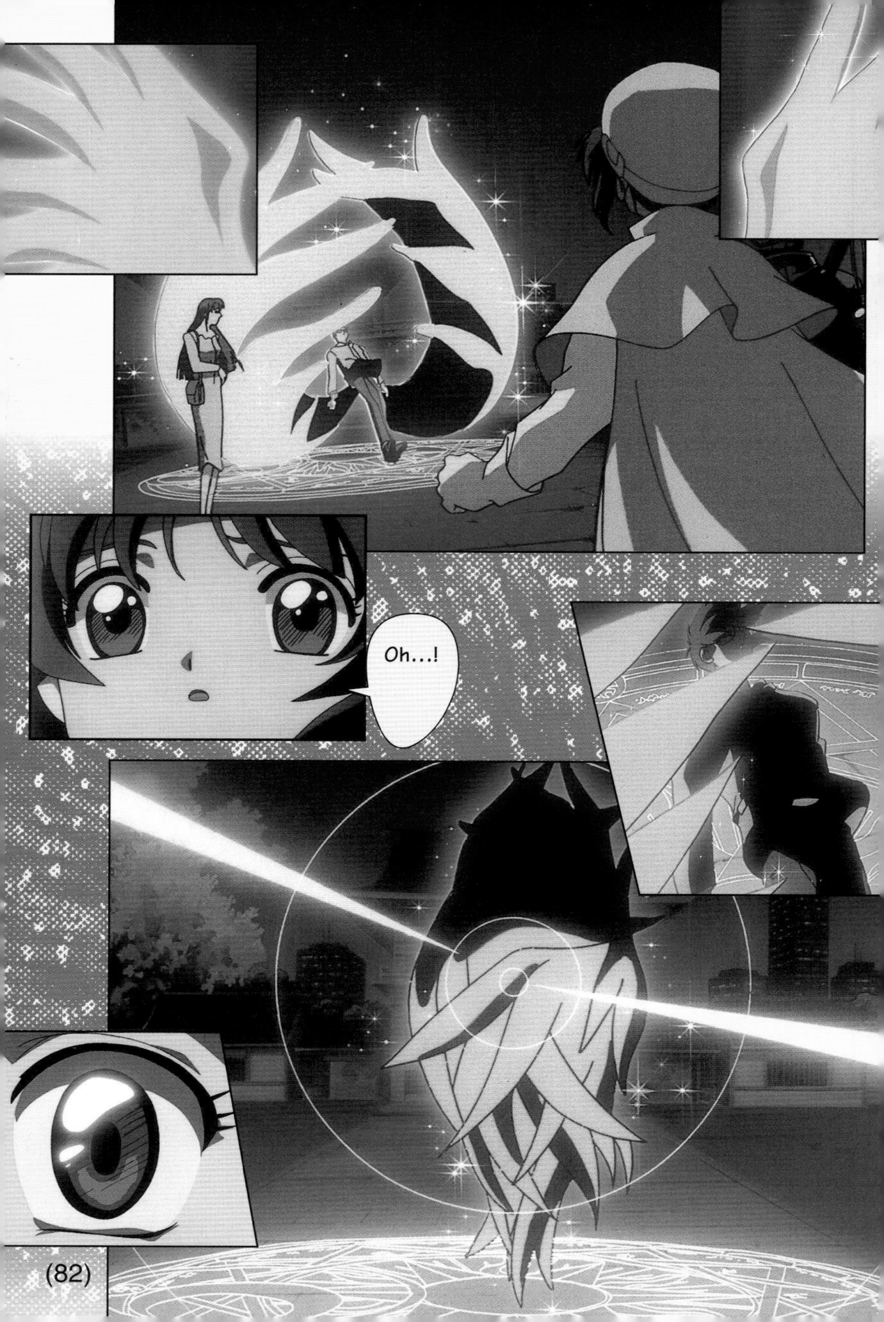
Oh...!

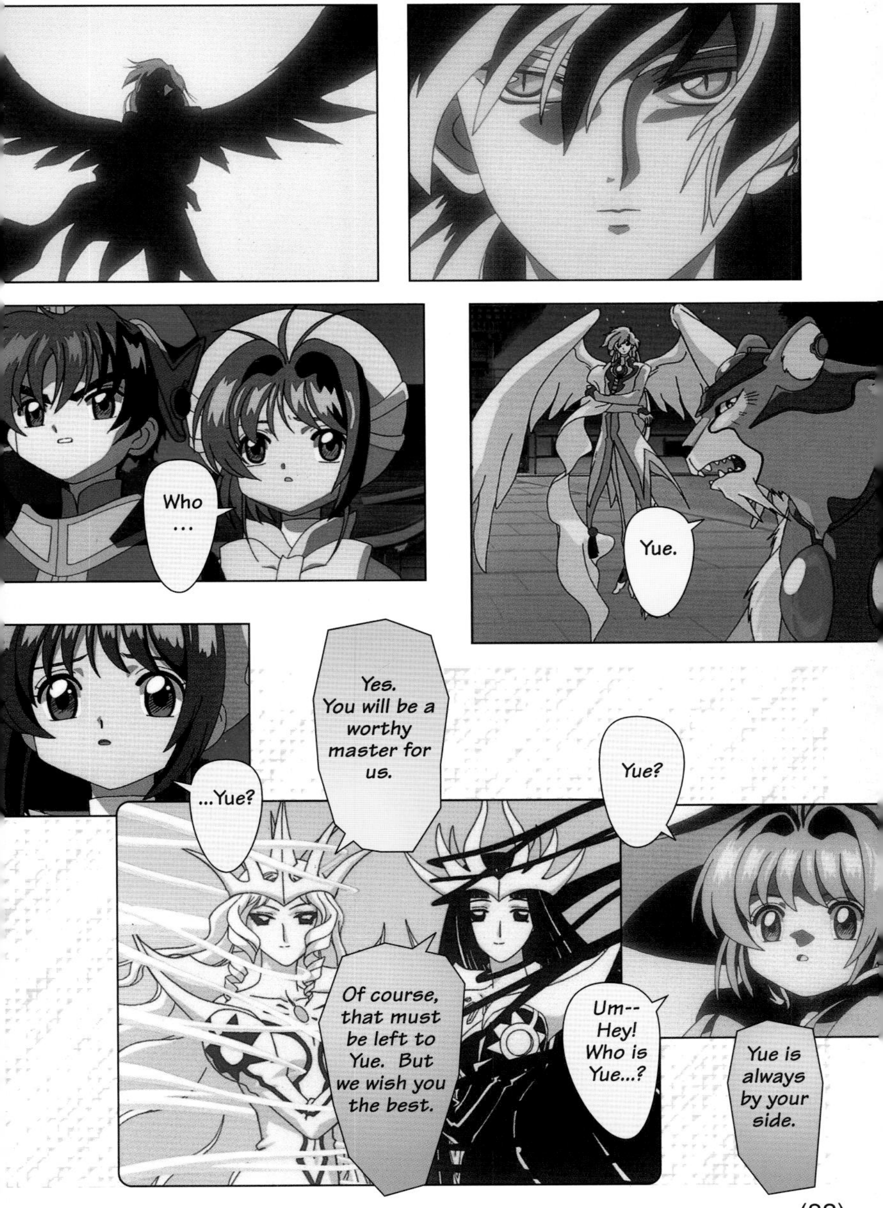

Who ...
Yue.
...Yue?
Yes. You will be a worthy master for us.
Yue?
Of course, that must be left to Yue. But we wish you the best.
Um-- Hey! Who is Yue...?
Yue is always by your side.

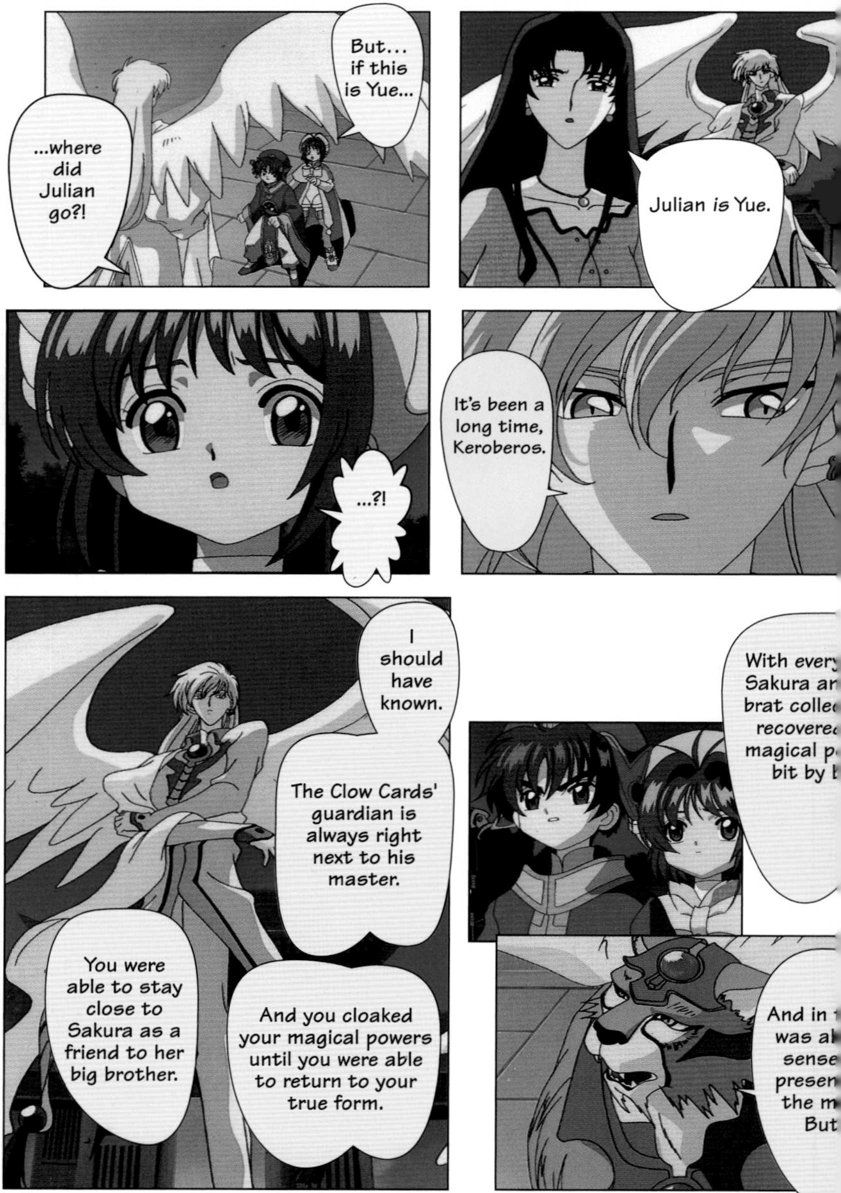
But... if this is Yue...
...where did Julian go?!
Julian *is* Yue.
...?!
It's been a long time, Keroberos.
I should have known.
The Clow Cards' guardian is always right next to his master.
You were able to stay close to Sakura as a friend to her big brother.
And you cloaked your magical powers until you were able to return to your true form.
With every Sakura ar brat colle recovere magical p bit by
And in was al sense presen the m But

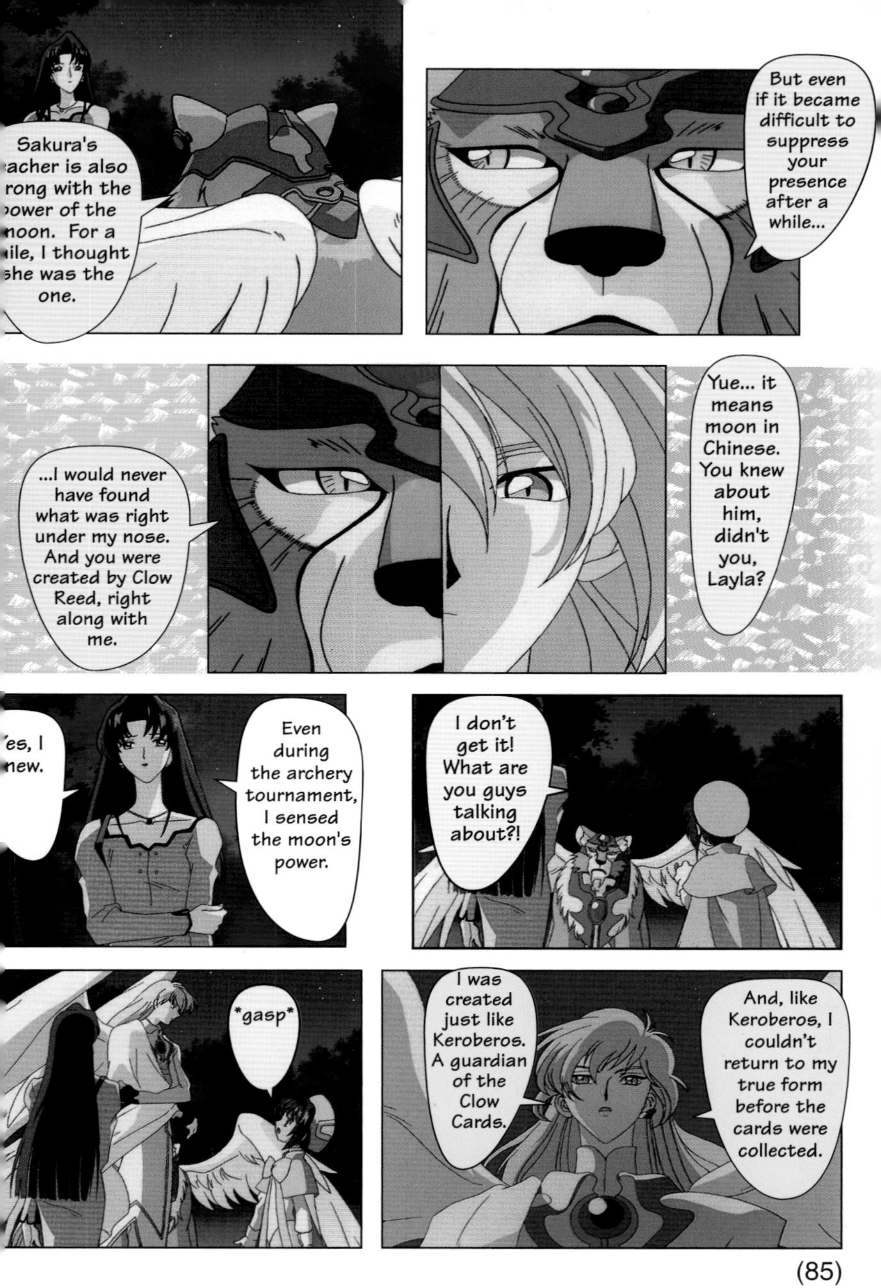
Sakura's acher is also rong with the ower of the moon. For a ile, I thought she was the one.
But even if it became difficult to suppress your presence after a while...
...I would never have found what was right under my nose. And you were created by Clow Reed, right along with me.
Yue... it means moon in Chinese. You knew about him, didn't you, Layla?
es, I new.
Even during the archery tournament, I sensed the moon's power.
I don't get it! What are you guys talking about?!
gasp
I was created just like Keroberos. A guardian of the Clow Cards.
And, like Keroberos, I couldn't return to my true form before the cards were collected.

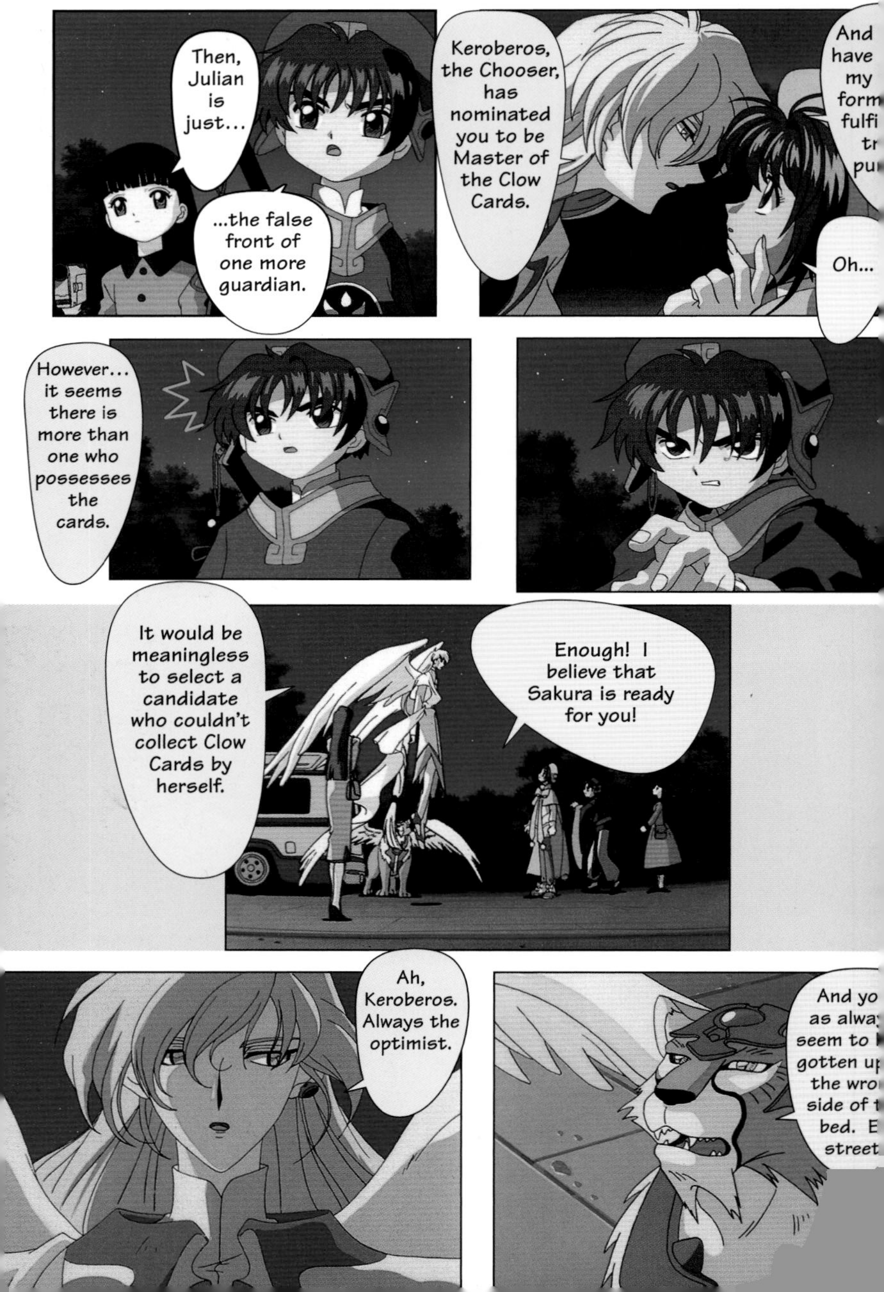
Then, Julian is just...
...the false front of one more guardian.
Keroberos, the Chooser, has nominated you to be Master of the Clow Cards.
And have my form fulfi tr pu
Oh...
However... it seems there is more than one who possesses the cards.
It would be meaningless to select a candidate who couldn't collect Clow Cards by herself.
Enough! I believe that Sakura is ready for you!
Ah, Keroberos. Always the optimist.
And yo as alwa seem to gotten up the wro side of bed. E street

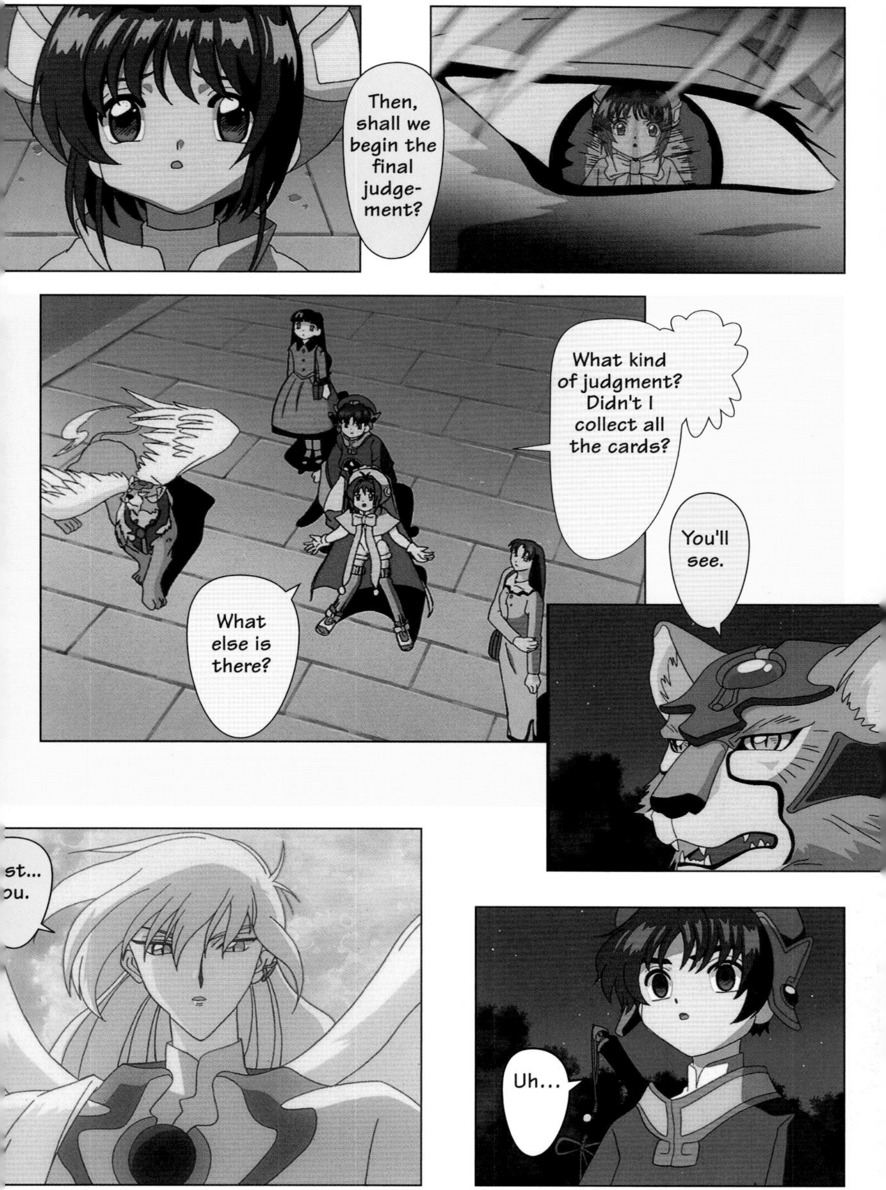
Then, shall we begin the final judge-ment?
What kind of judgment? Didn't I collect all the cards?
What else is there?
You'll see.
st...
ou.
Uh...

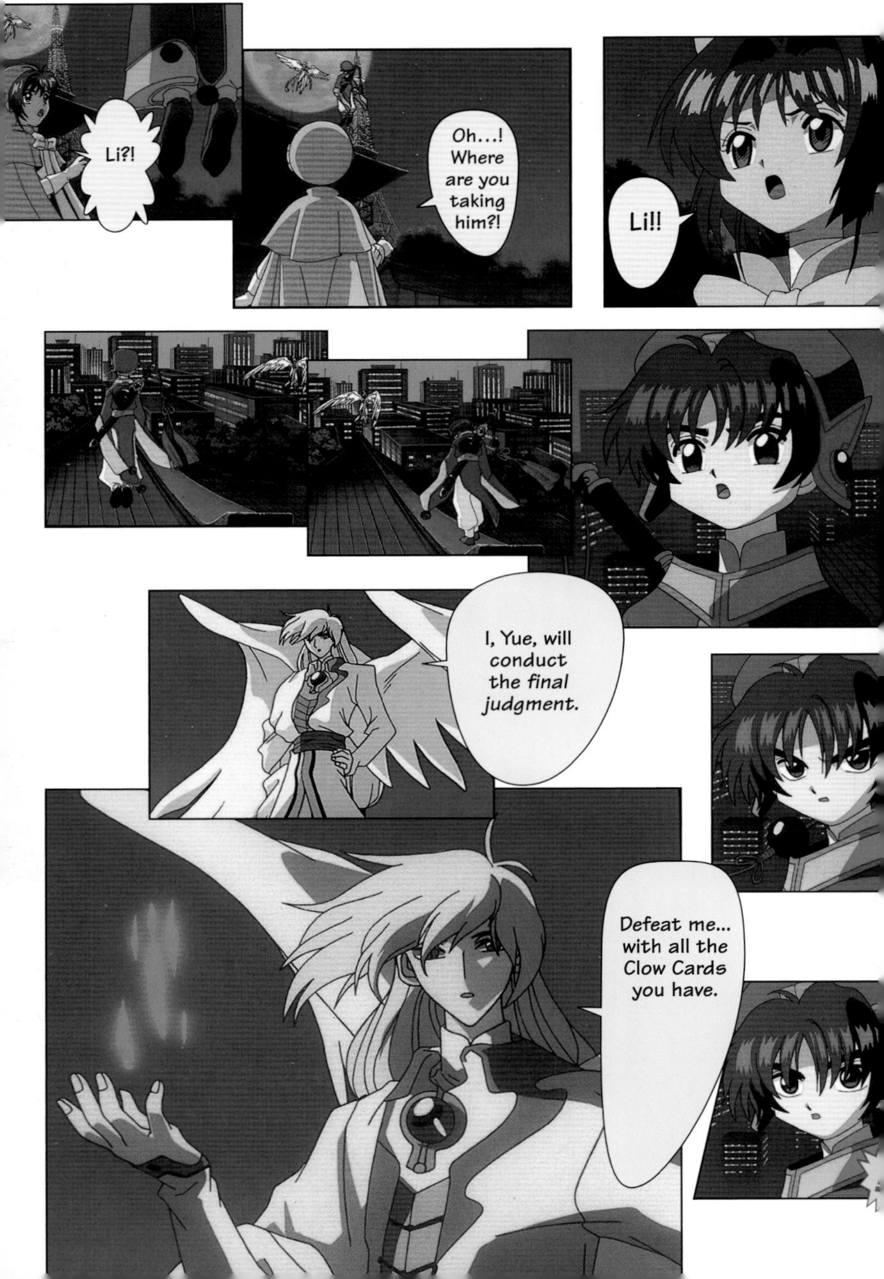

Li?!
Oh…! Where are you taking him?!
Li!!
I, Yue, will conduct the *final* judgment.
Defeat me... with all the Clow Cards you have.

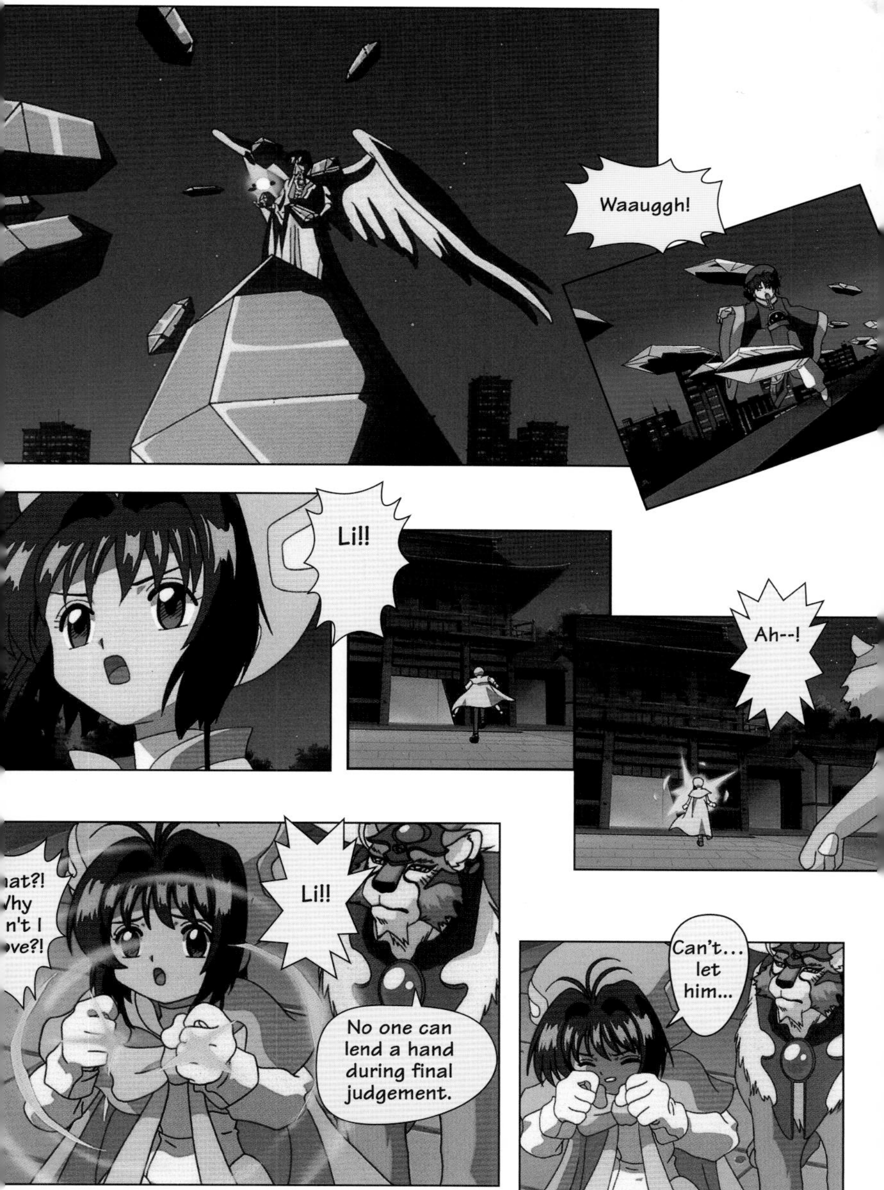

Waauggh!
Li!!
Ah--!
Li!!
No one can lend a hand during final judgement.
Can't... let him...

Bring forth Raging Fire!

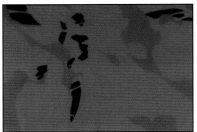

T-t

The Judge cannot be defeated with Fire.

Oh.

...ery
...ell...

Bring
forth
Wind
Fl--

Tut,
tut...

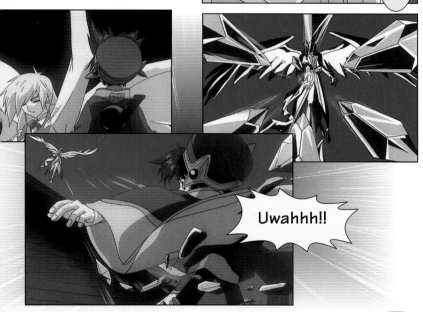

Uwahhh!!

Huff

Huff

You were able
to capture
Clow Cards
with that
degree of
magic?

Grr...

TIME!

!?

W-where'd he go?

This is the end, young Cardcaptor...

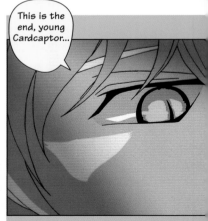

Time, like all your cards, must bow to me.

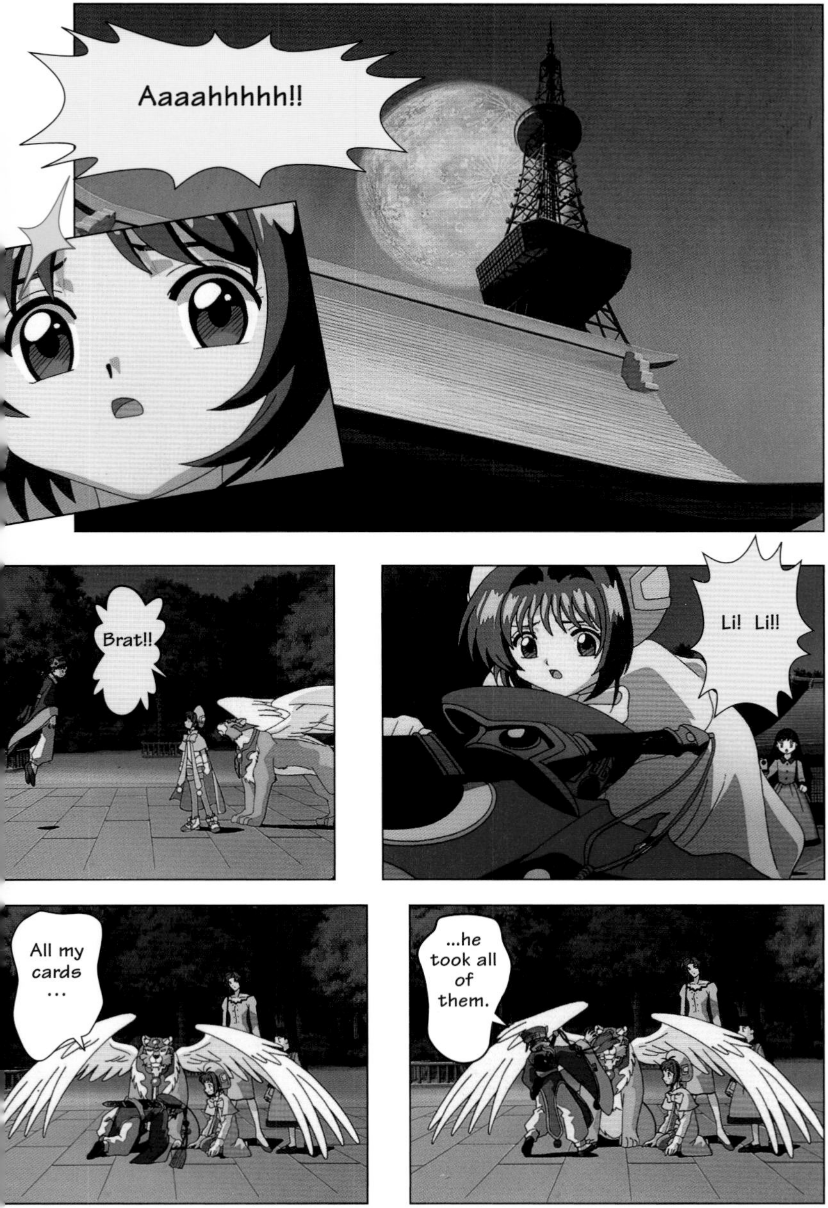

Aaaahhhhh!!
Brat!!
Li! Li!!
All my cards ...
...he took all of them.

Be careful...

He's stronger than you think.

Now for the next candidate... Sakura Avalon.

Sakura!

· · · ·

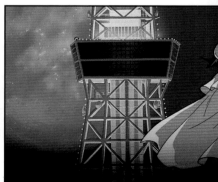

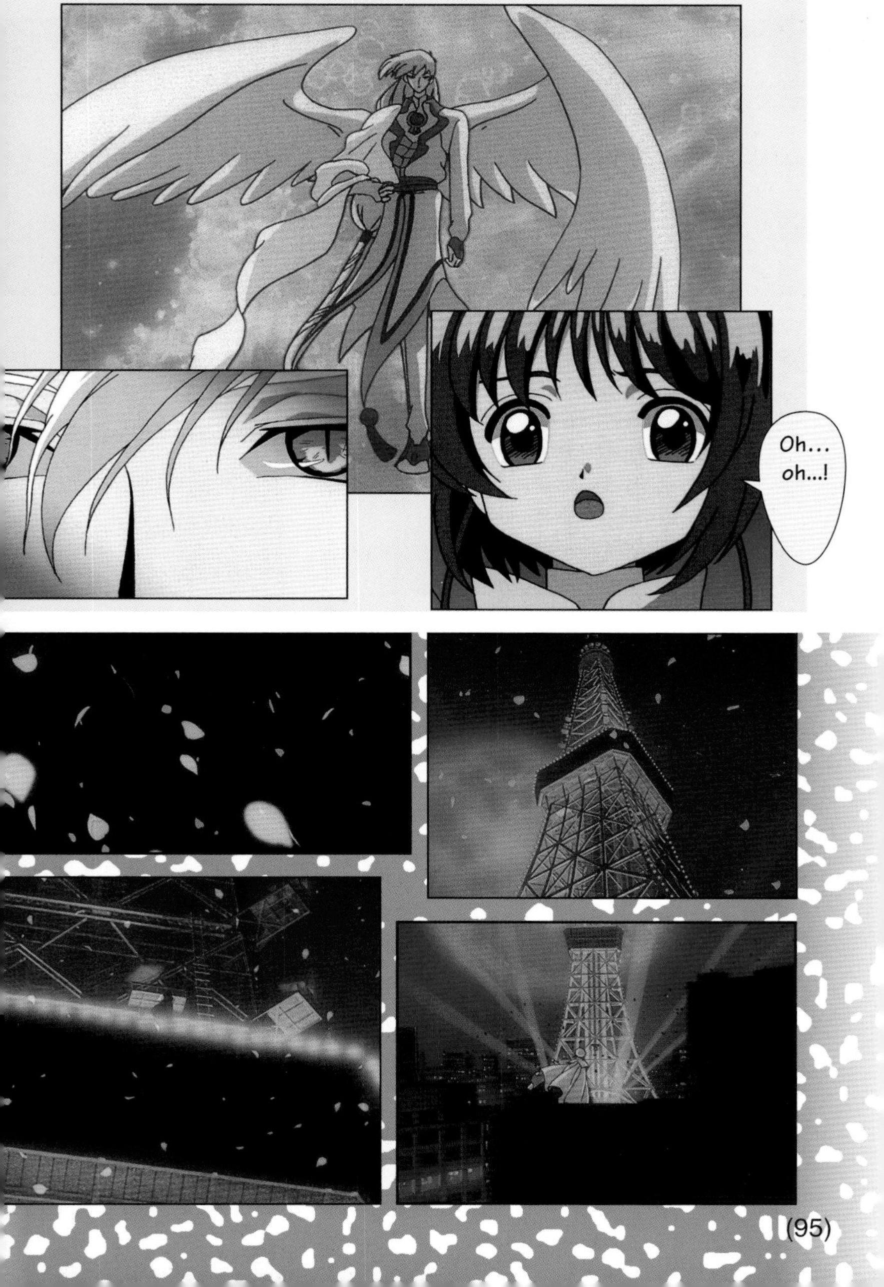
Oh... oh...!

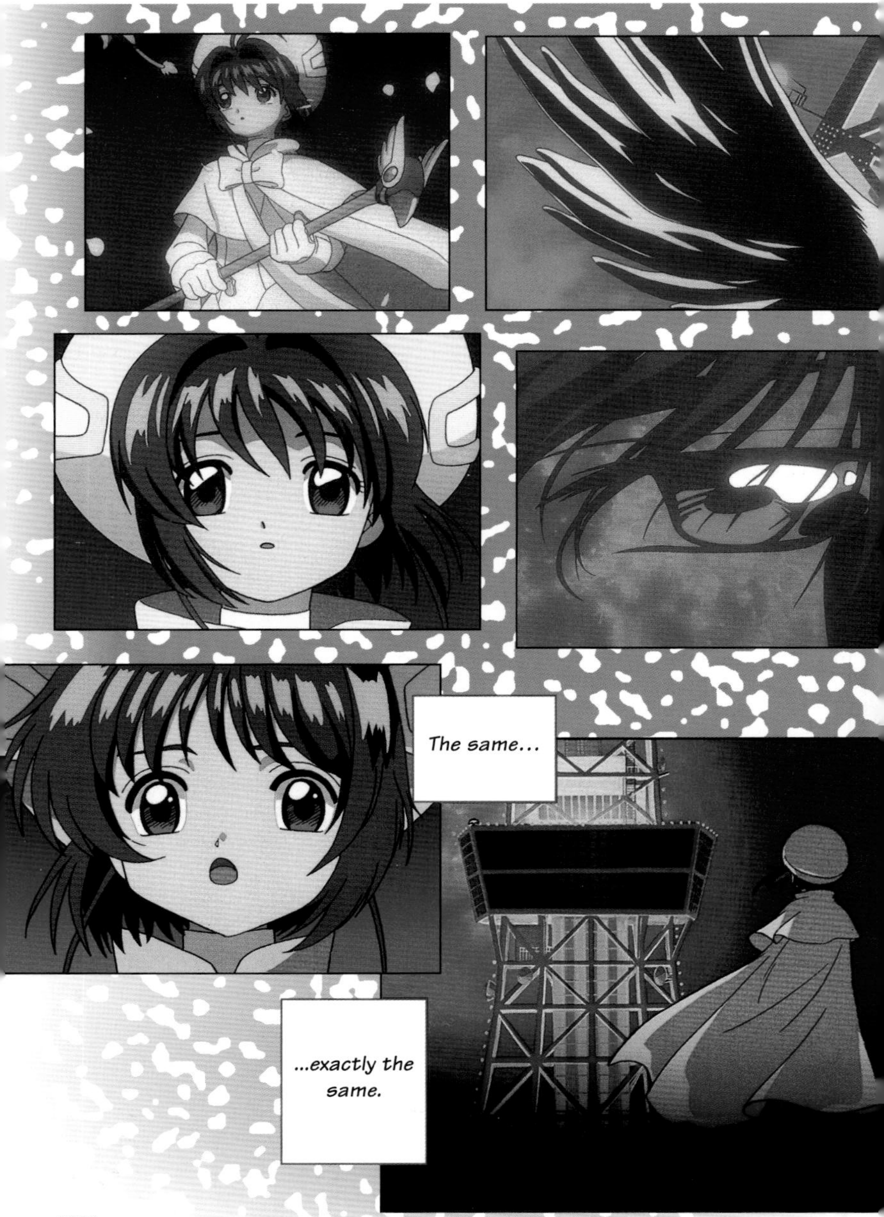
The same...
...exactly the same.

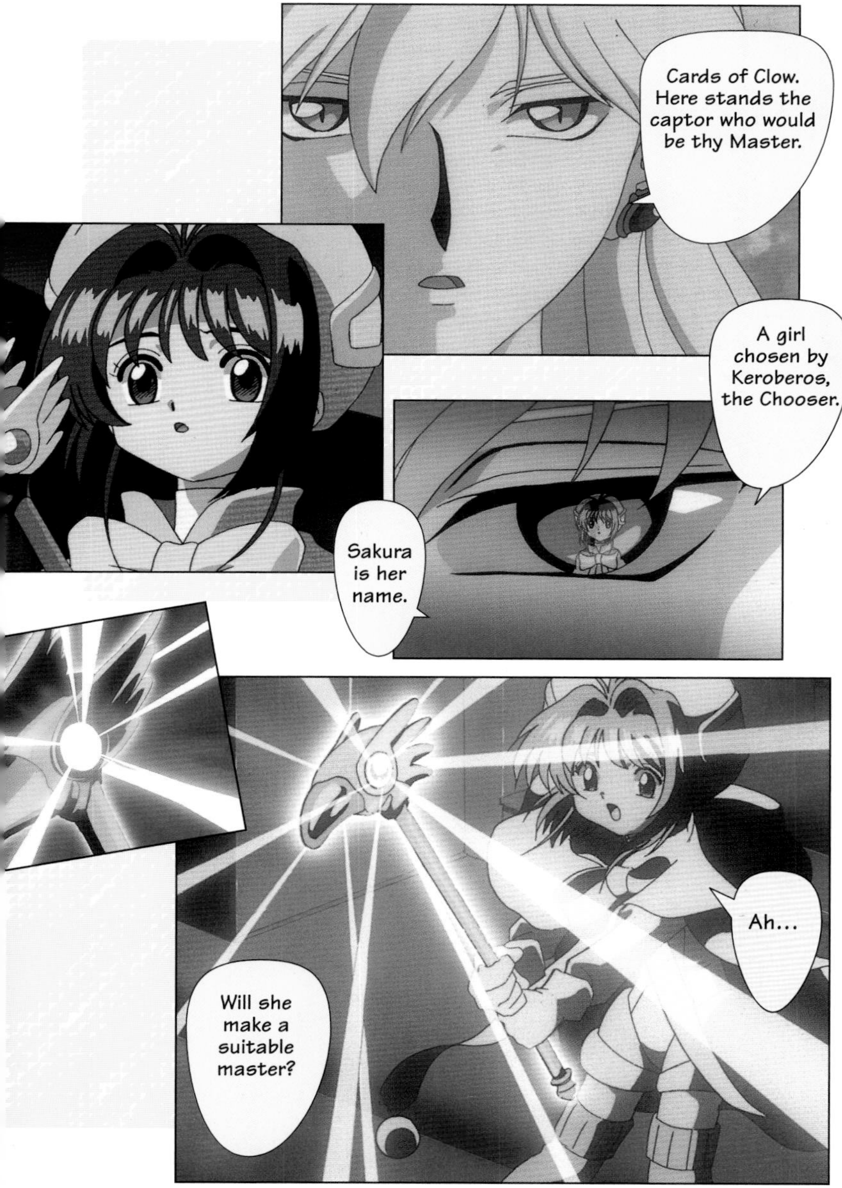
Cards of Clow. Here stands the captor who would be thy Master.
A girl chosen by Keroberos, the Chooser.
Sakura is her name.
Ah...
Will she make a suitable master?

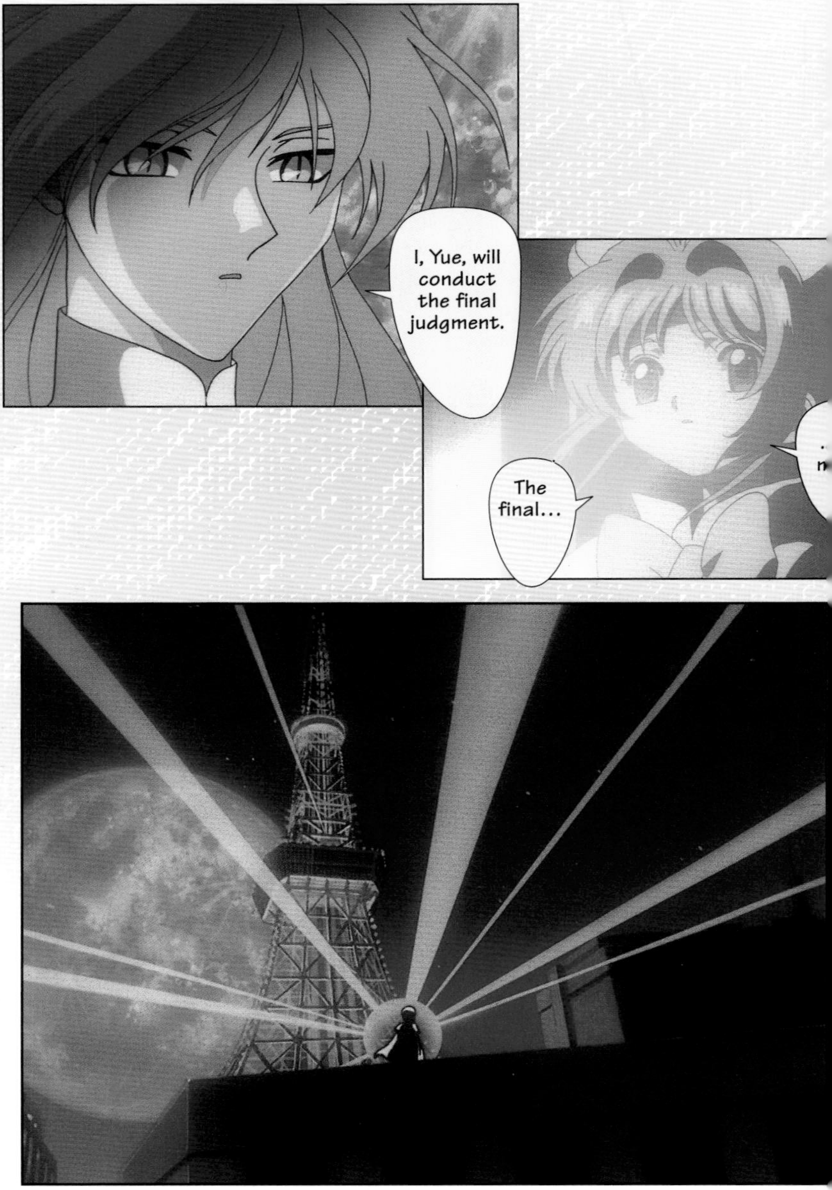
I, Yue, will conduct the final judgment.
The final...

The Last Card - The End

Episode 46

The Final Judgment

CARDCAPTORS™

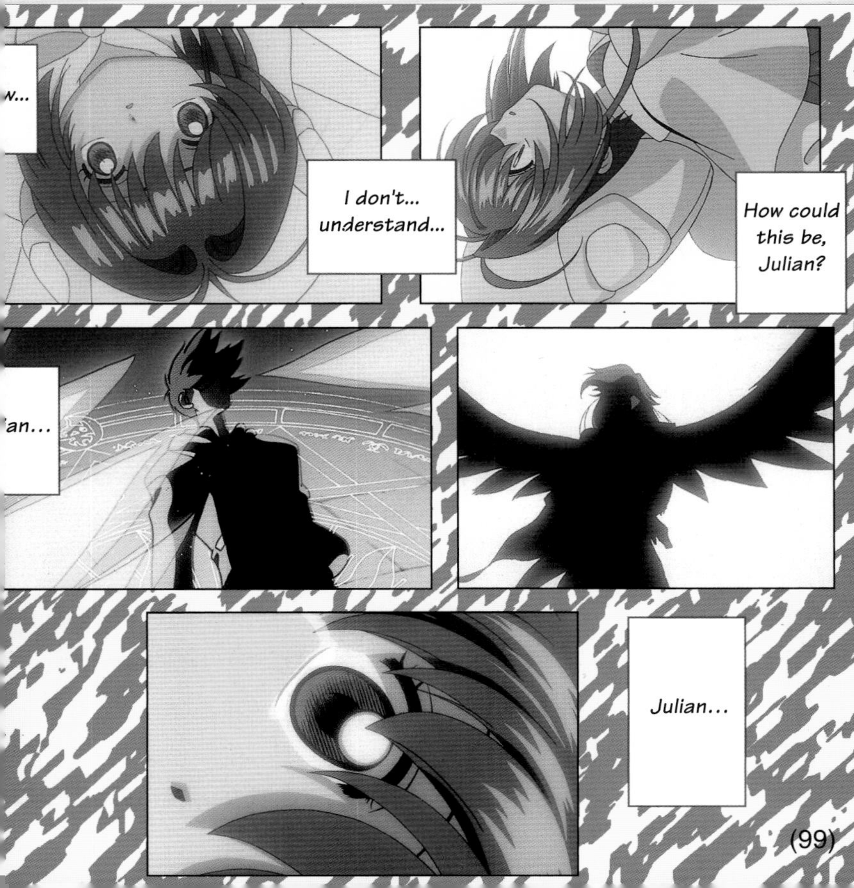
w...
I don't... understand...
How could this be, Julian?
an…
Julian…

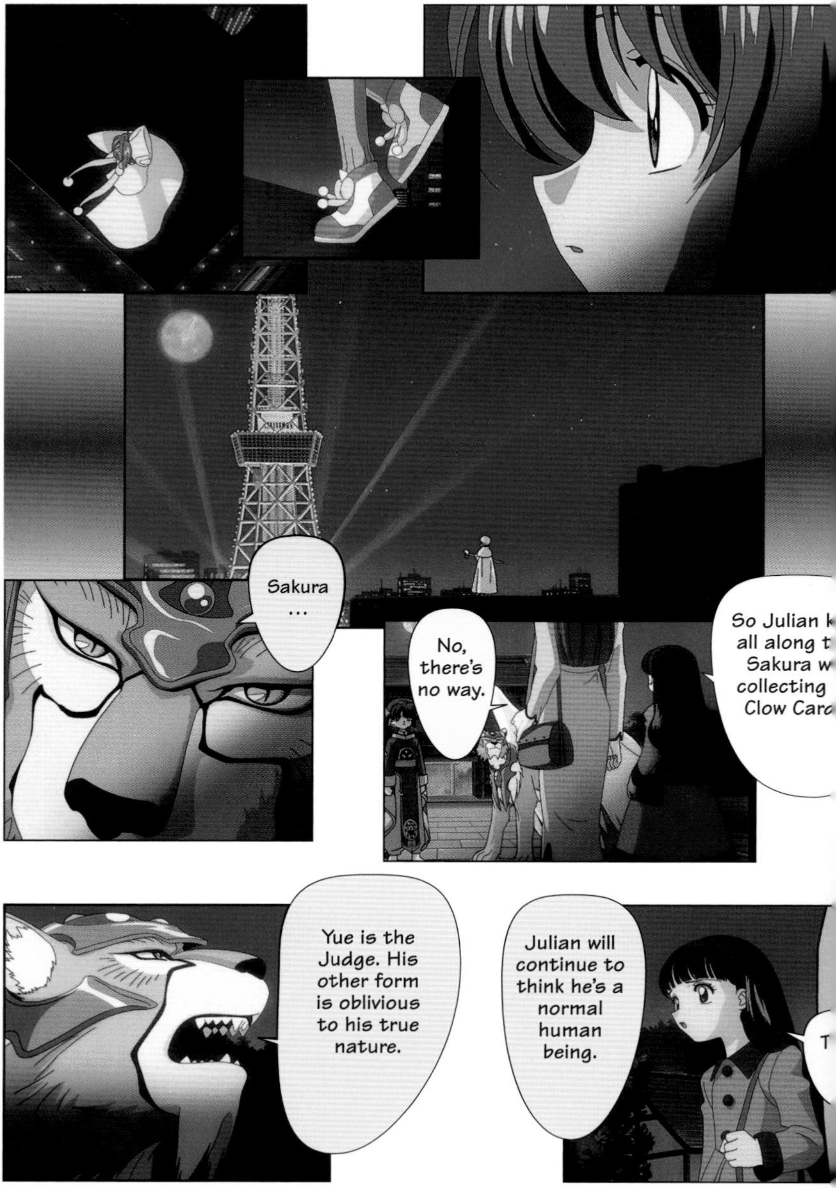

Sakura ...
No, there's no way.
So Julian all along Sakura collecting Clow
Yue is the Judge. His other form is oblivious to his true nature.
Julian will continue to think he's a normal human being.

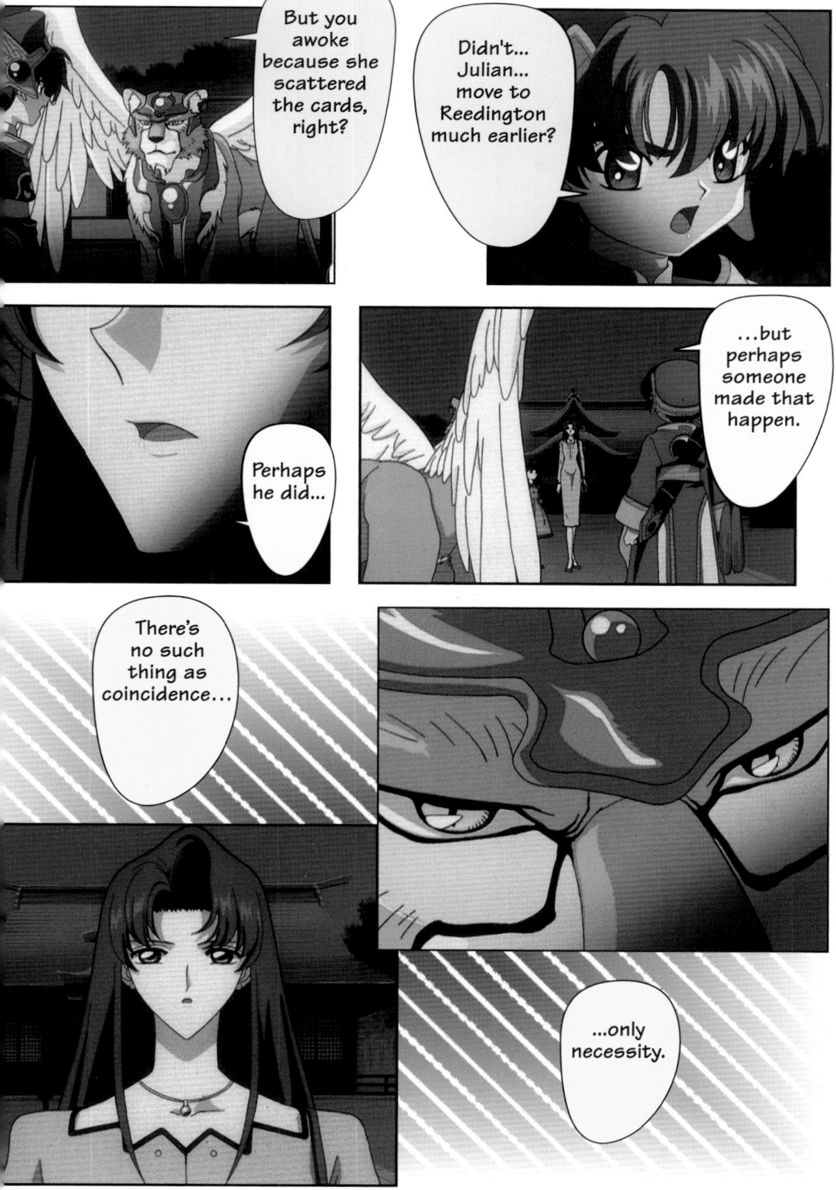
But you awoke because she scattered the cards, right?
Didn't... Julian... move to Reedington much earlier?
Perhaps he did...
...but perhaps someone made that happen.
There's no such thing as coincidence...
...only necessity.

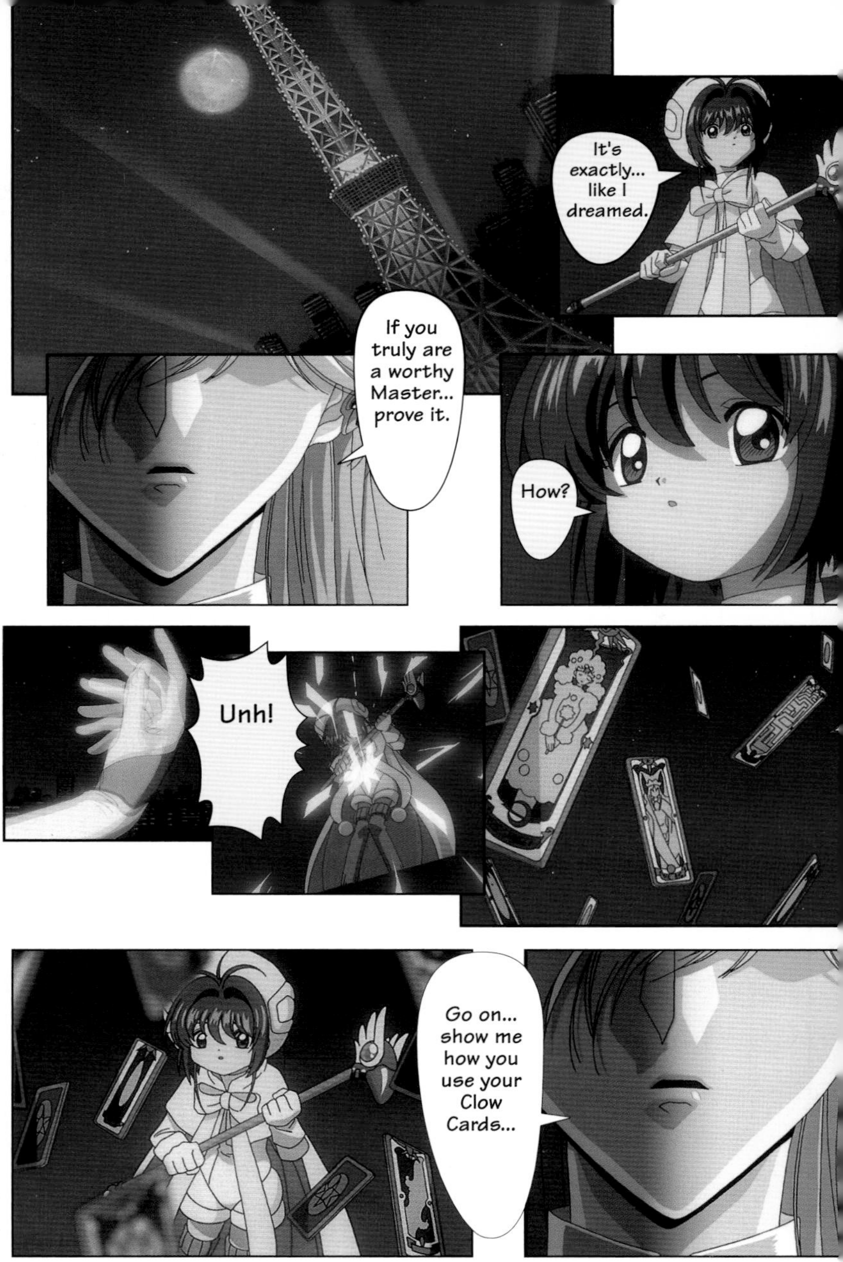

It's exactly... like I dreamed.
If you truly are a worthy Master... prove it.
How?
Unh!
Go on... show me how you use your Clow Cards...

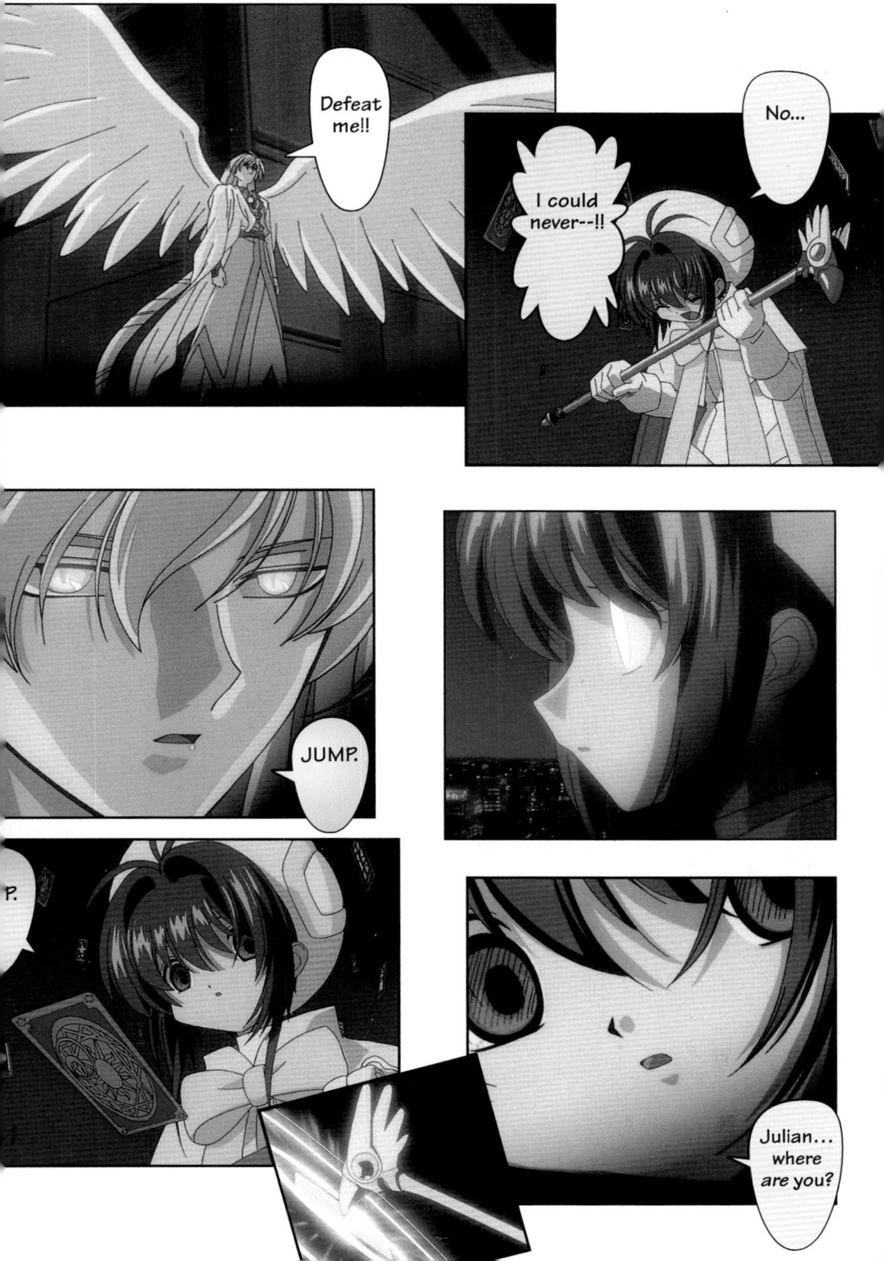
Defeat me!!
No...
I could never--!!
JUMP.
P.
Julian... where are you?

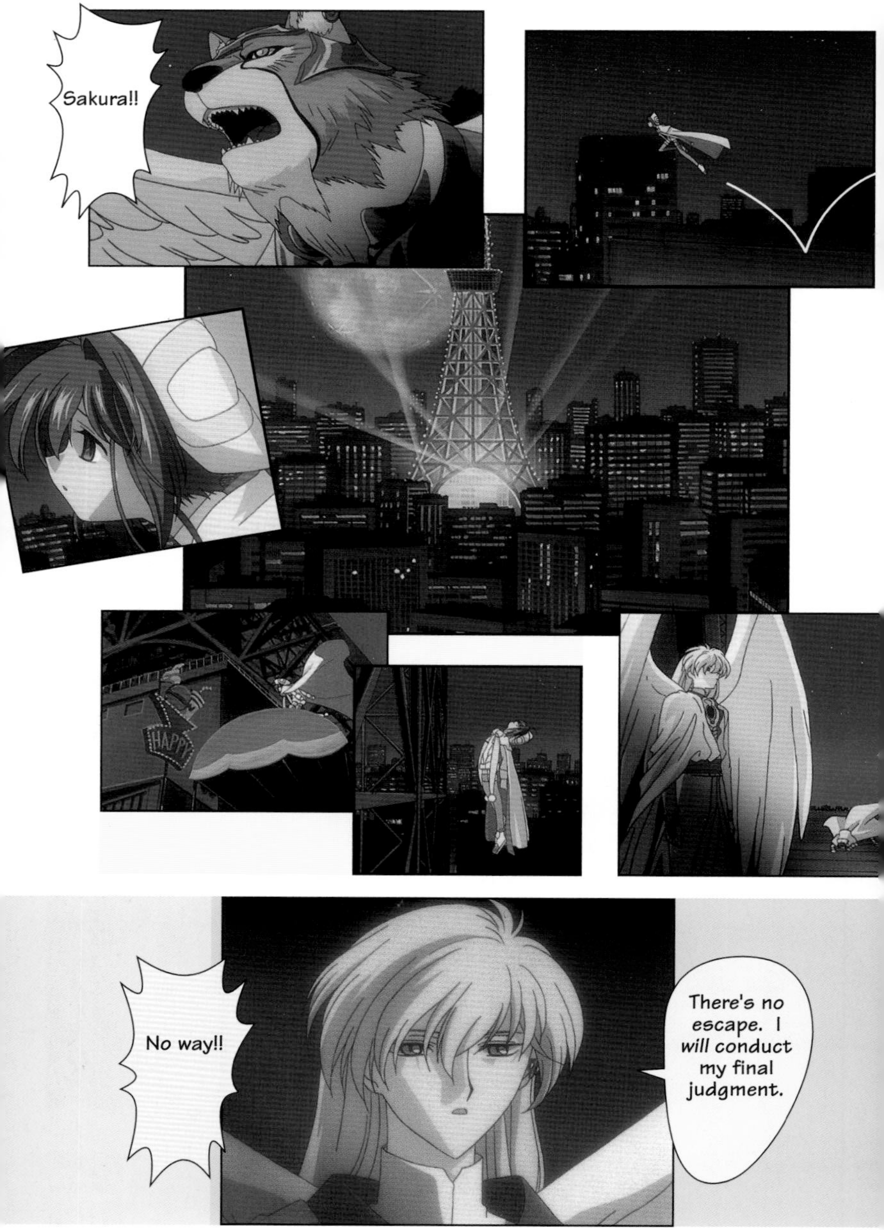
Sakura!!
HAPPY
No way!!
There's no escape. I *will* conduct my final judgment.

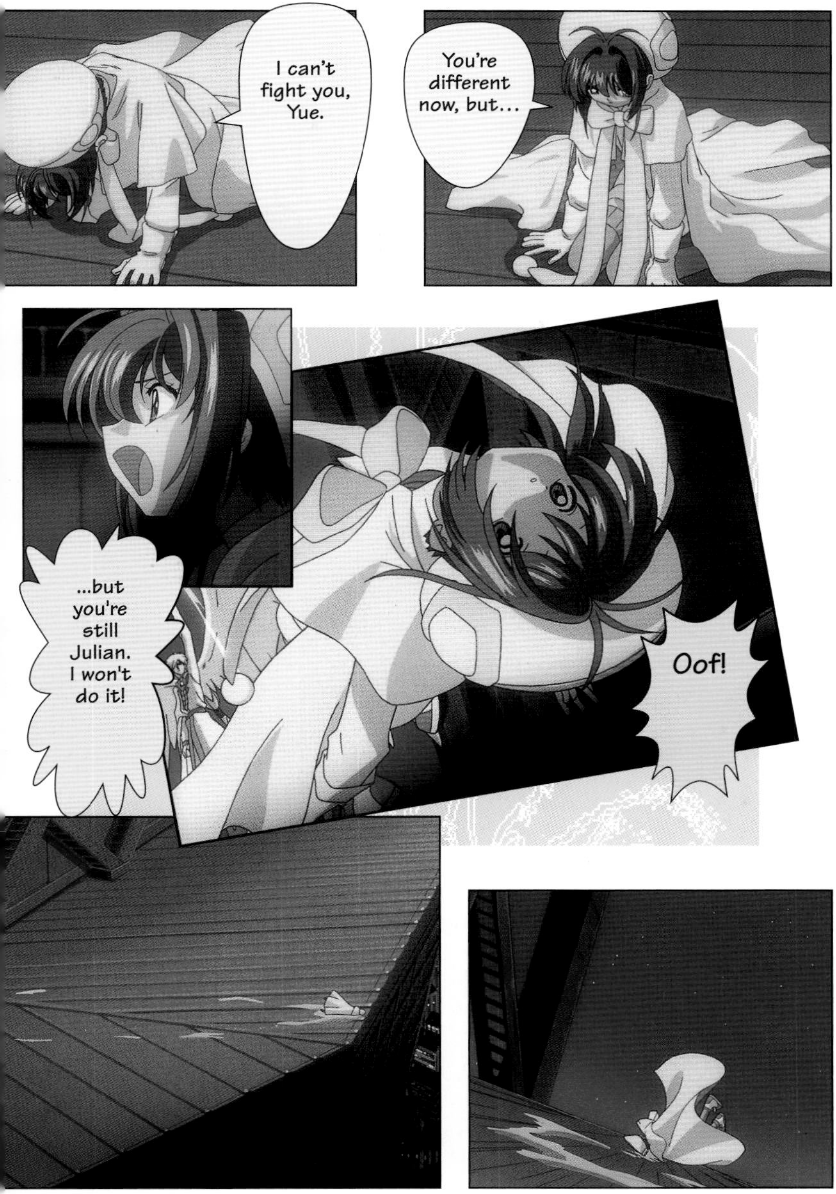

I can't fight you, Yue.
You're different now, but...
...but you're still Julian. I won't do it!
Oof!

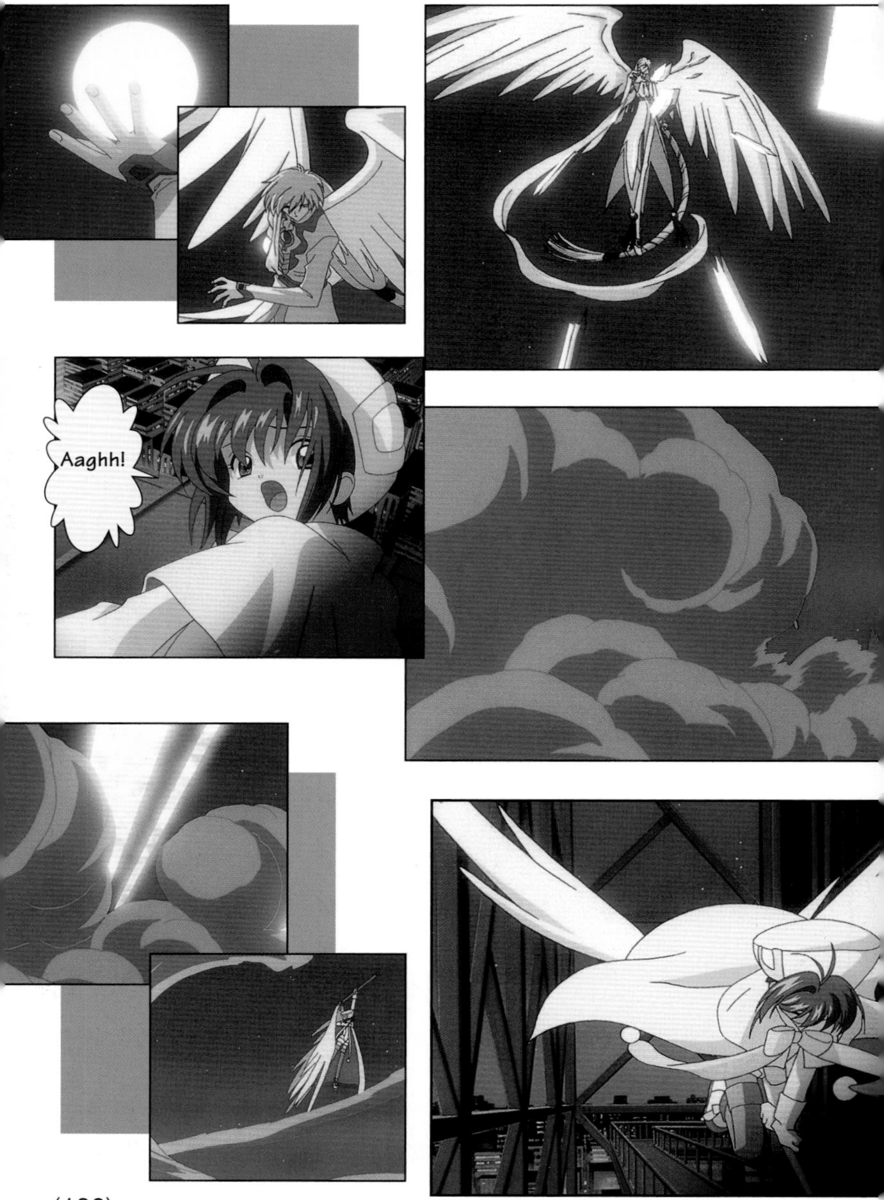
Aaghh!

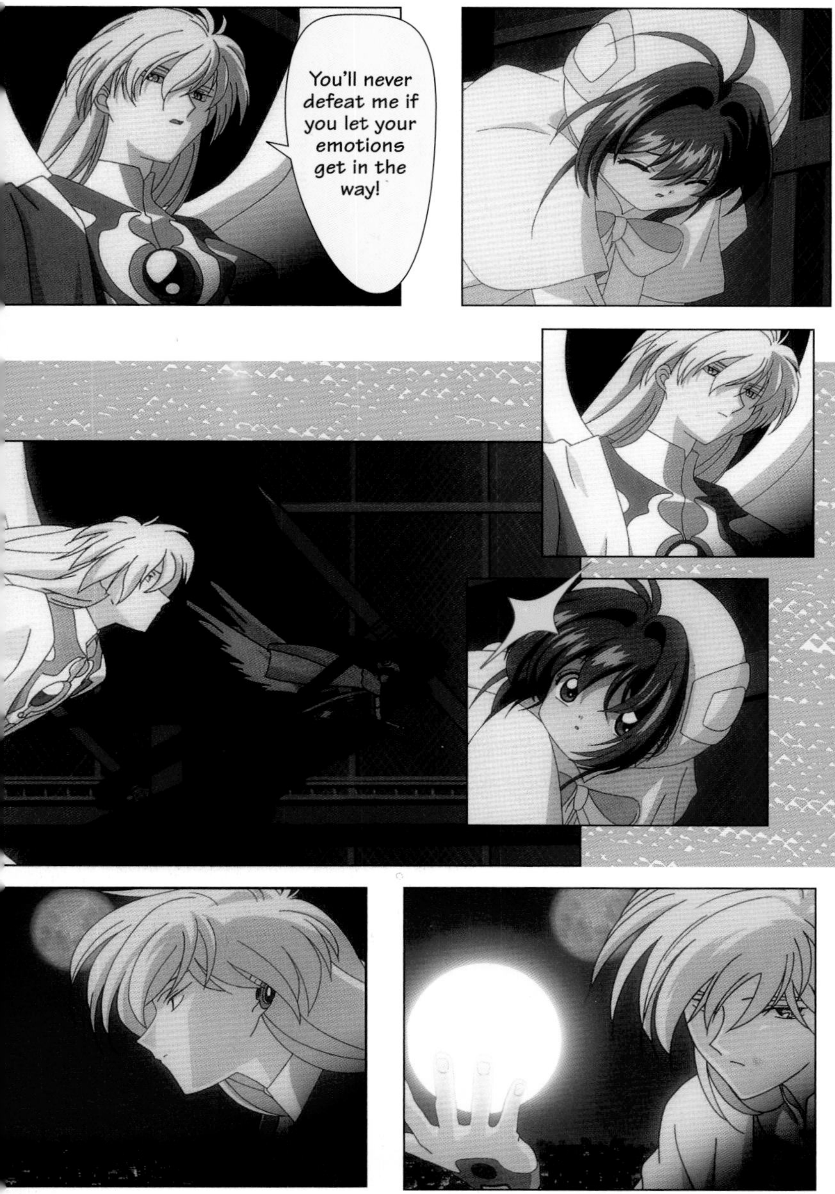
You'll never defeat me if you let your emotions get in the way!

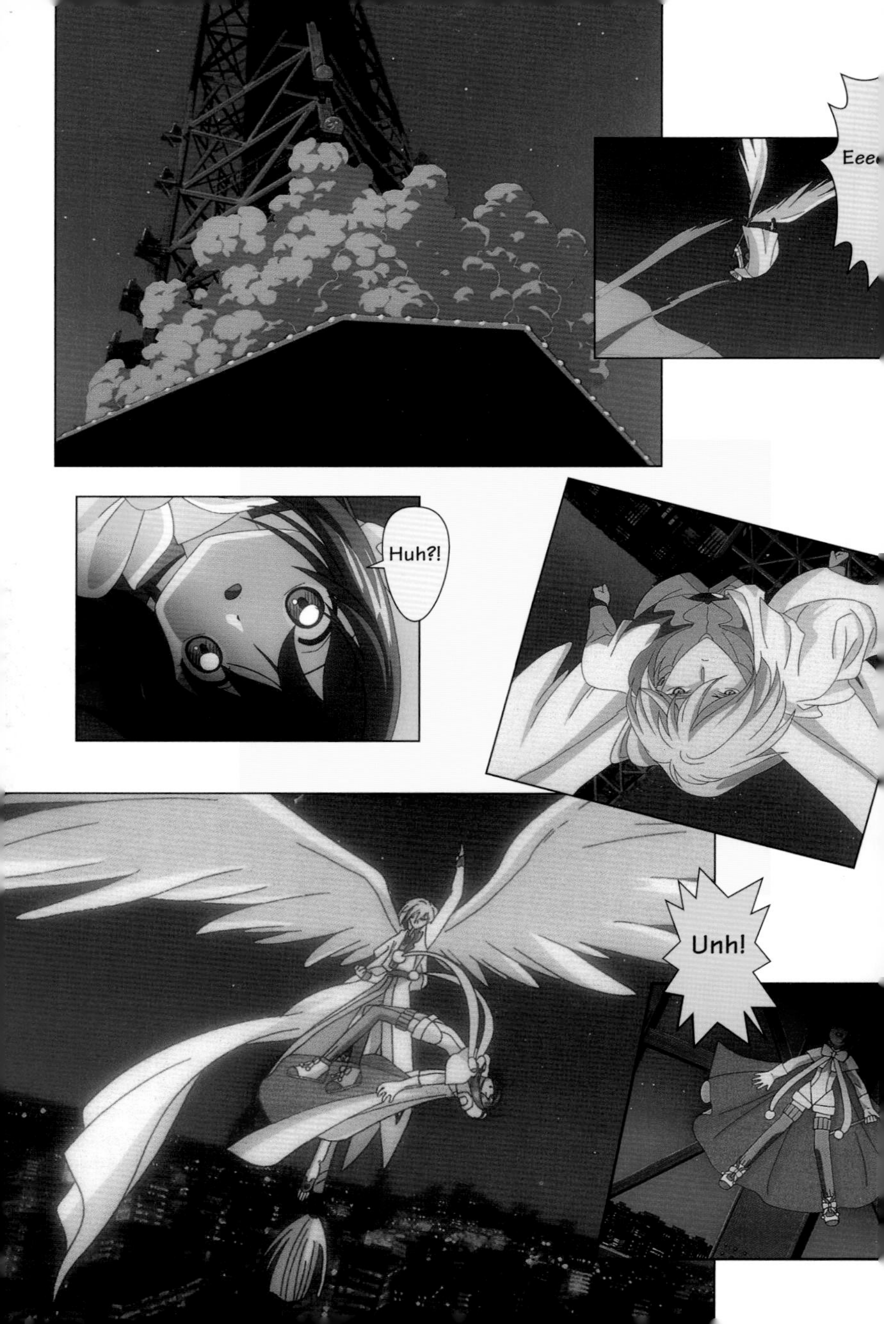
Eee
Huh?!
Unh!

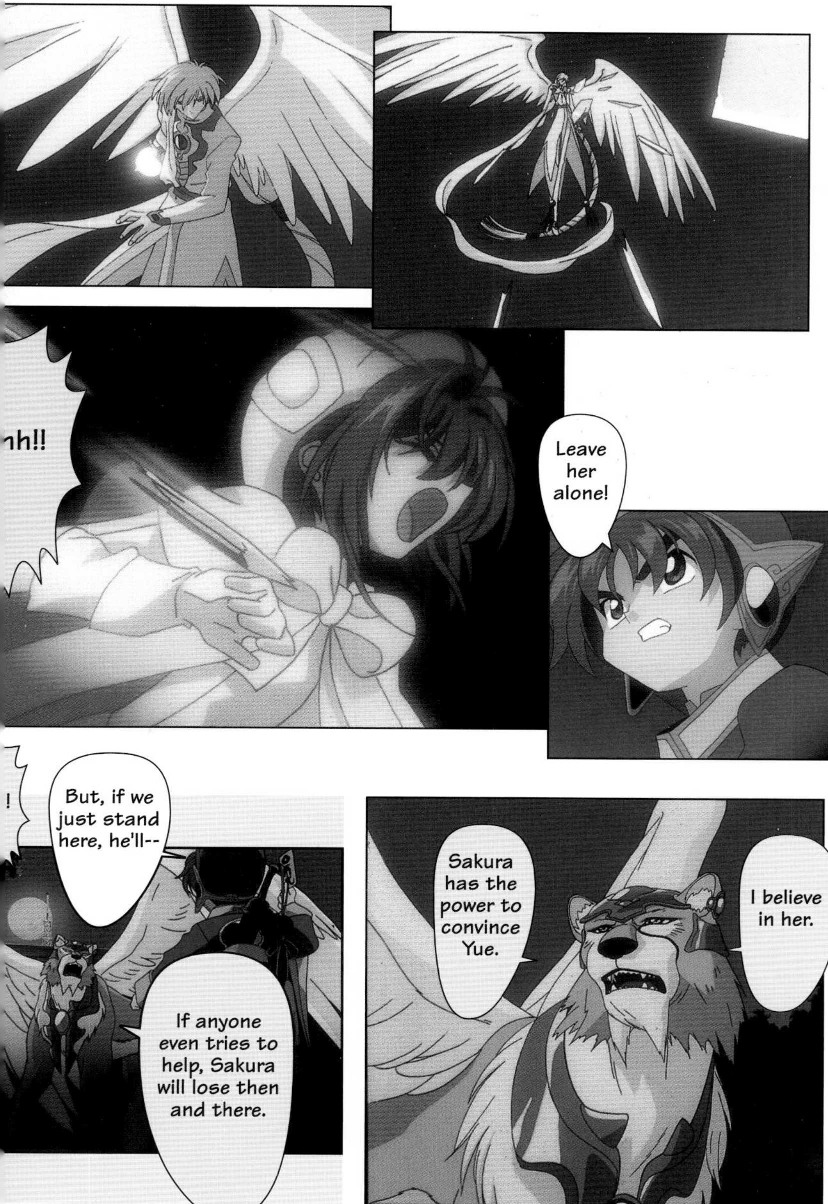
nh!!
Leave her alone!
!
But, if we just stand here, he'll--
If anyone even tries to help, Sakura will lose then and there.
Sakura has the power to convince Yue.
I believe in her.

Come now, Sakura. If you don't try, you will most certainly fail.

Someh there's to be a

tha hu

Think! A non-offensive card...

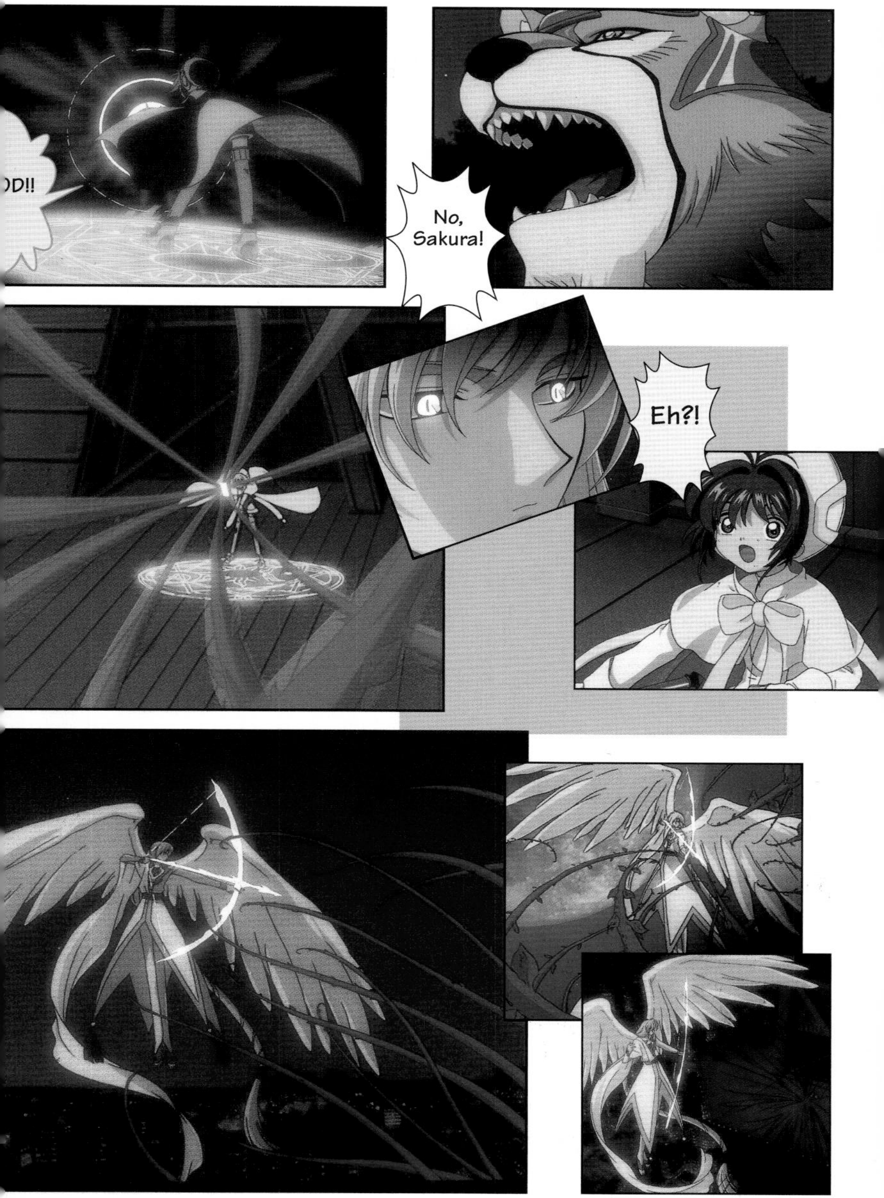
No, Sakura!
Eh?!

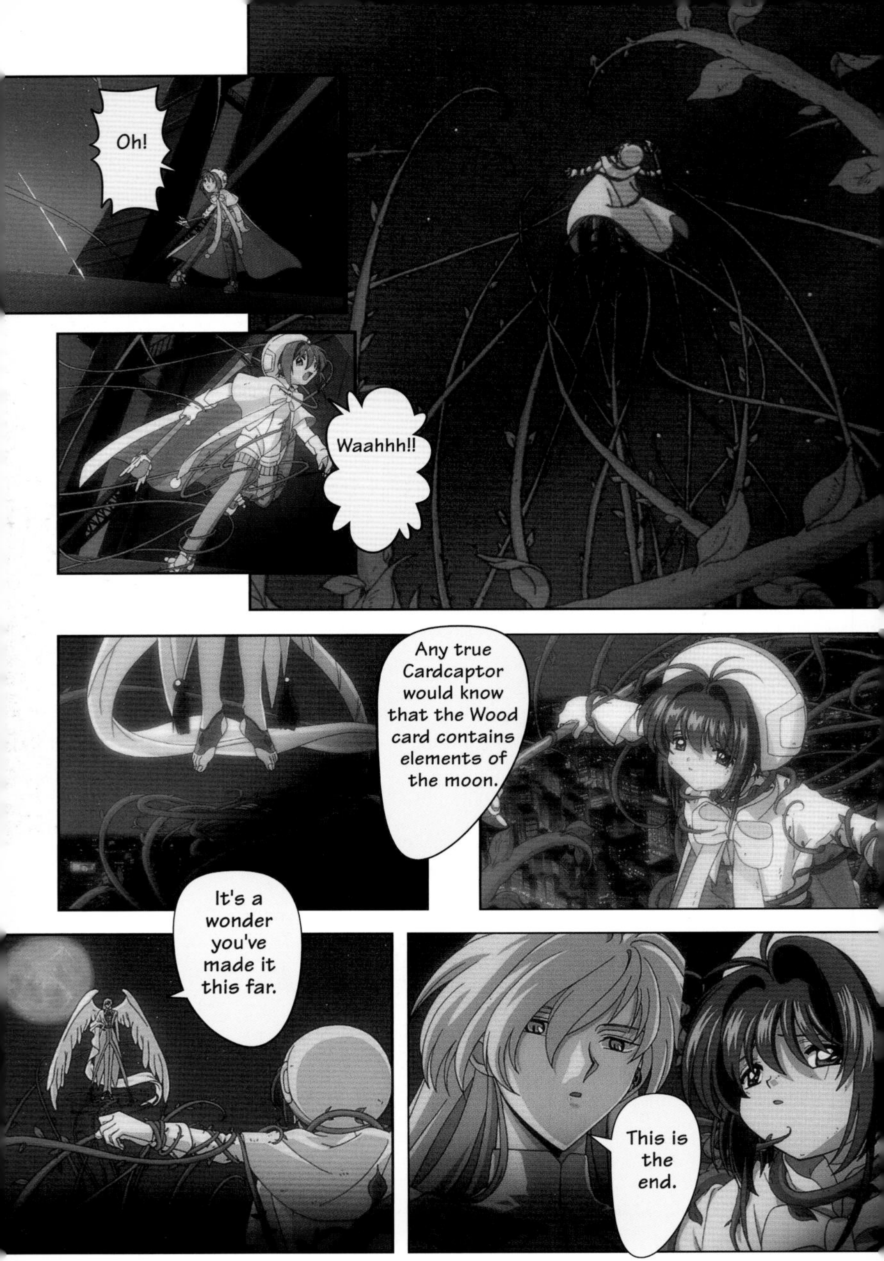

Oh!
Waahhh!!
Any true Cardcaptor would know that the Wood card contains elements of the moon.
It's a wonder you've made it this far.
This is the end.

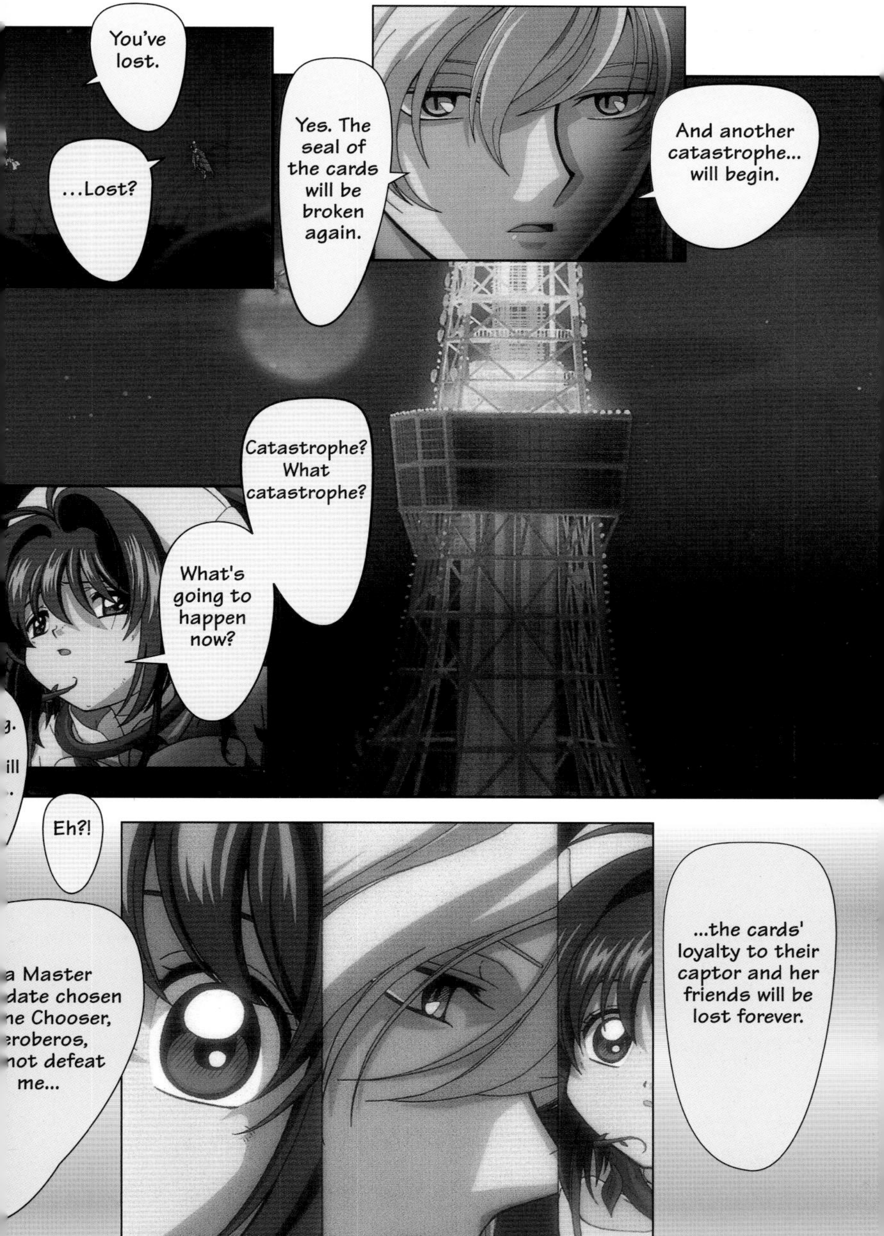
You've lost.
...Lost?
Yes. The seal of the cards will be broken again.
And another catastrophe... will begin.
Catastrophe? What catastrophe?
What's going to happen now?
Eh?!
a Master
date chosen
ne Chooser,
eroberos,
not defeat
me...
...the cards' loyalty to their captor and her friends will be lost forever.

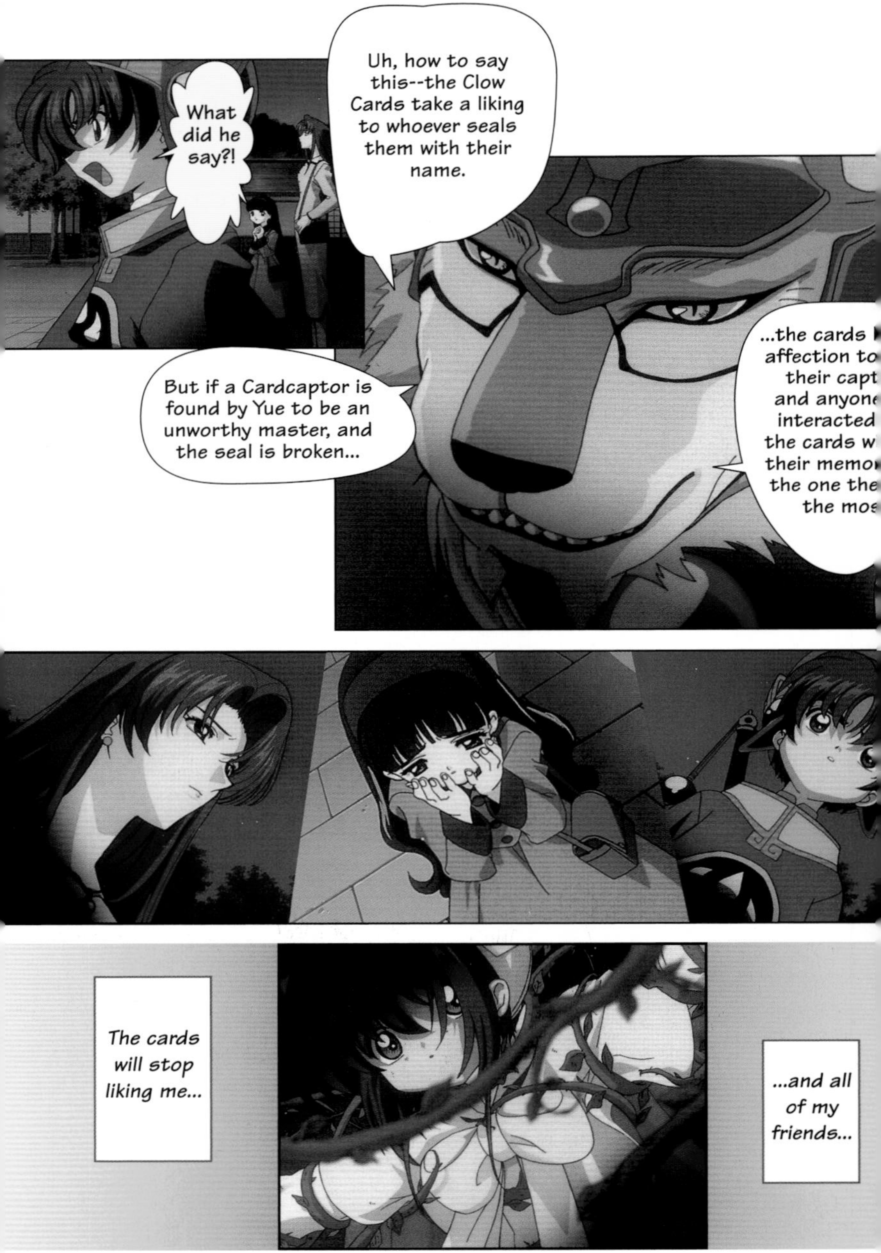
What did he say?!
Uh, how to say this--the Clow Cards take a liking to whoever seals them with their name.
But if a Cardcaptor is found by Yue to be an unworthy master, and the seal is broken...
...the cards affection to their capt and anyone interacted the cards w their memo the one the the mos
The cards will stop liking me...
...and all of my friends...

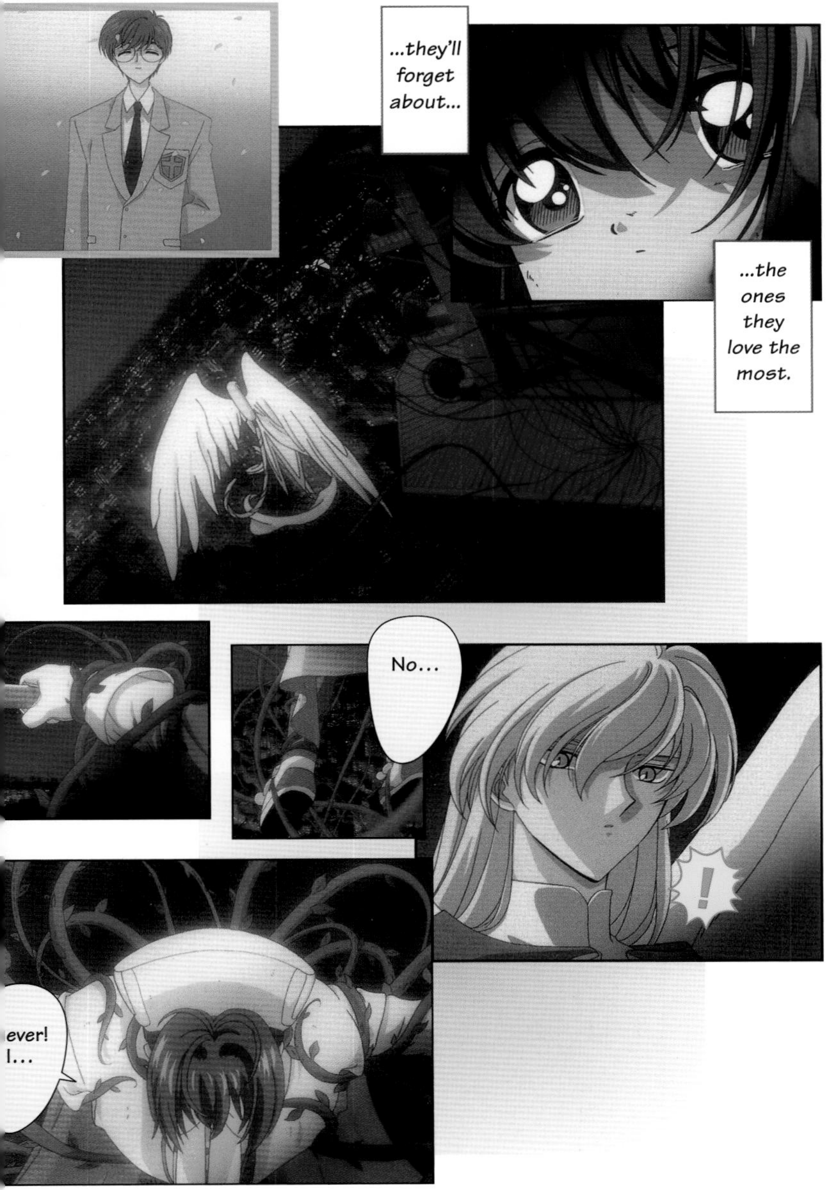
...they'll forget about...
...the ones they love the most.
No...
!
ever!
I...

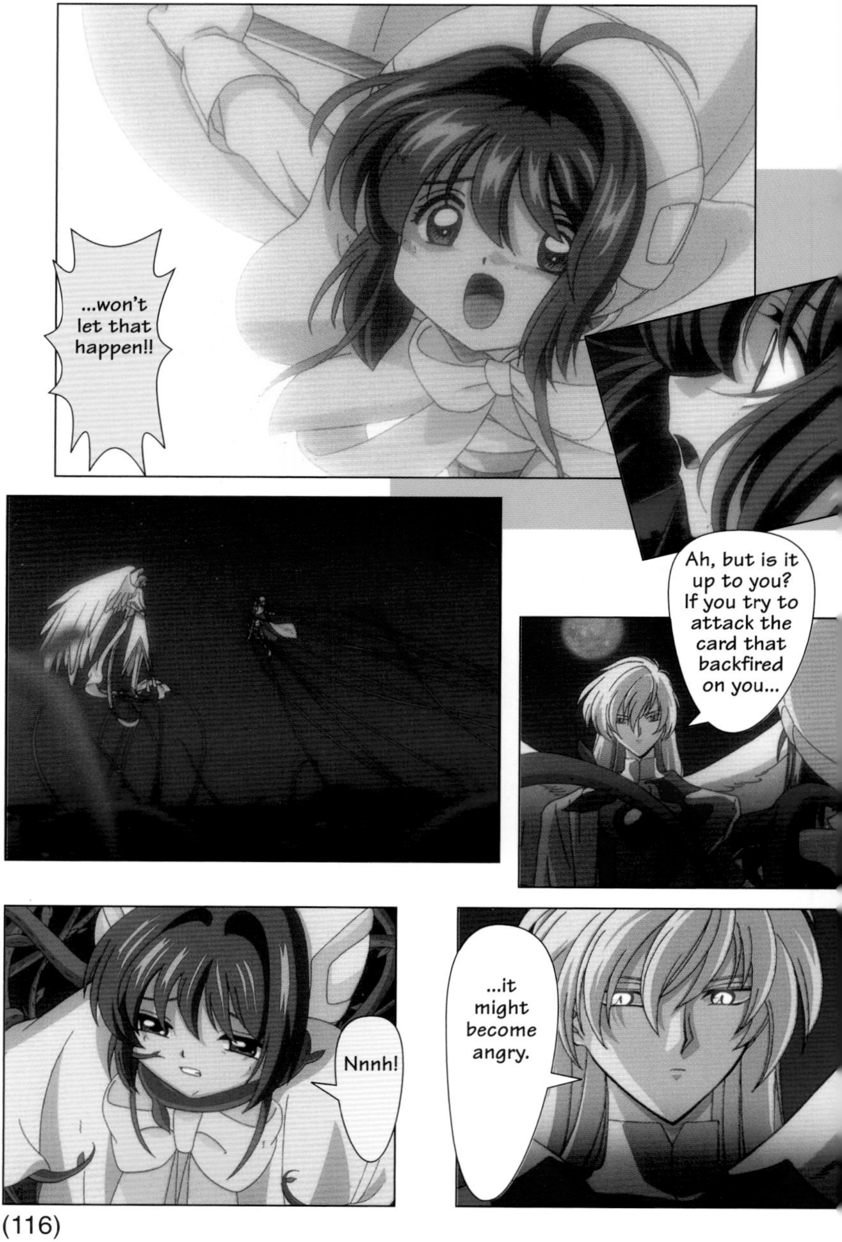
...won't let that happen!!
Ah, but is it up to you? If you try to attack the card that backfired on you...
Nnnh!
...it might become angry.

Ugh! Ngh!!

So has it ever been. Only Clow Reed can defeat me.

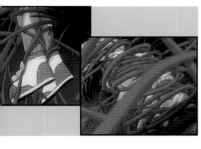

No!!

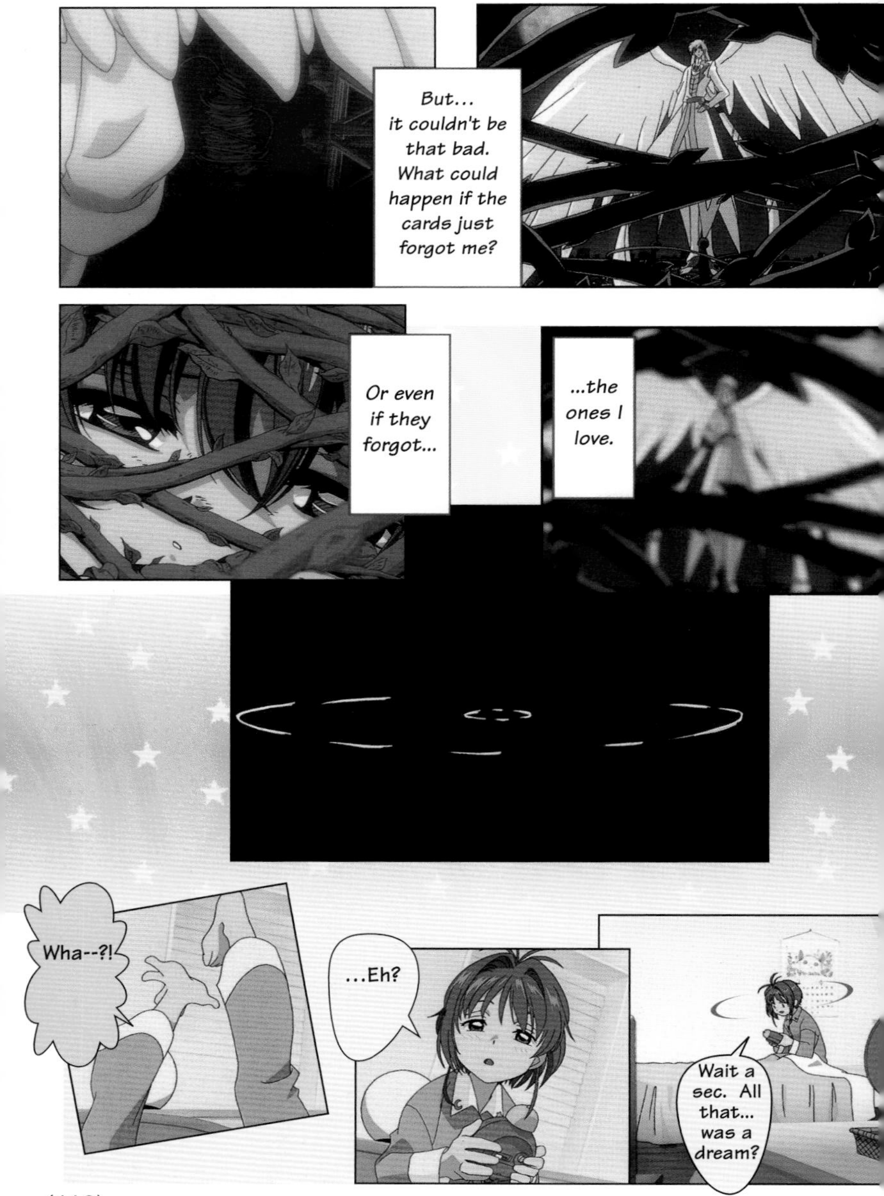

But… it couldn't be that bad. What could happen if the cards just forgot me?
Or even if they forgot...
...the ones I love.
Wha--?!
…Eh?
Wait a sec. All that... was a dream?

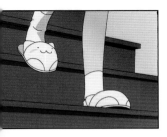

Good morning!

G'morning, Dad.

Good morning!

. . . . .

Morning, mo--

Sakura? Anything the matter?

Nah... it's nothing.

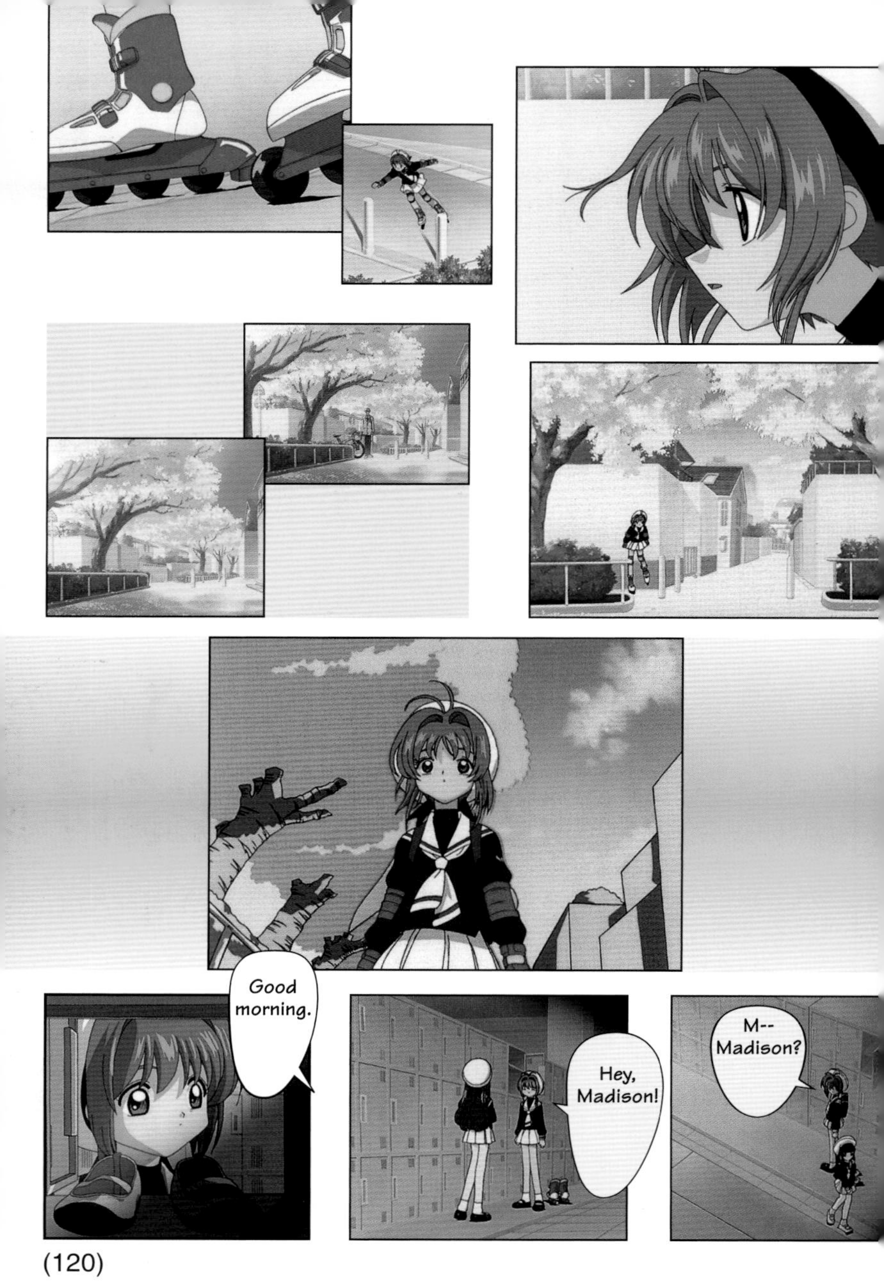
Good morning.
Hey, Madison!
M-- Madison?

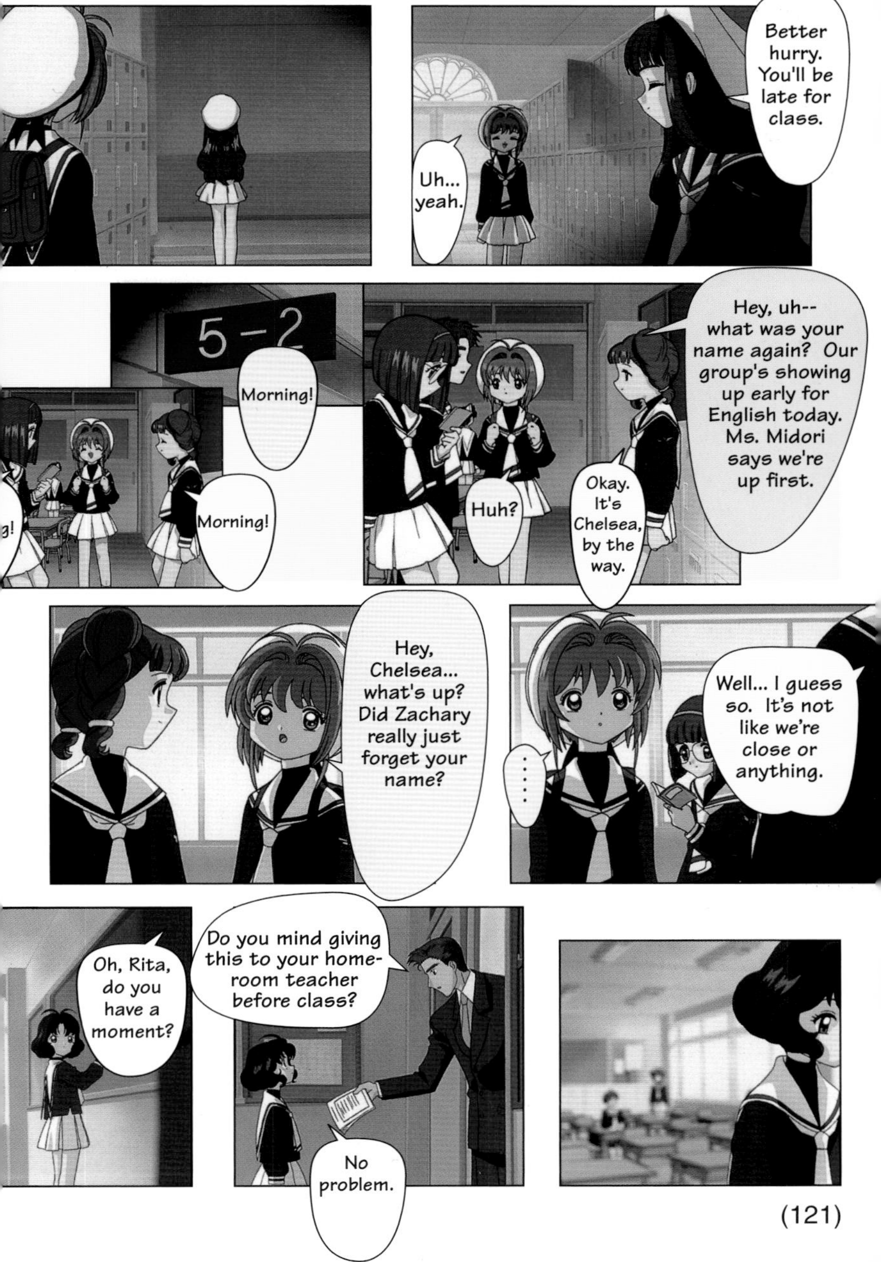
Better hurry. You'll be late for class.
Uh... yeah.
5-2
Morning!
Morning!
Hey, uh-- what was your name again? Our group's showing up early for English today. Ms. Midori says we're up first.
Huh?
Okay. It's Chelsea, by the way.
Hey, Chelsea... what's up? Did Zachary really just forget your name?
.....
Well... I guess so. It's not like we're close or anything.
Oh, Rita, do you have a moment?
Do you mind giving this to your home-room teacher before class?
No problem.

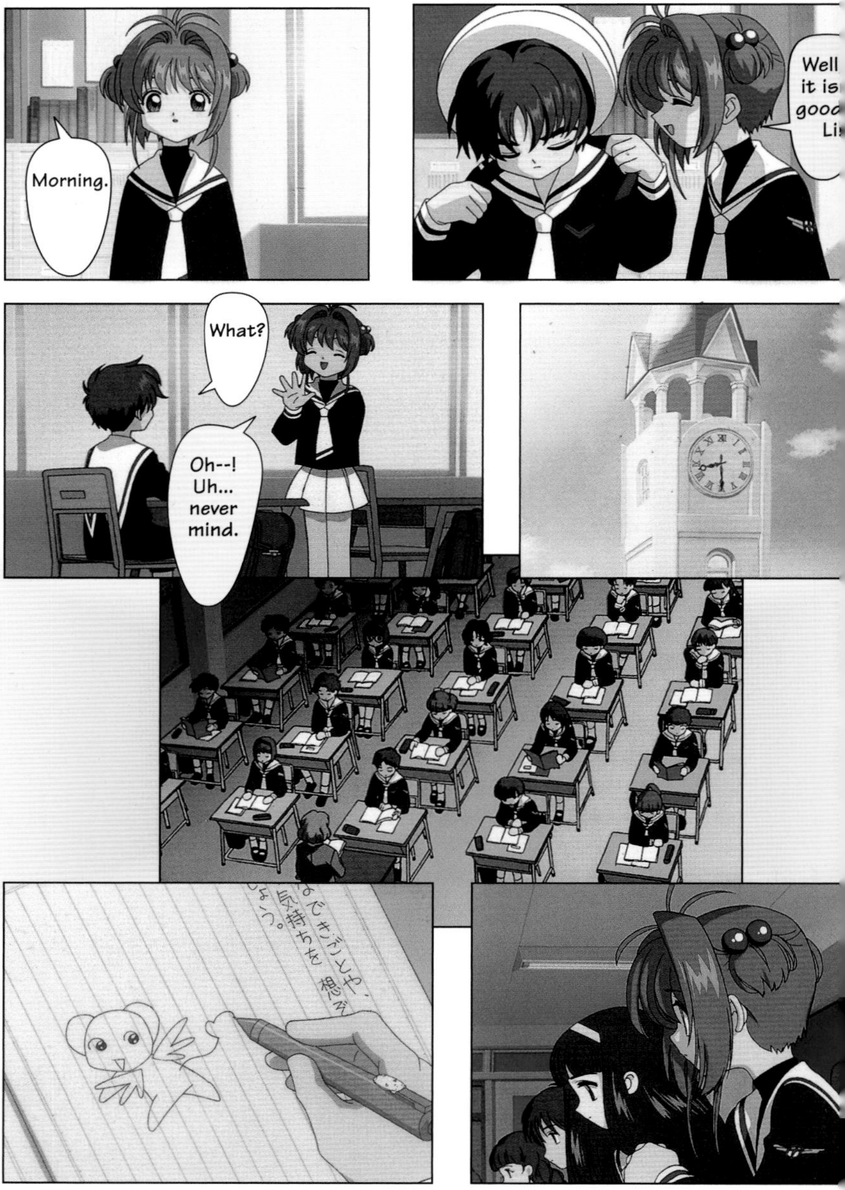
Morning.
Well it is good Li
What?
Oh--! Uh... never mind.
なできごとや、
気持ちを
しょう。

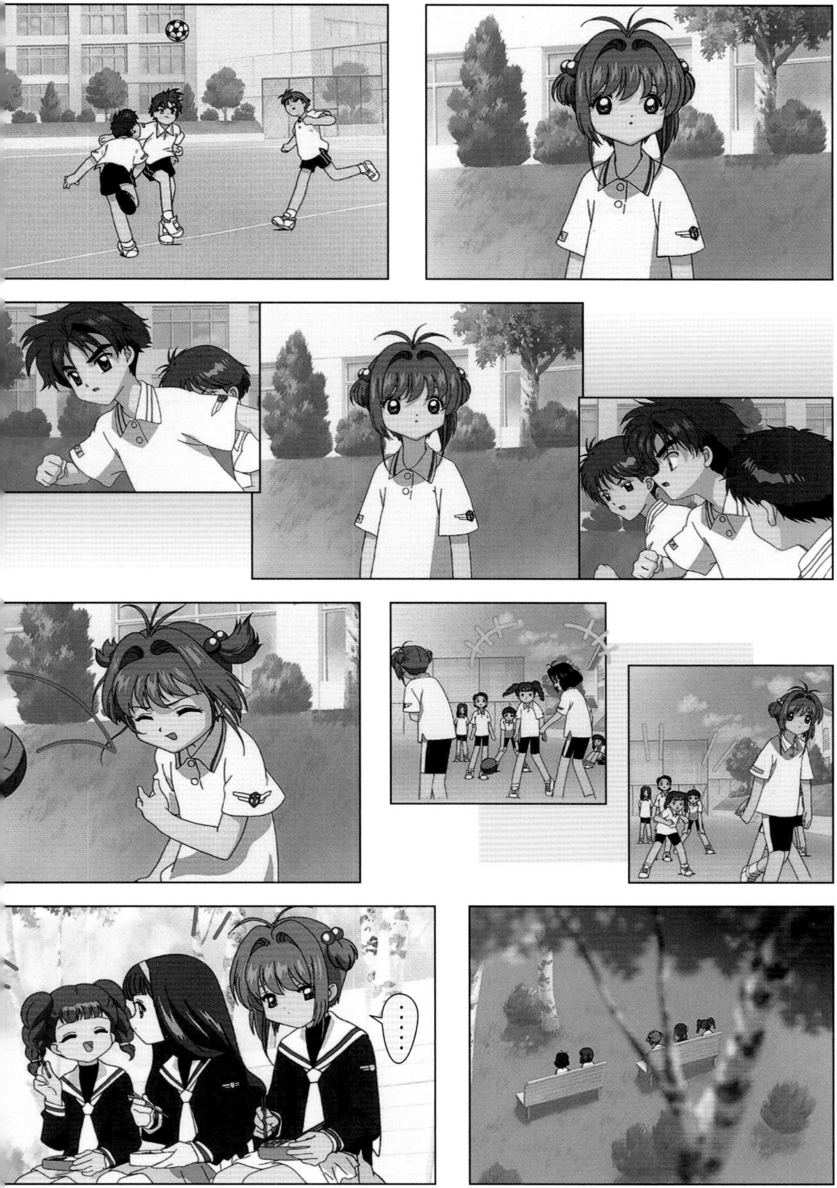
.....

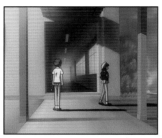

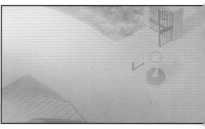

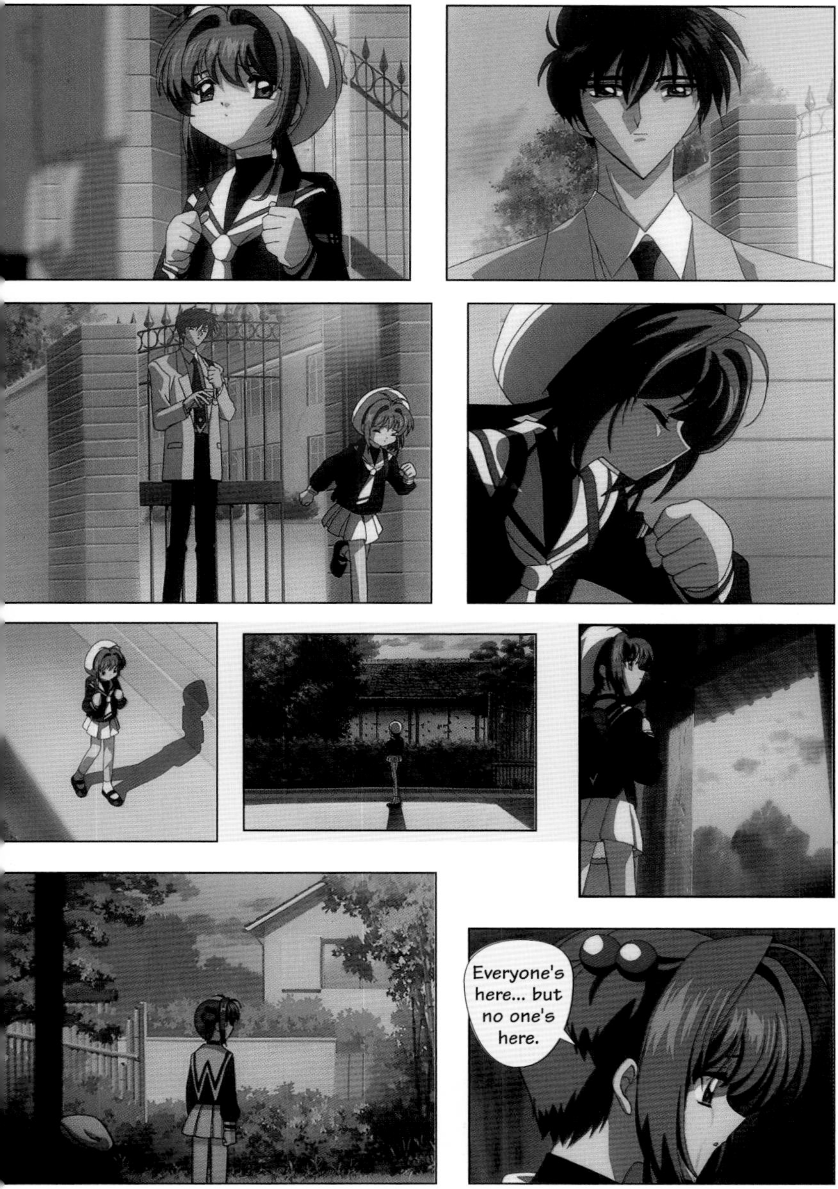
Everyone's here... but no one's here.

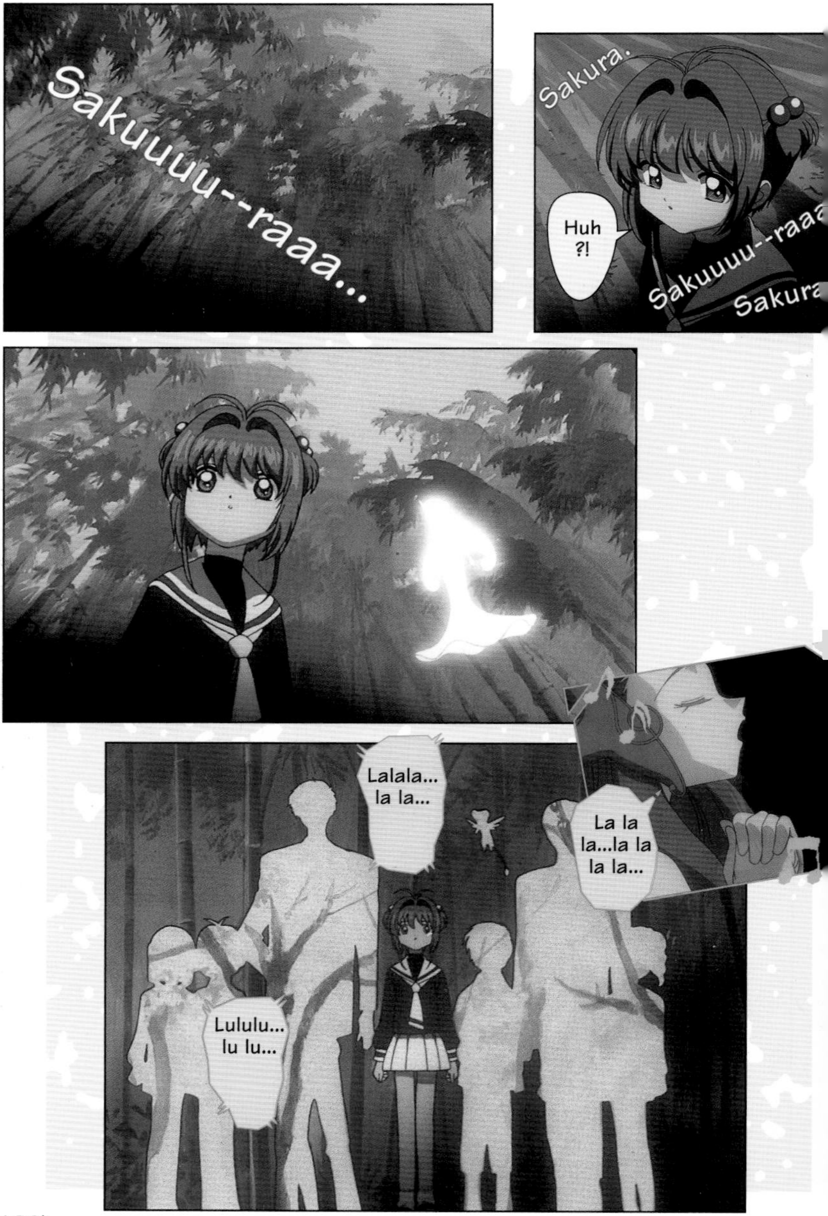
Sakuuuuu--raaa...
Sakura.
Huh ?!
Sakuuuu--raaa
Sakura
Lalala... la la...
La la la...la la la la...
Lululu... lu lu...

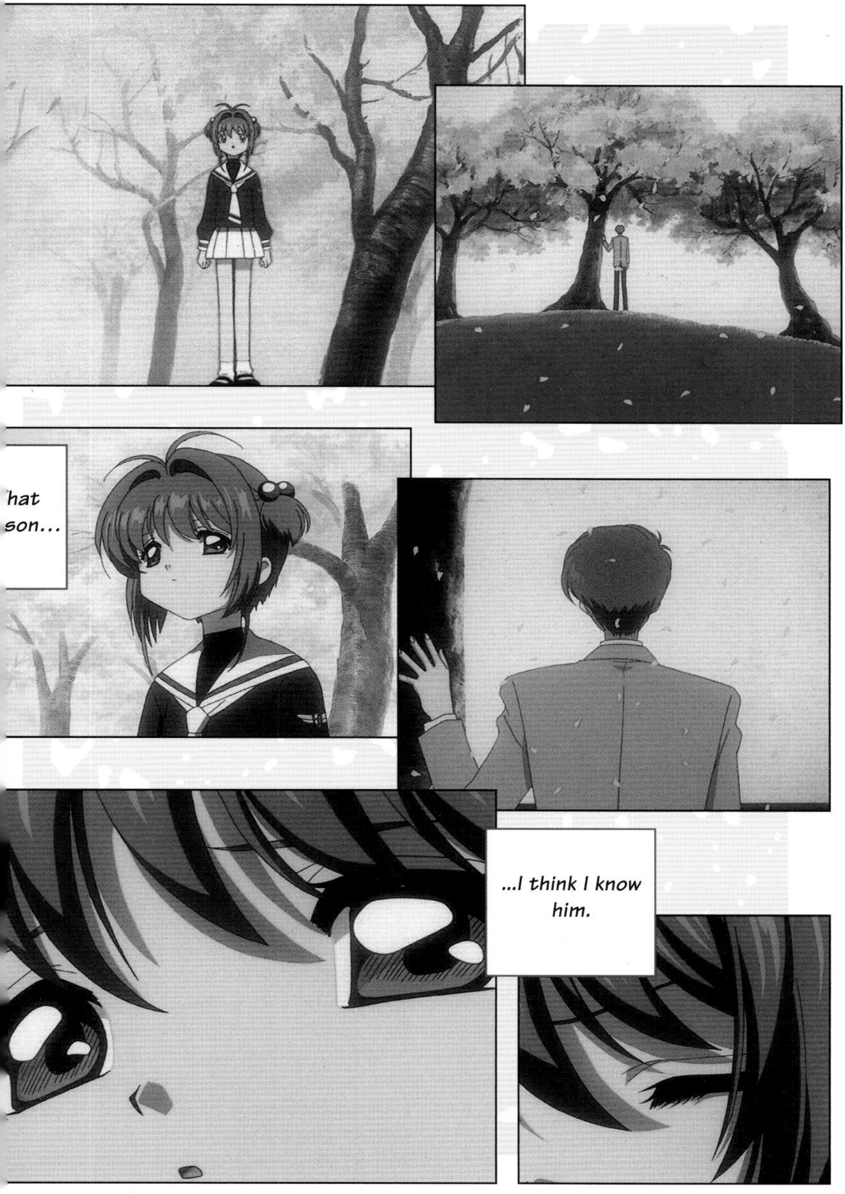
hat
son...
...I think I know
him.

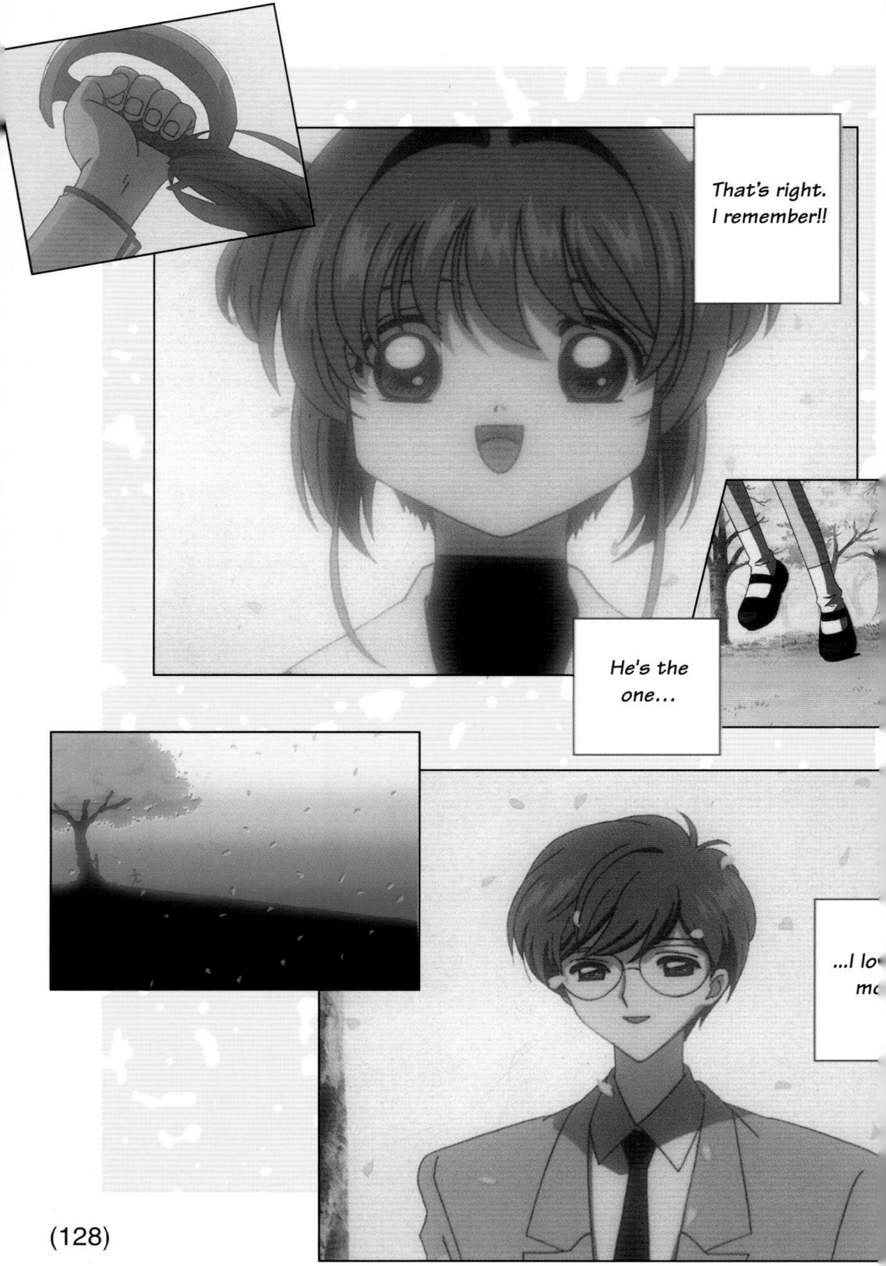
That's right.
I remember!!
He's the
one...
...I lo

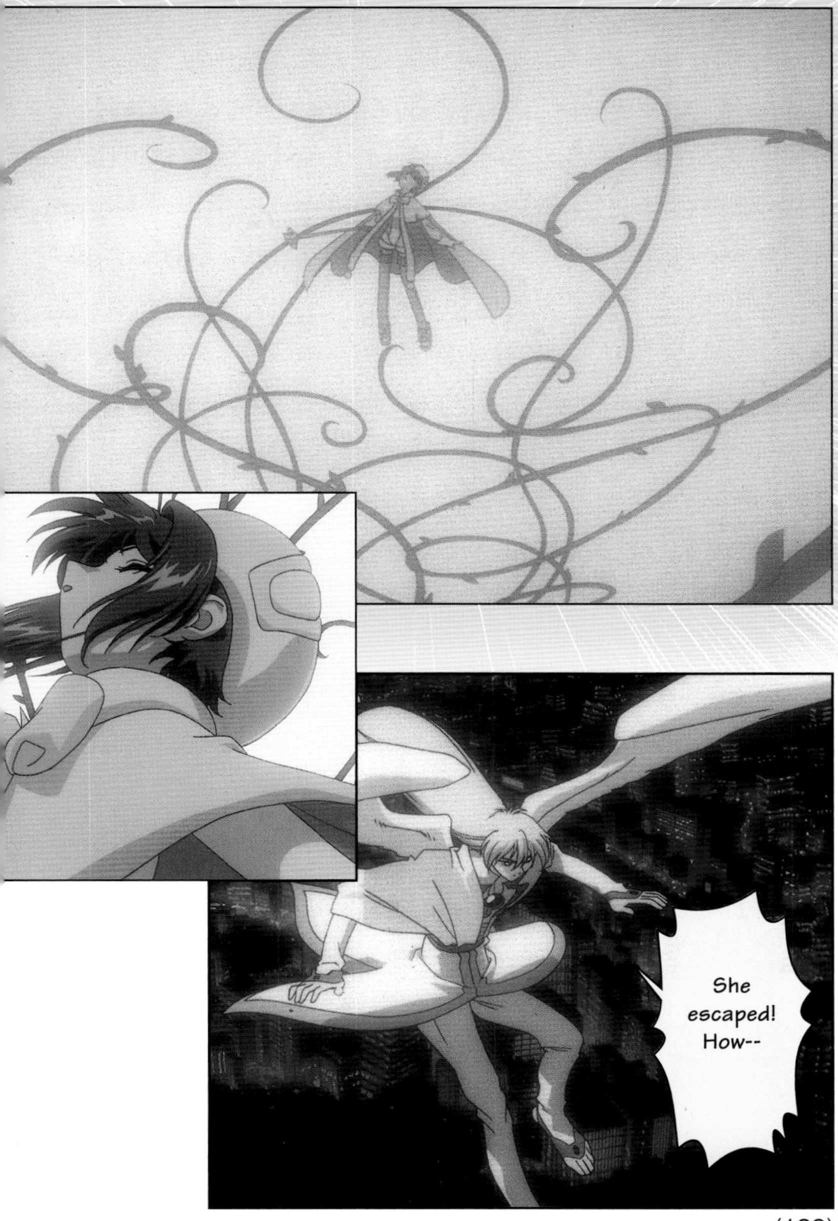
She escaped! How--

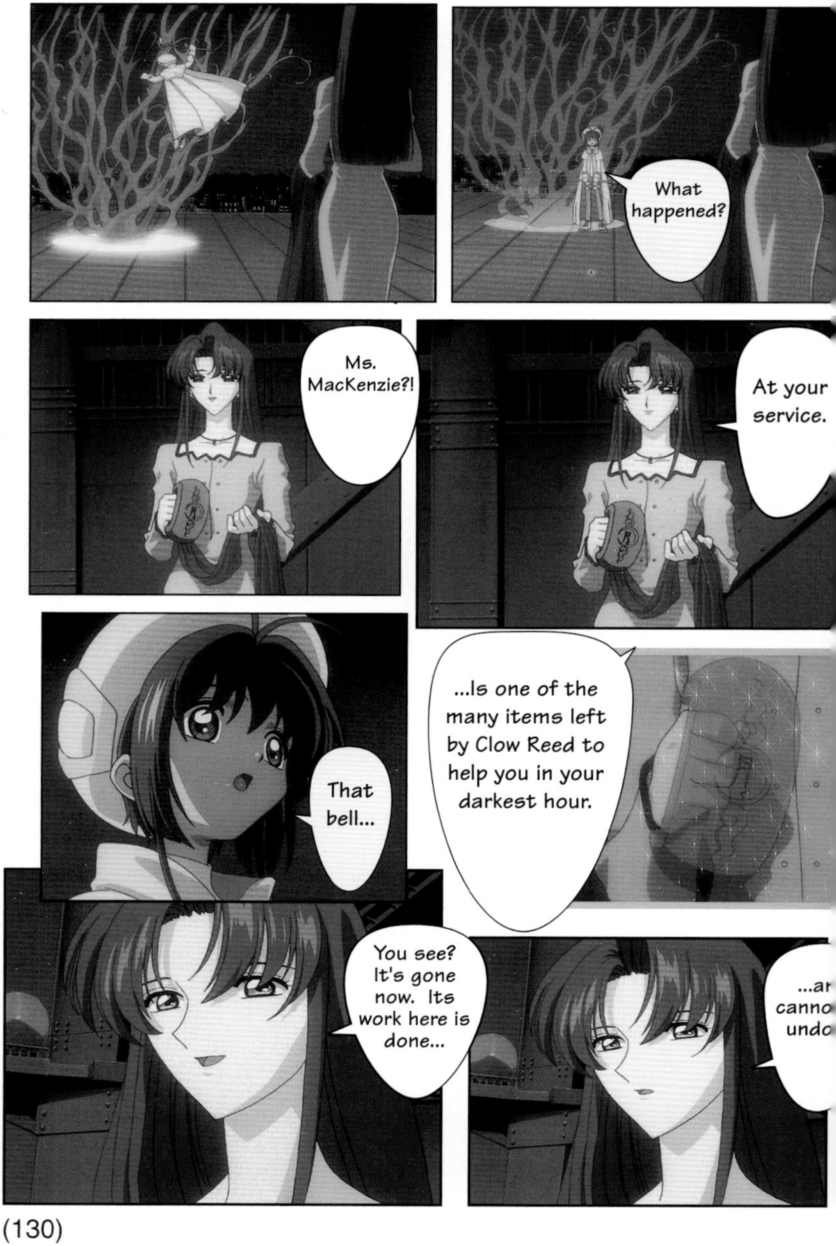
What happened?
Ms. MacKenzie?!
At your service.
That bell...
...Is one of the many items left by Clow Reed to help you in your darkest hour.
You see? It's gone now. Its work here is done...
...ar canno undo

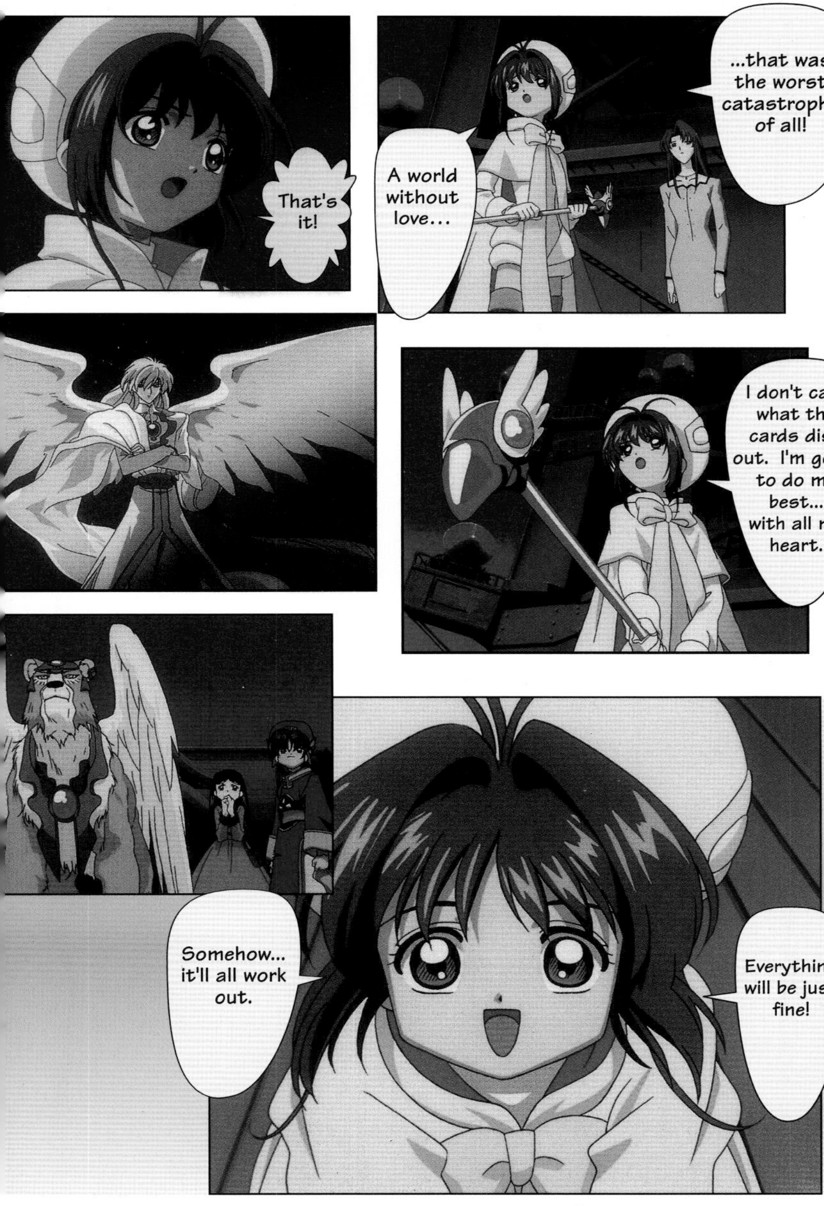
That's it!
A world without love...
...that was the worst catastrophe of all!
I don't care what the cards dish out. I'm going to do my best... with all my heart.
Somehow... it'll all work out.
Everything will be just fine!

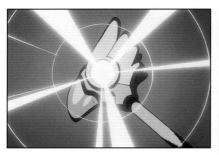

It is done... release the seal.

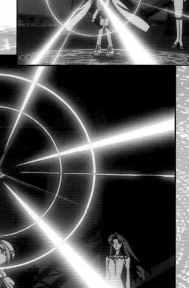

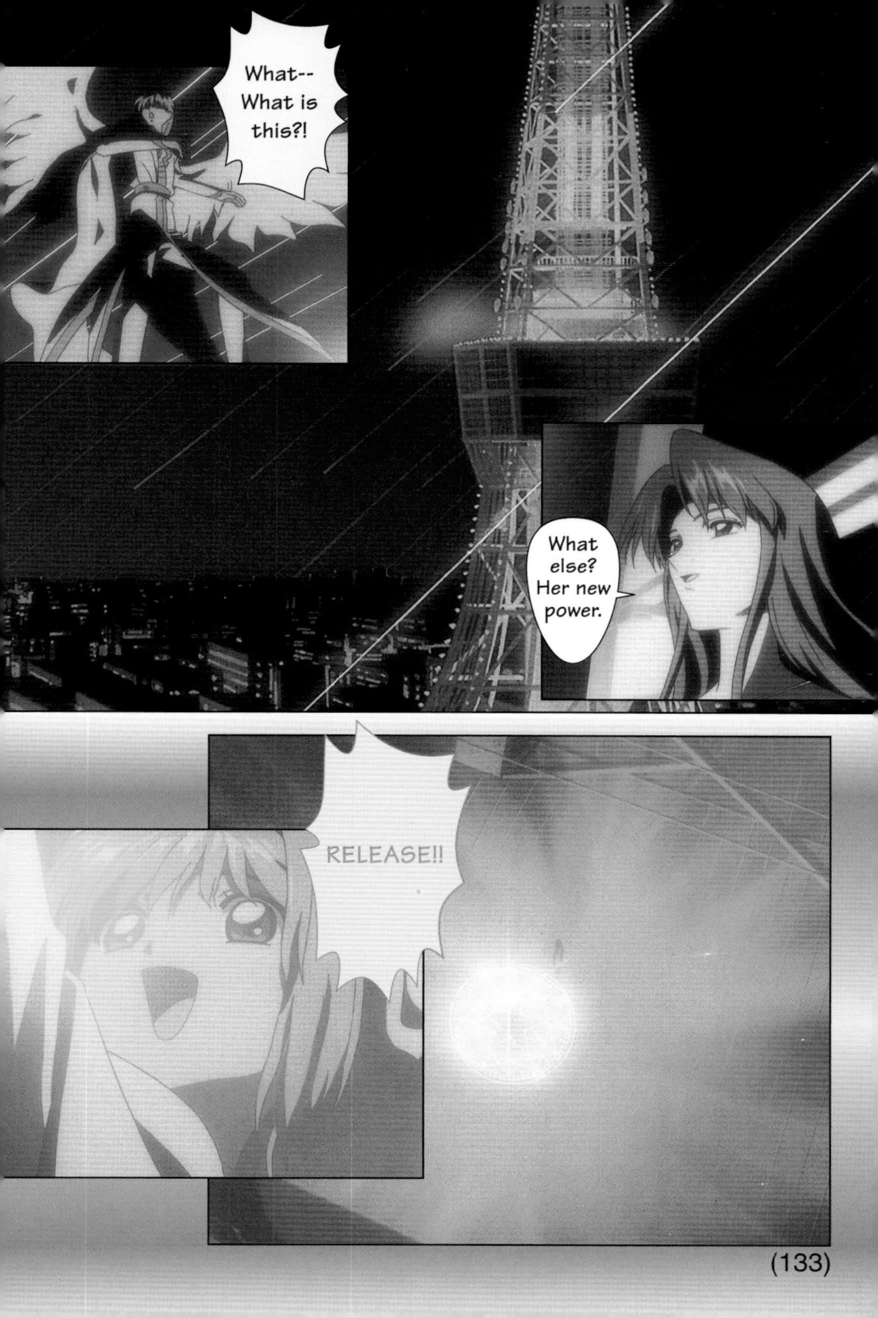
What-- What is this?!
What else? Her new power.
RELEASE!!

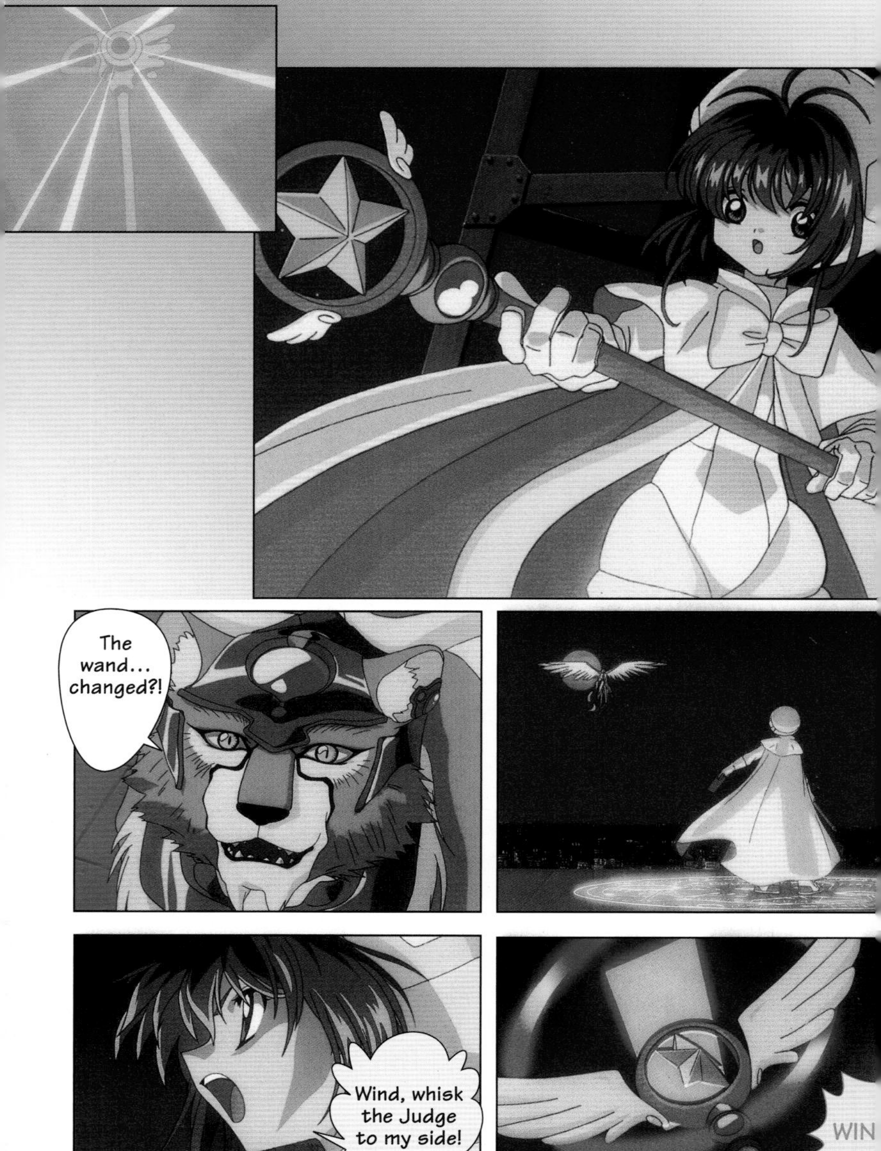
The wand... changed?!
Wind, whisk the Judge to my side!
WIN

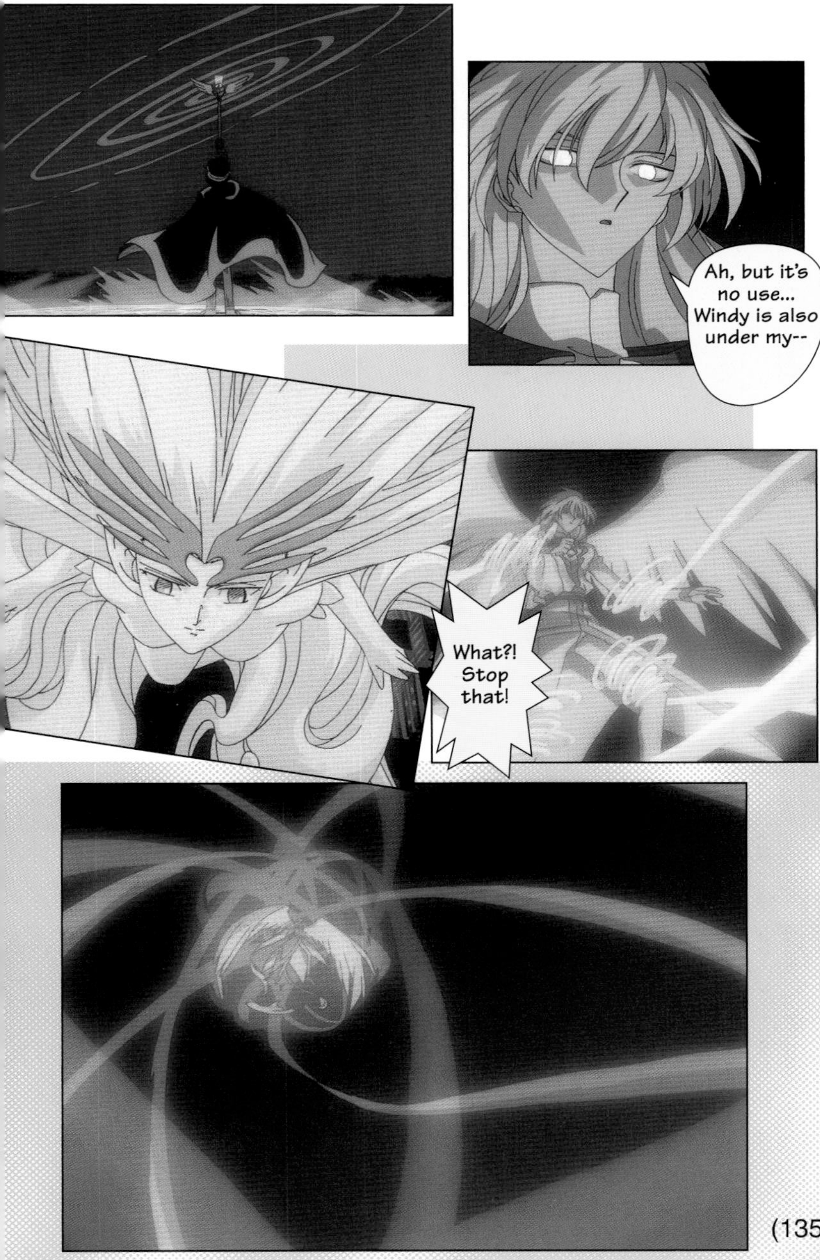
Ah, but it's no use... Windy is also under my--
What?! Stop that!

Yue, you were close to Clow Reed, weren't you?

If so, maybe you'd understand what it would be like to forget the one you loved most, too.

I may be just a kid, and don't have great powers like Clow Reed, but...

...I'll always have the power to do my best!

(136)

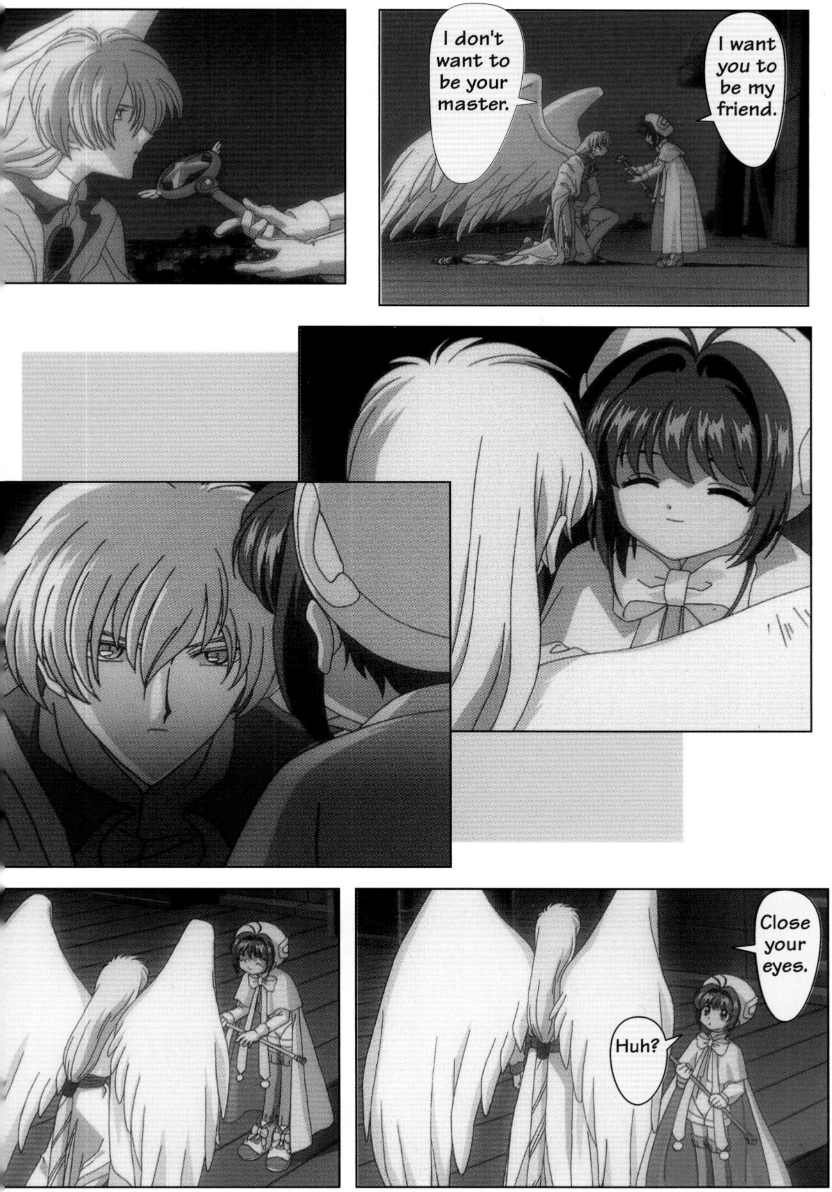
I don't want to be your master.
I want you to be my friend.
Huh?
Close your eyes.

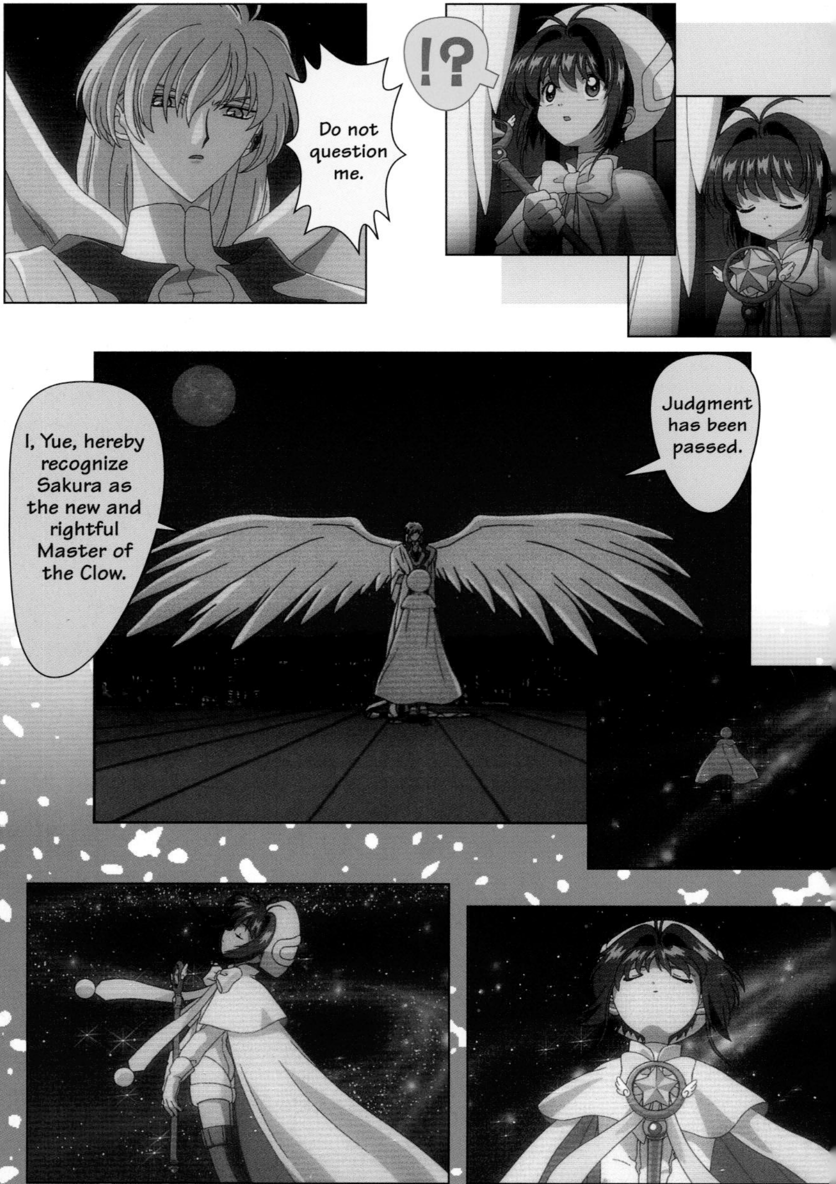
Do not question me.
!?
I, Yue, hereby recognize Sakura as the new and rightful Master of the Clow.
Judgment has been passed.

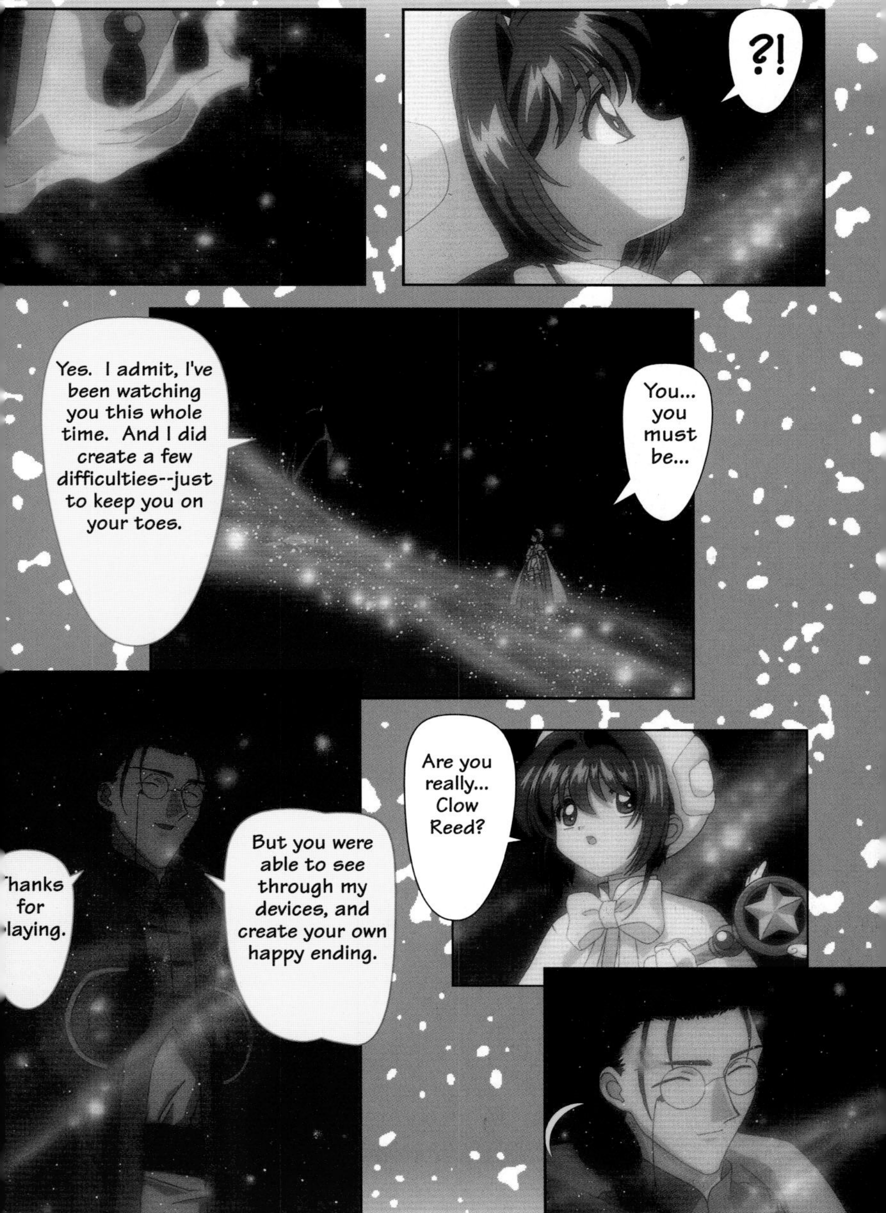
?!
Yes. I admit, I've been watching you this whole time. And I did create a few difficulties--just to keep you on your toes.
You... you must be...
But you were able to see through my devices, and create your own happy ending.
Thanks for playing.
Are you really... Clow Reed?

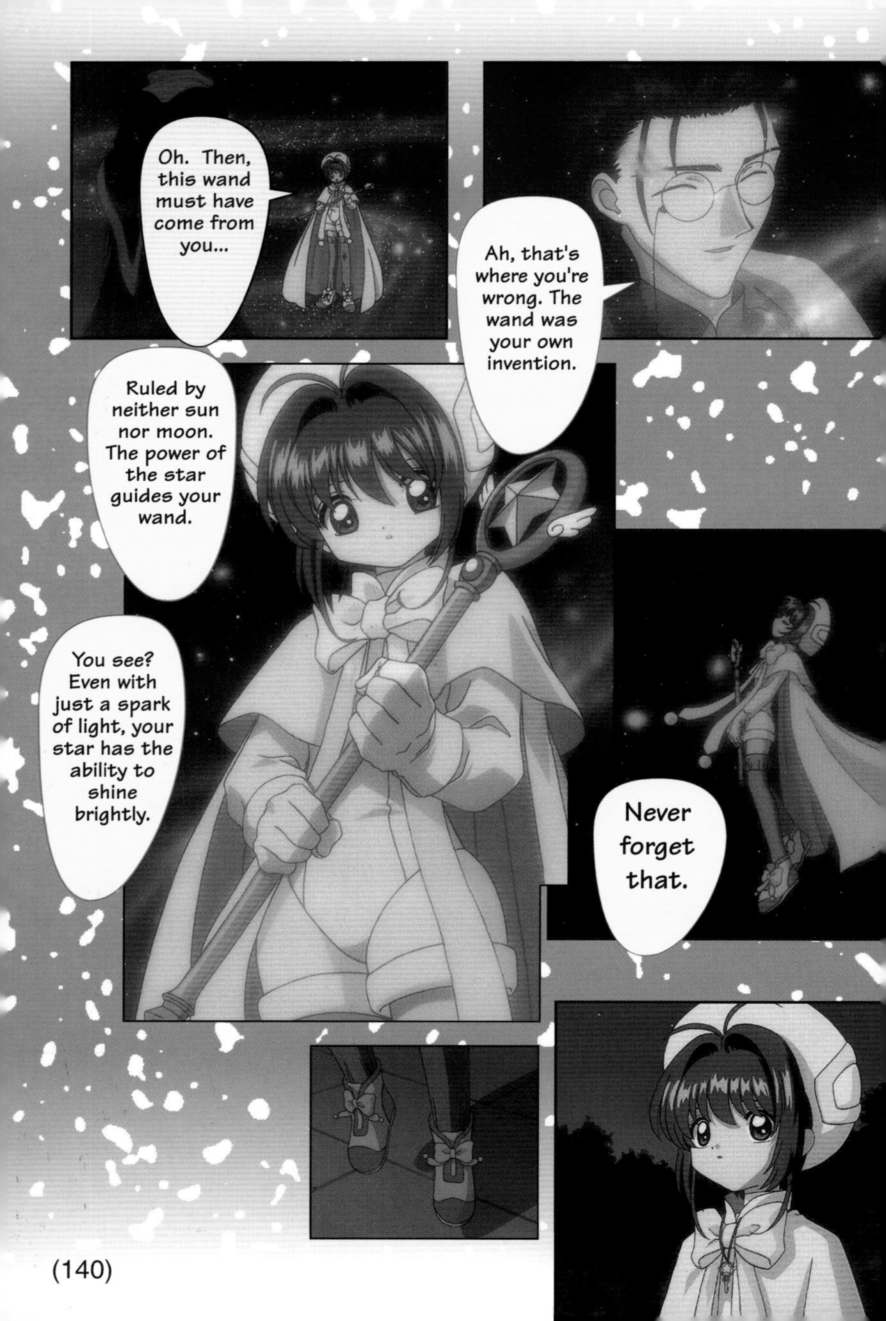

Oh. Then, this wand must have come from you...
Ah, that's where you're wrong. The wand was your own invention.
Ruled by neither sun nor moon. The power of the star guides your wand.
You see? Even with just a spark of light, your star has the ability to shine brightly.
Never forget that.

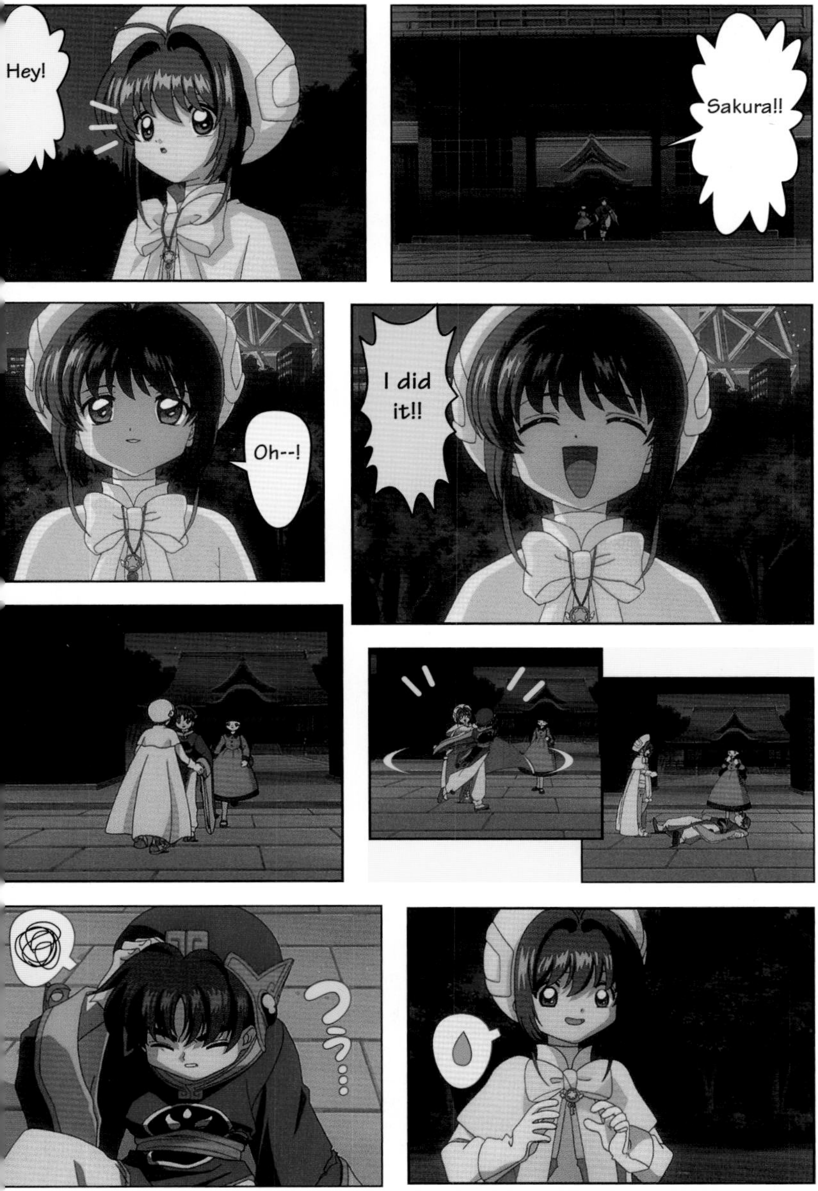
Hey!
Sakura!!
Oh--!
I did it!!
つう...

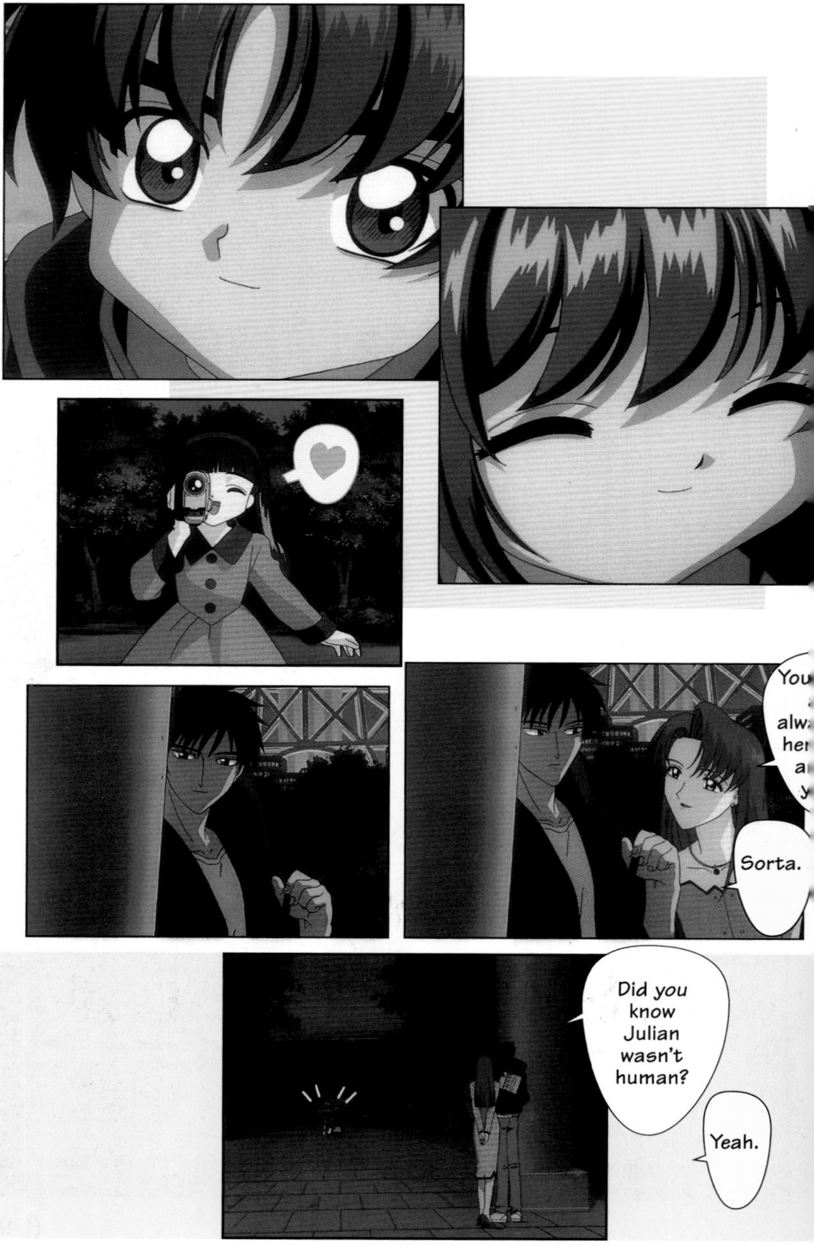

Sorta.
Did you know Julian wasn't human?
Yeah.

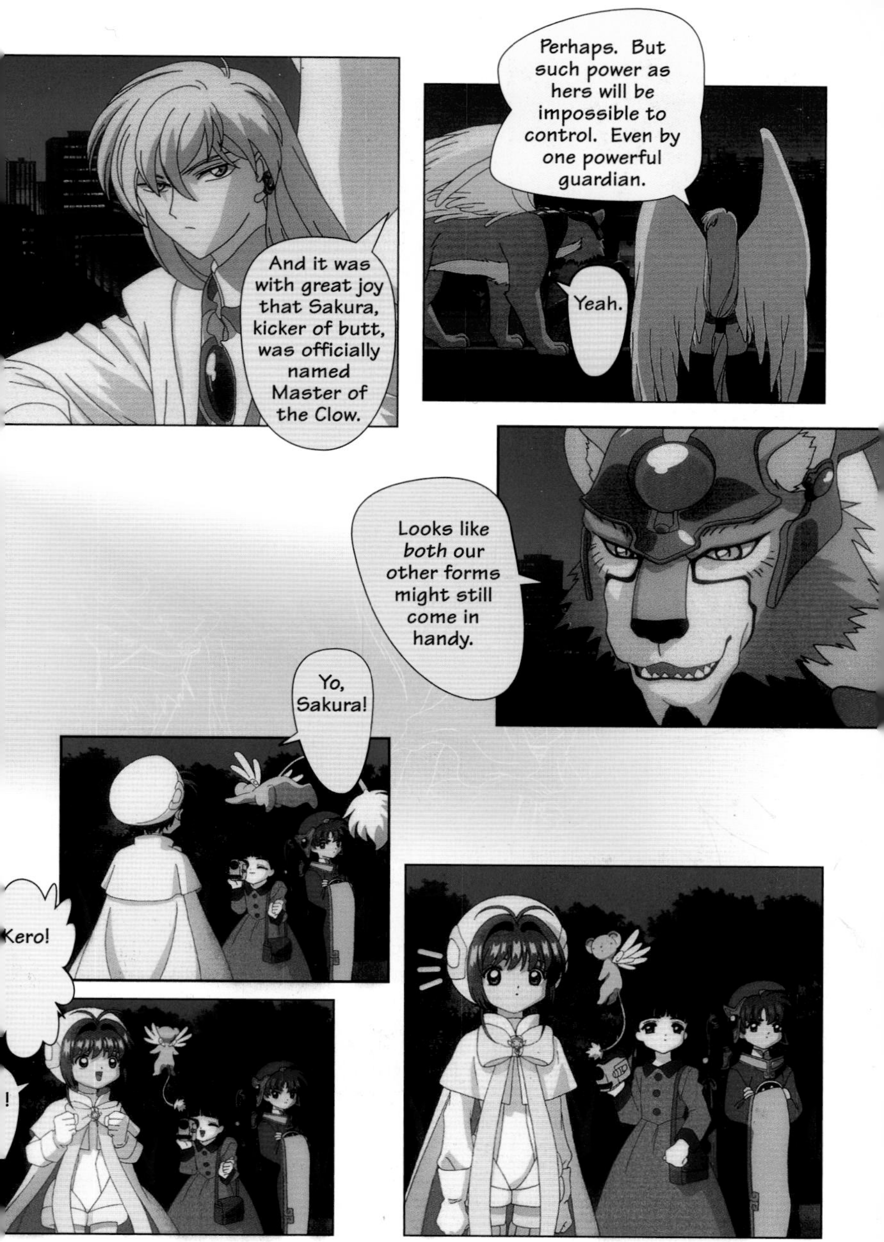
And it was with great joy that Sakura, kicker of butt, was officially named Master of the Clow.
Perhaps. But such power as hers will be impossible to control. Even by one powerful guardian.
Yeah.
Looks like *both* our other forms might still come in handy.
Yo, Sakura!
Kero!
!

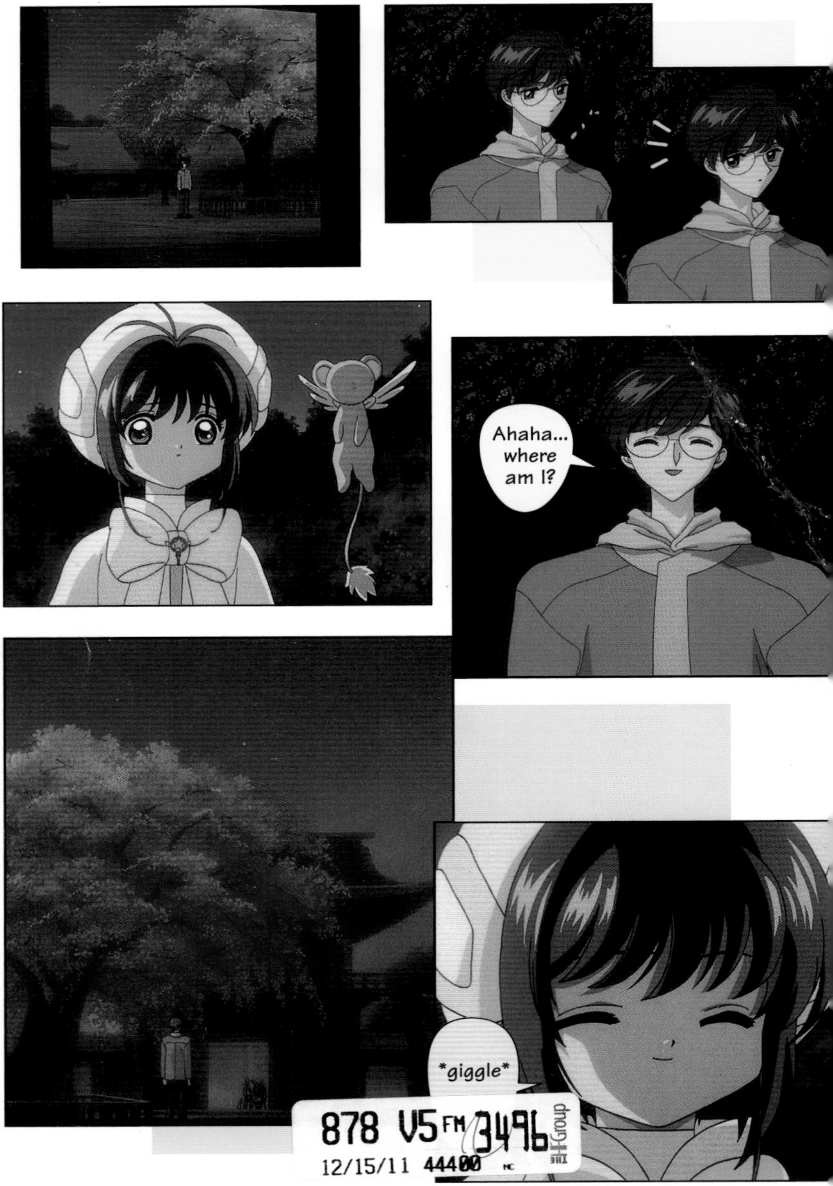
Ahaha... where am I?
giggle

The Final Judgment - The End